A Handbook of
Business Law Terms

Bryan A. Garner
Editor

David W. Schultz
Lance A. Cooper
Elizabeth C. Powell
Assistant Editors

WEST
GROUP

St. Paul, Minnesota
1999

PREFACE

In this *Handbook of Business Law Terms*, you'll find the most up-to-date, reliable treatment of law-related terms that businesspeople need to know.

The business world and the legal universe around it are more complex than ever—and the constantly expanding vocabulary of business law reflects this complexity. In real estate there are *synthetic leases*, and in construction financing there are *bankruptcy-remote entities*. In intellectual-property law, it's important to know the difference between *trademark* and *trade dress*. If you're dealing in securities, it can be important to know what your partners mean when they talk about a *short sale against the box*. And it can be critical to know the difference between a *debt ratio* and a *debt-to-equity ratio*. These are only a few of hundreds of possible examples.

My colleagues and I thank our business-law consultant, Professor Marc I. Steinberg of Southern Methodist University School of Law. He reviewed the entire manuscript, commenting with the insight of one who has taught Business Enterprises for many years.

Whatever your terminological quandary, we hope that this book will help answer your questions.

BRYAN A. GARNER

Dallas, Texas
March 1999

*

iii

A Handbook of Business Law Terms

A

AAA. *abbr.* **1.** AMERICAN ARBITRATION ASSOCIATION. **2.** AMERICAN ACCOUNTING ASSOCIATION. **3.** AMERICAN ACADEMY OF ACTUARIES.

abandonment. 1. The relinquishing of a right or interest with the intention of never again claiming it. **2.** In bankruptcy law, the trustee's court-approved release of property that is burdensome or of inconsequential value to the estate, or the trustee's release of nonadministered property to the debtor after the case has been closed. **3.** See RESCISSION (2).

abatement. Reduction or cancellation of a tax, charge, or debt.

above-the-line, *adj.* (Of a deduction) taken after calculating gross income and before calculating adjusted gross income. ● Examples of above-the-line deductions are IRA contributions and moving expenses. Formerly, individual tax returns had a dark line above which these deductions were written. Cf. BELOW-THE-LINE.

absolute defense. See *real defense* under DEFENSE.

1

absolute delivery. See DELIVERY.

absolute liability. See *strict liability* under LIABILITY.

absolute-priority rule. In bankruptcy law, the rule that a confirmable reorganization plan must provide for full payment to a class of dissenting unsecured creditors before a junior class of claimants will be allowed to receive or retain anything under the plan.

absorbable risk. See RISK.

absorption. 1. The act or process of including or incorporating (a thing) into something else. **2.** The rate at which property will be leased or sold on the market at a given time. **3.** A sales method by which a manufacturer pays the seller's freight costs, which the manufacturer accounts for before quoting the seller a price. **4.** In a post-merger collective-bargaining agreement, a provision allowing seniority for union members in the resulting entity.

abstract of judgment. A copy or summary of a judgment that, when filed with the appropriate public office, creates a lien on the judgment debtor's nonexempt property. See *judgment lien* under LIEN.

abstract of title. A concise statement, usu. prepared for a mortgagee or purchaser of real property, summarizing the history of a piece of land, including all conveyances, interests, liens, and encumbrances that affect title to the property.

Accelerated Cost Recovery System. An accounting method that is used to calculate asset depreciation and that allows for the faster recovery of costs by assigning the asset a shorter useful life than what was previously permitted under the Internal Revenue Code. • This system applies to property put into service from 1981 to 1986. It was replaced in 1986 by the Modified Accelerated Cost Recovery System.—Abbr. ACRS.

accelerated-depreciation method. See DE-PRECIATION METHOD.

acceleration. 1. The advancing of a loan agreement's maturity date so that payment of the entire debt is due immediately. **2.** In securities law, the SEC's expediting of a registration statement's effective date so that the registrant bypasses the required 20-day waiting period.

acceleration clause. A loan-agreement provision requiring the debtor to pay off the balance sooner than the regular payment date if some specified event occurs, such as failure to timely pay installments or to maintain insurance. Cf. INSECURITY CLAUSE.

acceptance. 1. An agreement, either by express act or by implication from conduct, to the terms of an offer so that a binding contract is formed. • If an acceptance modifies the terms or adds new ones, it generally operates as a counteroffer. **2.** A buyer's assent that the goods are to be taken in performance of a contract for sale. • Under the UCC, a buyer's acceptance consists in (1) signifying to the seller that the goods are conforming ones or that the buyer will take them in spite of nonconformities, (2) not making an effective rejection, or (3) taking any action inconsistent with the seller's ownership (assuming that the action is not wrongful against the seller). **3.** The formal receipt of a negotiable instrument, together with an agreement to pay it. **4.** A negotiable instrument, esp. a bill of exchange, that has been accepted for payment.

banker's acceptance. A bill of exchange drawn on and accepted by a commercial bank. • Banker's acceptances are often issued to finance the sale of goods in international trade.

trade acceptance. A bill of exchange for the amount of a specific purchase, drawn on and accepted by the buyer for payment at a specified time.

acceptor. A person or entity who accepts a negotiable instrument and agrees to be primarily responsible for its payment or performance.

accident insurance. See INSURANCE.

accommodation. 1. A loan or other financial favor. **2.** The act of signing an accommodation paper as surety for another. See ACCOMMODATION PAPER.

accommodation loan. See LOAN.

accommodation paper. A negotiable instrument that one party cosigns, without receiving any consideration in return, in order to act as surety for another party who remains primarily liable. ● Accommodation paper is typically used when the cosigner is more creditworthy than the principal debtor.—Also termed *accommodation note*.

accommodation party. A person who, without recompense or other benefit, signs a negotiable instrument for the purpose of being a surety for another party (called the *accommodated party*) to the instrument. ● The accommodation party can sign in any capacity (i.e., as maker, drawer, acceptor, or indorser) <the father served as an accommodation party by cosigning the bank note with his daughter>. See SURETY.

accord, *n.* An offer to give or to accept a stipulated performance in the future to satisfy an obligor's existing duty, together with an acceptance of that offer. • The performance becomes what is known as a *satisfaction*. See SATISFACTION.

accord and satisfaction. An agreement to substitute for an existing debt some alternative form of discharging that debt, coupled with the actual discharge of the debt by the substituted performance. • The new agreement is called the *accord*, and the discharge is called the *satisfaction*. Cf. NOVATION.

account, *n.* **1.** A detailed statement of the debits and credits between parties to a contract or to a fiduciary relationship; a reckoning of monetary dealings <the trustee balanced the account at the end of each month>. **2.** A course of business dealings or other relations for which records must be kept <open a brokerage account>. **3.** See ACCOUNTING (2) <the principal filed an action for account against his agent>. **4.** See ACCOUNTING (3) <the contractor filed an action for account against the nonpaying customer>.

account payable. (*usu. pl.*) An account reflecting a balance owed to a creditor; a debt owed by an enterprise in the normal course of business dealing.—Often shortened to *payable*. Pl. *accounts payable*.

account receivable. (*usu. pl.*) An account reflecting a balance owed by a debtor; a debt owed by a customer to an enterprise for goods or services.—Often shortened to *receivable*. Pl. *accounts receivable*.

account rendered. An account produced by the creditor and presented for the debtor's examination and acceptance.

account settled. An account with a paid balance.

account stated. **a.** A balance that parties to a transaction or settlement agree on, either expressly or by implication. • The phrase also refers to the agreement itself or to the assent giving rise to the agreement. **b.** A plaintiff's claim in a suit for such a balance.

assigned account. A pledge of an account receivable to a bank or factor as security for a loan.

book account. A detailed statement of debits and credits giving a history of an enterprise's business transactions.

capital account. An account on a partnership's balance sheet representing a partner's share of the partnership capital.

closed account. An account that no further credits and debits may be added to, but that remains open for adjustment or setoff.

escrow account. **a.** A bank account, generally held in the name of the depositor and an escrow agent, that is returnable to the depositor or paid to a third person on the fulfillment of specified conditions. See ESCROW (2). **b.** See *impound account.*

impound account. An account of accumulated funds held by a lender for payment of taxes, insurance, or other periodic debts against real property.—Also termed *escrow*; *escrow account.* See ESCROW (2).

margin account. A brokerage account that allows an investor to buy or sell securities on credit, with the securities usu. serving as collateral for the broker's loan.

open account. **a.** An unpaid or unsettled account. **b.** An account that is left open for ongoing debit and credit entries and that has a fluctuating balance until either party finds it convenient to settle and close, at which time there is a single liability.

pledged account. A mortgagor's account pledged to a lender in return for a loan bearing interest at a below-market rate.

running account. An open, unsettled account that exhibits the reciprocal demands between the parties.

accountant. A person authorized under applicable law to practice public accounting; a person whose business is to keep books or accounts, to perform financial audits, to design and control accounting systems, and to give tax advice. • For some purposes, the term includes a professional accounting association, a corporation, and a partnership, if they are so authorized.

certified public accountant. An accountant who has satisfied the statutory and administrative requirements to be registered or licensed as a public accountant.—Abbr. CPA.

accountant-client privilege. The protection afforded to a client from unauthorized disclosure by his or her accountant of materials submitted to or prepared by the accountant. • This privilege has been adopted in only a few states.

accounting. 1. The act or a system of making up or settling financial accounts; esp., the process of recording transactions in the financial records of a business and periodically extracting, sorting, and summarizing the recorded transactions to produce a set of financial records.—Also termed *financial accounting*. Cf. BOOKKEEPING. **2.** A legal action commenced by one who has given another money or other property to be applied in a particular way, the action being designed to compel the recipient to provide details of the debts owed to the plaintiff. **3.** More broadly, an action for the recovery of money for services performed, property sold and delivered, money loaned, or damages for the nonperformance of simple contracts. ● Such an action is available when the rights of parties will be adequately protected by the payment of money.—Also termed *action on account*. **4.** In partnership law, an equitable proceeding for a complete settlement of all partnership affairs, usu. in connection with partner misconduct or with a winding up. See WINDING UP.

accounting method. A system for determining income and expenses for tax purposes.

   accrual accounting method. An accounting method that records entries of debits and credits when the liability arises, not when the income or expense is received or disbursed.

10

capitalization accounting method. A method of determining an asset's present value by discounting its stream of expected future benefits at an appropriate rate.

cash-basis accounting method. The accounting system that considers only cash actually received as income, and only cash actually paid out as an expense.

completed-contract accounting method. A method of reporting profit or loss on certain long-term contracts by recognizing gross income and expenses in the tax year that the contract is completed.

cost accounting method. The practice of recording the value of assets in terms of their cost.—Also termed *cost accounting*.

direct charge-off accounting method. A system of accounting for bad debts allowing for a deduction when an account becomes partially or completely worthless.

equity accounting method. A method of accounting for long-term investment in common stock based on acquisition cost, investor income, net losses, and dividends.

fair-value accounting method. The valuation of assets at present actual or market value.

installment accounting method. A method by which a taxpayer can spread the recognition of gains from a sale of property over the payment period by computing the gross-profit percentage from the sale and applying it to each payment.

physical-inventory accounting method. A method of counting a company's goods at the close of an accounting period.

accounting period. A regular span of time used for accounting purposes; esp., a period used by a taxpayer in determining income and related tax liability.

account payable. See ACCOUNT.

account receivable. See ACCOUNT.

account rendered. See ACCOUNT.

account settled. See ACCOUNT.

account stated. See ACCOUNT.

accredited investor. An investor that is treated under the Securities Act of 1933 as being knowledgeable and sophisticated about financial matters, esp. because of its large net worth. • In a securities offering that is exempt from registration, an accredited investor (which can be a person or an entity) is not entitled to protection under the Act's disclosure provisions, although the investor does keep its remedies for fraud.

accredited representative. See REPRESENTATIVE.

accrual accounting method. See ACCOUNTING METHOD.

accrual bond. See BOND (1).

accrue, *vb.* **1.** To come into existence as an enforceable claim; to arise <the plaintiff's cause of action for silicosis did not accrue until the plaintiff knew or had reason to know of the disease>. **2.** To accumulate periodically <the savings-account interest accrues monthly>.

accrued compensation. See COMPENSATION.

accrued expense. See EXPENSE.

accrued income. See INCOME.

accrued interest. See INTEREST.

accumulated-earnings tax. See TAX.

acknowledgment. 1. A formal declaration made in the presence of an authorized officer, such as a notary public, by someone who signs a document and says that the signature is authentic. ● In most states, the officer certifies that (1) he or she personally knows the document signer or has established the signer's identity through satisfactory evidence, (2) the signer appeared before the officer on the date and in the place (usu. the county) indicated, and (3) the signer acknowledged signing the document freely. Cf. VERIFICATION (1). **2.** The officer's certificate that is affixed to the document.—Also termed (loosely) *verification*.

acquired surplus. See SURPLUS.

acquisition. 1. The gaining of possession or control over something <acquisition of the target company's assets>. **2.** Something acquired <a valuable acquisition>.

acquittance, *n.* A document by which one is discharged from a debt or other obligation; a receipt or release indicating payment in full.

ACRS. *abbr.* ACCELERATED COST RECOVERY SYSTEM.

action on account. See ACCOUNTING (3).

active trust. See TRUST.

14

act of God. An overwhelming, unpreventable event caused exclusively by forces of nature, such as an earthquake, flood, or tornado. Cf. FORCE MAJEURE.

actual authority. See AUTHORITY.

actual bailment. See BAILMENT.

actual damages. See DAMAGES.

actual delivery. See DELIVERY.

actual eviction. See EVICTION.

actual fraud. See FRAUD.

actual knowledge. Direct and clear awareness or understanding of a fact or circumstance <the employer, having witnessed the accident, had actual knowledge of the worker's injury>. Cf. CONSTRUCTIVE KNOWLEDGE.

actual loss. See LOSS.

actual notice. See NOTICE.

actuarial table. An organized chart of statistical data indicating life expectancies for people falling within various categories (such as age, family history, or exposure to chemicals).—Also termed *mortality table*.

15

actuary. A statistician who determines the present effects of future contingent events; esp., one who calculates insurance and pension rates on the basis of empirically based tables.

ADA. *abbr.* AMERICANS WITH DISABILITIES ACT.

additional standard deduction. See DEDUCTION.

adequate protection. In bankruptcy law, the protection afforded to a holder of a secured claim against the debtor, such as a periodic cash payment or an additional lien <the bankruptcy court permitted the lender to foreclose on the debtor's home after finding a lack of adequate protection of the lender's property interest>.

adhesion contract. See CONTRACT.

adjustable-rate mortgage. See MORTGAGE.

adjusted basis. See BASIS.

adjusted gross income. See INCOME.

adjusted present value. See PRESENT VALUE.

adjusting entry. An accounting entry made at the end of an accounting period to record previously unrecognized revenue and expenses, as well as changes in assets and liabilities.

adjustment board. An administrative agency charged with the duty of hearing and deciding zoning appeals.—Also termed *board of zoning appeals*.

adjustment bond. See BOND (1).

adjustment security. See SECURITY.

administration. The management or performance of the executive duties of a government, institution, or business.

administrative adjudication. The process used by an administrative agency to issue regulations through an adversary proceeding.

administrative agency. See AGENCY (3).

administrative hearing. An administrative-agency proceeding in which evidence is offered for argument or trial.

administrative law. The law governing the organization and operation of the executive branch of government (including independent agencies) and the relations of the executive with the legislature, the judiciary, and the public.

administrative-law judge. An official who presides at an administrative hearing, with the power to administer oaths, take testimony, rule on questions of evidence, and make factual determinations.—Abbr. ALJ.—Also termed *administrative judge*; *hearing officer*.

administrative remedy. See REMEDY.

administrator. A person who manages a business, public office, or agency.

admiralty law. See MARITIME LAW.

adoption. In contract law, the process by which a person agrees to assume a contract previously made for that person's benefit, such as a newly formed corporation's acceptance of a preincorporation contract.

ADR. *abbr.* **1.** ALTERNATIVE DISPUTE RESOLUTION. **2.** AMERICAN DEPOSITORY RECEIPT. **3.** ASSET-DEPRECIATION RANGE.

ad valorem tax. See TAX.

adversary proceeding. In bankruptcy law, a lawsuit brought within a bankruptcy proceeding and based on conflicting claims usu. between the debtor (or the trustee) and a creditor or other interested party <the Chapter 7 trustee filed an adversary proceeding against

the party who received $100,000 from the debtor one week before the bankruptcy filing>.

adverse opinion. An outside auditor's statement that a company's financial statements do not conform with generally accepted accounting principles or do not accurately reflect the company's financial position.

advertising substantiation. A doctrine of the Federal Trade Commission making it an unfair and deceptive act to issue an advertisement unless the advertiser has a reasonable basis for believing that each claim in the advertisement is true.

advising bank. See BANK.

affidavit. A voluntary declaration of facts written down and sworn to by the declarant before an officer authorized to administer oaths. ● A great deal of evidence is submitted by affidavit, esp. in pretrial matters such as summary-judgment motions.

affiliate (ə-**fil**-ee-ət), *n.* **1.** A corporation that is related to another corporation by shareholdings or other means of control; a subsidiary, parent, or sibling corporation. **2.** In securities law, one who controls, is controlled by, or is under common control with an issuer of a security. See CONTROL PERSON.

affiliated group. A chain of corporations that can choose to file a consolidated tax return because at least 80% of each corporation is owned by others in the group.

affirmative action. A set of actions designed to eliminate existing and continuing discrimination, to remedy lingering effects of past discrimination, and to create systems and procedures to prevent future discrimination. See *reverse discrimination* under DISCRIMINATION.

AFL-CIO. *abbr.* AMERICAN FEDERATION OF LABOR AND CONGRESS OF INDUSTRIAL ORGANIZATIONS.

after-acquired property. 1. A debtor's property that is acquired after a secured transaction and becomes additional security for payment of the debt. **2.** In bankruptcy law, property that the bankruptcy estate acquires after commencement of the bankruptcy proceeding.

after-acquired-title doctrine. In property law, the principle that title to property automatically vests in a person who bought the property from a seller who acquired title only after purporting to sell the property to the buyer.

Age Discrimination in Employment Act.
A federal law prohibiting job discrimination
based on a person's age. ● Passed in 1967, the
Act applies to businesses with more than 20
employees and to governmental entities.

agency. 1. A fiduciary relationship created by
express or implied contract or by law, in which
one party (the *agent*) may act on behalf of
another party (the *principal*) and bind that
other party by words or actions. See AUTHORITY.

> *agency by estoppel.* An agency created by
> operation of law and established by a princi-
> pal's actions that would lead a reasonable
> third party to conclude that an agency ex-
> ists.—Also termed *apparent agency*.

> *exclusive agency.* The right to represent a
> principal—esp. either to sell the principal's
> products or to act as the seller's real-estate
> agent—within a particular market free from
> competition.

> *general agency.* A principal's delegation to
> an agent, without restriction, to take any
> action connected with a particular trade,
> business, or employment.

> *special agency.* An agency in which the
> agent is authorized only to conduct a single
> transaction or a series of transactions not
> involving continuous service.

undisclosed agency. A relationship between an agent and a third party who has no knowledge that the agent is acting on a principal's behalf. ● The fact that the agency is undisclosed does not prohibit the third party from seeking redress from the principal or the agent.

2. An agent's place of business. **3.** A governmental body charged with implementing and administering particular legislation, such as the Federal Communications Commission.— Also termed (in sense 3) *administrative agency*.

independent agency. A federal agency, commission, or board that is not under the direction of the executive, such as the Federal Trade Commission or the Environmental Protection Agency.

agency by estoppel. See AGENCY (1).

agency security. See *government security* under SECURITY.

agency shop. A business in which a union acts as an agent for the employees, regardless of their union membership.

agent. One who is authorized to act for or in place of another; a representative <a profes-

sional athlete's agent>. Cf. PRINCIPAL (1); EM-PLOYEE.

> ***apparent agent.*** A person who reasonably appears to have authority to act for another, regardless of whether actual authority has been conferred. See *apparent authority* under AUTHORITY.

> ***bargaining agent.*** A labor union in its capacity of representing employees in collective bargaining.

> ***co-agent.*** A person who shares with another agent the authority to act for the principal.

> ***corporate agent.*** An agent authorized to act on behalf of a corporation; broadly, all employees and officers who have the power to bind the corporation.

> ***del credere agent.*** An agent who guarantees the solvency of the third party with whom the agent makes a contract for the principal. • A del credere agent receives possession of the principal's goods for purposes of sale and guarantees that anyone to whom the agent sells the goods on .credit will pay promptly for them. For this guaranty, the agent receives a higher commission for sales.

> ***general agent.*** An agent authorized to transact all the principal's business of a

particular kind or in a particular place. •
Among the common types of general agents
are factors, brokers, and partners.

independent agent. An agent who exercises his or her own judgment and is subject to
the principal only for the results of the work
performed.

local agent. An agent appointed to act as
another's (esp. a company's) representative
and to transact business within a specified
district.

managing agent. A person with general
power involving the exercise of judgment
and discretion, as opposed to an ordinary
agent who acts under the direction and control of the principal.

public agent. A person appointed to act for
the public in matters pertaining to governmental administration or public business.

registered agent. A person authorized to
accept service of process for another person,
esp. a corporation, in a particular jurisdiction.—Also termed *resident agent.*

special agent. An agent employed to conduct a particular transaction or to perform a
specified act.

statutory agent. An agent designated by law to receive litigation documents and other legal notices for a nonresident corporation. ● In most states, the secretary of state is the statutory agent for such corporations.

stock-transfer agent. An organization that oversees and maintains records of transfers of shares for a corporation.

subagent. A person appointed by an agent to perform some duty relating to the agency.

transfer agent. An organization, usu. a bank or trust company, responsible for transferring title to a publicly traded company's securities. ● Transfer agents are often appointed to maintain lists of a company's shareholders and to mail out dividend payments.

universal agent. An agent authorized to perform all acts that the principal could personally perform.

aggregate concept. An approach to taxing business organizations (esp. partnerships) whereby the organization is viewed as a collection of its individual owners, not as a separate taxable entity.

aggregate supply. See SUPPLY.

25

aggressor corporation. See CORPORATION.

agreement. A mutual understanding between two or more persons about their relative rights and duties regarding past or future performances.

airbill. A bill of lading for goods transported by air.

aleatory contract. See CONTRACT.

alien, *n.* A person who resides within the borders of a country but is not a citizen or subject of that country; a person not owing allegiance to a particular nation. • In the United States, an alien is a person who is born outside the jurisdiction of the United States, who is subject to some foreign government, and who has not been granted citizenship under U.S. law.

> *illegal alien.* An alien who enters a country at the wrong time or place, eludes an examination by officials, obtains entry by fraud, or enters into a sham marriage to evade immigration laws.—Also termed *undocumented alien.*

alienation. Conveyance or transfer of property to another <alienation of one's land>.

ALJ. *abbr*. ADMINISTRATIVE-LAW JUDGE.

all-events test. A requirement that all events fixing an accrual-method taxpayer's right to receive income or incur expense must occur before the taxpayer can report an item of income or expense.

all-holders rule. 1. An SEC rule that prohibits a public offering by the issuer of shares to some, but less than all, of the holders of a class of shares. **2.** An SEC rule requiring a tender offeror to make its offer to all of the subject company's shareholders.

allocation. A designation or apportionment for a specific purpose; esp., the crediting of a receipt or the charging of a disbursement to an account <allocation of funds>.

allograph (**al**-ə-graf *or* **al**-oh-graf). An agent's writing or signature for the principal.

allonge (ə-**lonj**). A slip of paper sometimes attached to a negotiable instrument for the purpose of receiving further indorsements when the original paper is filled with indorsements.

all-or-none offering. See OFFERING.

allotment. A share or portion of something, such as property previously held in common or shares in a corporation.

allowance. 1. The sum awarded by a court to a fiduciary as payment for services. **2.** A share or portion, esp. of money that is assigned or granted. **3.** A deduction.

all-risk insurance. See INSURANCE.

alter ego. A corporation used by an individual in conducting personal business, the result being that a court may impose liability on the individual by piercing the corporate veil when fraud has been perpetrated on someone dealing with the corporation. See PIERCING THE CORPORATE VEIL.

alter-ego rule. The doctrine that shareholders will be treated as the owners of a corporation's property, or as the real parties in interest, whenever it is necessary to do so to prevent fraud or to do justice.

alternative constituency. See NONSHAREHOLDER CONSTITUENCY.

alternative contract. See CONTRACT.

alternative dispute resolution. A procedure for settling a dispute by means other than litigation, such as arbitration, mediation, or minitrial.—Abbr. ADR.

alternative minimum tax. See TAX.

amalgamation (ə-mal-gə-**may**-shən). The act of combining or uniting; consolidation <amalgamation of two small companies to form a new corporation>. Cf. MERGER.

ambiguity (am-bi-**gyoo**-ə-dee). An uncertainty of meaning or intention, esp. in a contractual term.

   latent ambiguity. An ambiguity that does not readily appear in the language of a document, but instead arises from a collateral matter when the document's terms are applied or executed <the contract contained a latent ambiguity because the shipping terms stated the goods would arrive on the ship *Peerless*, but two ships have that name>.

   patent ambiguity (**pay**-tənt). An ambiguity that clearly appears on the face of a document, arising from the language itself <the nonperformance was excused because the two different prices expressed in the contract created a patent ambiguity>.

amended return. See TAX RETURN.

American Academy of Actuaries. A national organization of actuaries who must meet specified educational requirements and have at least three years of actuarial work experience. ● Created in 1965, the Academy promotes public awareness of the actuarial profession, represents the profession before federal and state governments, and sponsors continuing-education conferences.—Abbr. AAA. See ACTUARY.

American Accounting Association. An organization of accounting practitioners, educators, and students. ● The Association, founded in 1916, promotes accounting as an academic discipline by sponsoring research projects and continuing-education seminars.—Abbr. AAA.

American Arbitration Association. A national organization that maintains a panel of arbitrators to hear labor and commercial disputes.—Abbr. AAA.

American depository receipt. A receipt issued by an American bank as a substitute for stock shares in a foreign-based corporation.—Abbr. ADR.

American Federation of Labor and Congress of Industrial Organizations. A voluntary affiliation of more than 100 labor unions that operate autonomously yet benefit from the affiliation's establishment of broad policies for the national labor movement.—Abbr. AFL-CIO.

American rule. The requirement that each litigant must pay its own attorney's fees, even if the party prevails in the lawsuit. ● The rule is subject to bad faith and other statutory and contractual exceptions. Cf. ENGLISH RULE.

American Stock Exchange. An organized stock exchange, located in New York City, for trading national corporate stocks. ● It often trades in the securities of new or small companies because its listing requirements are less strict than those of the New York Stock Exchange.—Abbr. AMEX; ASE.

Americans with Disabilities Act. A federal statute that prohibits discrimination against physically or mentally disabled persons in employment, public services, and public accommodations (including those operated by private entities).—Abbr. ADA.

AMEX. *abbr.* AMERICAN STOCK EXCHANGE.

amortization (am-ərd-ə-**zay**-shən *or* -ərt-). **1.** The act or result of gradually extinguishing a debt, such as a mortgage, usu. by contributing payments of principal each time a periodic interest payment is due.

negative amortization. An increase in a loan's principal balance caused by monthly payments insufficient to pay accruing interest.

2. The act or result of apportioning the initial cost of a usu. intangible asset, such as a patent, over the asset's useful life. Cf. DEPRECIATION.

amortized loan. See LOAN.

amortized mortgage. See MORTGAGE.

annual exclusion. See EXCLUSION.

annual meeting. See MEETING.

annual percentage rate. See INTEREST RATE.

annual report. A yearly corporate financial report for shareholders and other interested parties. ● An annual report typically includes a balance sheet, income statement, statement of changes in financial position, reconciliation of changes in owners' equity accounts, a summary of significant accounting principles, other explanatory notes, the auditor's report, and comments from management about prospects for the coming year. For publicly held companies, the SEC prescribes the information that must be included.

annuitant (ə-**n[y]oo**-ə-tənt). A beneficiary of an annuity.

annuity. 1. An obligation to pay a stated sum, usu. monthly or annually, to a stated recipient. ● These payments terminate upon the death of the designated beneficiary. **2.** A fixed sum of money payable periodically. **3.** A right, often acquired under a life-insurance contract, to receive fixed payments periodically for a specified duration. Cf. PENSION. **4.** A savings account with an insurance company or investment company, usu. established for retirement income. ● Payments into the account accumulate tax-free, and the account is taxed only when the annuitant withdraws money in retirement.

annuity certain. An annuity payable over a specified period, regardless of whether the annuitant dies.

annuity due. An annuity that makes payments at the beginning of each pay period. Cf. *ordinary annuity*.

contingent annuity. **a.** An annuity that begins making payments when some future event occurs, such as the death of a person other than the annuitant. **b.** An annuity that makes an uncertain number of pay-

33

ments, depending on the outcome of a future event.

deferred annuity. An annuity that begins making payments on a specified date if the annuitant is alive at that time.

fixed annuity. An annuity that guarantees fixed payments, either for life or for a specified period.

group annuity. An annuity payable to members of a group, esp. employees, who are covered by a single annuity contract, such as a group pension plan.

life annuity. An annuity payable only during the annuitant's lifetime, even if the annuitant dies prematurely.

nonrefund annuity. An annuity with guaranteed payments during the annuitant's life, but with no refund to anyone at death.— Also termed *straight life annuity*.

ordinary annuity. An annuity that makes payments at the end of each pay period. Cf. *annuity due*.

refund annuity. An annuity that, upon the annuitant's death, pays to the annuitant's estate the difference between the purchase price and the total payments received during the annuitant's lifetime.

straight annuity. An annuity that makes payments in fixed amounts at periodic intervals. Cf. *variable annuity.*

survivorship annuity. An annuity providing for continued payments to a survivor, usu. a spouse, after the original annuitant dies.

tax-deferred annuity. An annuity to which an educator and an employee of a nonprofit organization can make tax-deferred contributions to supplement a pension plan. ● Taxes are not due until the annuitant actually receives funds from the annuity.

variable annuity. An annuity that makes payments in varying amounts depending on the success of investment strategy. Cf. *straight annuity.*

annuity bond. See BOND (1).

annuity certain. See ANNUITY.

annuity due. See ANNUITY.

anomalous indorsement. See *irregular indorsement* under INDORSEMENT.

antecedent debt. See DEBT.

anticipatory breach. See BREACH OF CONTRACT.

anticipatory repudiation. See REPUDIATION.

antidilution provision. A convertible-security provision that safeguards the conversion privilege from share splits, share dividends, or other transactions that might affect the conversion ratio. See CONVERSION RATIO; DILUTION (1).

antidumping law. A statute designed to protect domestic companies by preventing the sale of foreign goods at a price below that of the domestic market. See DUMPING.

antitakeover statute. A state law that helps protect companies based in the state from hostile takeovers.

antitrust law. The body of law designed to protect trade and commerce from restraints, monopolies, price-fixing, and price discrimination. ● The principal federal antitrust laws are the Sherman Act and the Clayton Act.

apparent agency. See *agency by estoppel* under AGENCY (1).

apparent agent. See AGENT.

apparent authority. See AUTHORITY.

apportionment. 1. Division into proportionate shares. **2.** The act of allocating or attributing moneys or expenses in a given way, as when a taxpayer allocates part of profits to a particular tax year or part of the use of a car to a business.

appraisal. 1. The determination of what constitutes a fair price; valuation; estimation of worth. **2.** The report of such a determination. Cf. ASSESSMENT (3).

appraisal remedy. The statutory right of corporate shareholders who oppose some extraordinary corporate action (such as a merger) to have their shares judicially appraised and to demand that the corporation buy back their shares at the appraised value.—Also termed *appraisal right*; *dissenters' right*; *right of dissent and appraisal*.

appreciation. An increase in an asset's value, usu. because of inflation. Cf. DEPRECIATION.

appreciation surplus. See *reevaluation surplus* under SURPLUS.

appropriated retained earnings. See EARNINGS.

APR. See *annual percentage rate* under INTEREST RATE.

APV. See *adjusted present value* under PRESENT VALUE.

arbitrage (**ahr**-bə-trahzh). The simultaneous buying and selling of identical securities in different markets, with the hope of profiting from the price difference in those markets.

> **kind arbitrage.** Purchase of a security that, having no restriction other than the payment of money, is exchangeable or convertible within a reasonable time to a second security, with a simultaneous offsetting sale of the second security.—Also termed *convertible arbitrage.*

> **risk arbitrage.** Arbitrage of assets that are probably, but not necessarily, equivalent; esp., arbitrage of corporate stock in a potential merger or takeover, whereby the target company's stock is bought and the acquiring company's stock is sold simultaneously.

> **time arbitrage.** Purchase of a commodity against a present sale of the identical commodity for a future delivery; esp., the simultaneous buying and selling of securities for immediate delivery and future delivery, with the hope of profiting from the difference in prices.

arbitrage bond. See BOND (1).

arbitration. A method of dispute resolution involving one or more neutral third parties who are usu. agreed to by the disputing parties and whose decision is binding. Cf. MEDIATION.

arbitration clause. A contractual provision mandating arbitration—and thereby avoiding litigation—of disputes about the contracting parties' rights, duties, and liabilities.

arbitration of exchange. The simultaneous buying and selling of bills of exchange in different international markets, hoping to profit from the price difference of the currencies in those markets. See ARBITRAGE.

arbitrator. A neutral person chosen to resolve disputes between parties, esp. by means of formal arbitration.

Areeda-Turner test. In antitrust law, an economic test for predatory pricing whereby a price below average variable cost is presumed to be predatory and therefore illegal. • This test is widely accepted by federal courts.

ARM. See *adjustable-rate mortgage* under MORTGAGE.

arm's-length, *adj.* Of or relating to dealings between two parties who are not related or not on close terms and who are presumed to have roughly equal bargaining power; not involving a confidential relationship <an arm's-length transaction normally does not create fiduciary duties between the parties>.

arrangement with creditors. In bankruptcy law, a debtor's arrangement with creditors for the settlement, satisfaction, or extension of time for payment of debts. See BANKRUPTCY PLAN.

arrear, *n.* (*usu. pl.*) **1.** The state of being behind in the payment of a debt or the discharge of an obligation <the creditor filed a lawsuit against the debtor who was in arrears>.—Also termed *arrearage*. **2.** An unpaid or overdue debt <the creditor reached an agreement with the debtor on settling the arrears>.

articles of association. 1. See ARTICLES OF INCORPORATION. **2.** A document—similar to articles of incorporation—that legally creates a nonstock or nonprofit organization.

articles of dissolution. The document that a dissolving corporation must file with the appropriate governmental agency, usu. the secretary of state, after the corporation has settled all its debts and distributed all its assets.

articles of incorporation. The document that sets forth the basic terms of a corporation's existence, including the number and classes of shares and the purposes and duration of the corporation. ● In most states, the articles of incorporation are filed with the secretary of state as part of the process of forming the corporation. In some states, the articles serve as a certificate of incorporation and are the official recognition of the corporation's existence. In other states, the government issues a certificate of incorporation after approving the articles and other required documents.—Also termed *articles of association*. Cf. BYLAW; CHARTER (1).

artificial person. An entity, such as a corporation, created by law and given certain legal rights and duties of a human being.—Also termed *fictitious person*; *legal person*.

artisan's lien. See *mechanic's lien* under LIEN.

ASE. *abbr*. AMERICAN STOCK EXCHANGE.

as is, *adj. & adv.* In the existing condition without modification <the customer bought the car as is>. ● Under the UCC, a seller can disclaim all implied warranties by stating that the goods are being sold "as is" or "with all faults." Generally, a sale of property "as is" means that the property is sold in its existing condition, and use of the phrase *as is* relieves the seller from liability for defects in that condition.—Also termed *with all faults*.

asked price. See PRICE.

asking price. See PRICE.

assessment. 1. Determination of the rate or amount of something, such as a tax or damages <assessment of the losses covered by insurance>. **2.** Imposition of something, such as a tax or fine, according to an established rate; the tax or fine so imposed <assessment of a luxury tax>.

deficiency assessment. An assessment by the IRS—after administrative review and tax-court adjudication—of additional tax owed by a taxpayer who underpaid.

jeopardy assessment. An assessment by the IRS—without the usual review procedures—of additional tax owed by a taxpayer who underpaid, based on the IRS's belief that a delay would jeopardize its ability to collect the deficiency.

special assessment. The assessment of a tax on property that benefits in some important way from a public improvement.

3. Official valuation of property for purposes of taxation <assessment of the condominium>. Cf. APPRAISAL (1).

assessment bond. See BOND (1).

assessor. One who evaluates or makes assessments, esp. for purposes of taxation.

asset. 1. An item that is owned and has value. **2.** (*pl.*) The entries on a balance sheet showing the items of property owned, including cash, inventory, equipment, real estate, accounts receivable, and goodwill. **3.** (*pl.*) All the property of a person (esp. a bankrupt or deceased person) available for paying debts.

>*asset under management.* A securities portfolio for which an investment adviser provides ongoing, regular supervisory or management services.

>*capital asset.* **a.** A long-term asset used in operating a business or in producing goods or services, such as equipment, land, or an industrial plant.—Also termed *fixed asset.* **b.** For income-tax purposes, any of the assets held by a taxpayer except those specifically excluded by the Internal Revenue Code. • Excluded from the definition are, among other things, stock in trade, inventory, and property held by the taxpayer primarily for

sale to customers in the ordinary course of trade or business.

current asset. An asset that is readily convertible into cash, such as a marketable security, a note, or an account receivable.— Also termed *liquid asset*; *quick asset*.

dead asset. A worthless asset that has no realizable value, such as an uncollectible account receivable.

frozen asset. **a.** An asset that is difficult to convert into cash. **b.** An asset that cannot be used because of legal restrictions.

hidden asset. An asset carried on the books at a substantially reduced or understated value—considerably less than market value.

intangible asset. An asset that is not a physical object, such as a patent, a trademark, or goodwill.

nominal asset. An asset whose value is difficult to assess, such as a judgment or claim.

real asset. An asset in the form of land.

wasting asset. An asset exhausted through use or the loss of value, such as an oil well or a coal deposit.

asset acquisition. Acquisition of a corporation by purchasing all its assets directly from the corporation itself, rather than by purchasing shares from its shareholders. Cf. SHARE ACQUISITION.

asset allocation. The spreading of funds between different types of investments with the hope of decreasing risk and increasing return.

asset-based financing. See FINANCING.

asset-coverage test. In accounting, a bond-indenture restriction that permits additional borrowing only if the ratio of assets (typically net tangible assets) to debt (typically long-term debt) does not fall below a specified minimum.

asset-depreciation range. The IRS's range of depreciation lifetimes allowed for assets placed in service between 1970 and 1980 and for assets depreciated under the Modified Accelerated Cost Recovery System under the Tax Reform Act of 1986.—Abbr. ADR.

asset dividend. See DIVIDEND.

asset under management. See ASSET.

assigned account. See ACCOUNT.

45

assignee (as-ə-**nee** *or* ə-**sīn**-ee). One to whom property rights or powers are transferred by another.—Also termed *assign*.

assignment. 1. The transfer of rights or property <assignment of stock options>. **2.** The rights or property so transferred <the creditor took the assignment>. **3.** The instrument of transfer <the assignment was appended to the contract>.

assignment for the benefit of creditors. Assignment of a debtor's property to another person in trust so as to consolidate and liquidate the debtor's assets for payment to creditors, any surplus being returned to the debtor. ● This procedure serves as a state-law substitute for federal bankruptcy proceedings. The debtor is not discharged from unpaid debts by this procedure since creditors do not agree to any discharge.

assignment-of-rents clause. A mortgage provision or separate agreement that entitles the mortgagee to collect rents from the mortgaged premises if the mortgagor defaults.

assignor (as-ə-**nor** *or* ə-**sīn**-ər). One who transfers property rights or powers to another.

association. An unincorporated business organization that is not a legal entity separate from the persons who compose it. • If an association has sufficient corporate attributes, such as centralized management, continuity of existence, and limited liability, it may be classified and taxed as a corporation.—Also termed *unincorporated association*.

>   ***professional association.*** A group of professionals organized to practice their profession together, though not necessarily in corporate or partnership form.—Abbr. P.A.

assumed name. The name under which a business operates or by which it is commonly known <Antex Corporation's assumed name is Computer Warehouse>. • Many states require an individual or business operating under an assumed name to file an assumed-name certificate, usu. in the secretary of state's office or the county clerk's office where the principal place of business is located. See D/B/A. Cf. CORPORATE NAME.

assurance. A pledge or guarantee <adequate assurances of the borrower's solvency>.

attachment. 1. The creation of a security interest in property, occurring when the debtor agrees to the security, receives value from the secured party, and obtains rights in the collateral. Cf. PERFECTION. **2.** The seizing of one's property to secure a judgment or to be sold in satisfaction of a judgment. Cf. GARNISH-MENT; SEQUESTRATION. **3.** A writ ordering legal seizure of property, esp. to satisfy a creditor's claim.—Also termed (in sense 3) *writ of attachment*.

at-the-market price. See PRICE.

attorney. 1. Strictly, one who is designated to transact business for another; a legal agent.—Also termed *attorney-in-fact*. **2.** A person who practices law; a lawyer.—Also termed (in sense 2) *attorney-at-law*. Cf. COUNSEL.

attorney-client privilege. The client's right to refuse to disclose and to prevent any other person from disclosing confidential communications between the client and his or her attorney.

attractive-nuisance doctrine. In tort law, the rule that a person who owns property with a dangerous thing or condition that will foreseeably lure children to trespass is under a duty to protect those children from the danger.

attribution. The process—outlined in the Internal Revenue Code—by which a person's or entity's stock ownership is assigned to a related family member or entity for tax purposes.

auction, *n.* A sale of property to the highest bidder. • Under the UCC, a sale at auction is complete when the auctioneer so announces in a customary manner, such as the fall of a hammer.

audit, *n.* A formal examination of an individual's or organization's accounting records or financial situation. See GENERALLY ACCEPTED AUDITING STANDARDS.

correspondence audit. An IRS audit of a taxpayer's return conducted by mail or telephone.

field audit. An IRS audit conducted at the taxpayer's business premises or lawyer's offices.

independent audit. An audit conducted by an outside person or firm not connected with the organization being audited.

internal audit. An audit performed by an organization's personnel to ensure that internal procedures, operations, and accounting practices are being properly administered.

office audit. An IRS audit of a taxpayer's return conducted in the IRS agent's office.

post audit. An audit of funds spent on a completed capital project, the purpose being to assess the efficiency with which the funds were spent and to compare expected cash-flow estimates with actual cash flows.

tax audit. The review of a taxpayer's return by the IRS, including an examination of the taxpayer's books, vouchers, and records supporting the return.

auditor. A person or firm, usu. an accountant or an accounting firm, that formally examines an individual's or entity's financial records or status.

audit trail. The chain of evidence connecting account balances to original transactions and calculations.

authority. The right or permission to act on another's behalf; the power delegated by a principal to an agent <authority to sign the contract>. See AGENCY.

actual authority. Authority that a principal intentionally confers on an agent, including the authority that the agent reasonably believes he or she has as a result of the agent's dealings with the principal. • Actual authority can be either express or implied.

apparent authority. Authority that a third party reasonably believes an agent has, based on the third party's dealings with the principal. ● Apparent authority can be created by law even when no actual authority has been conferred.

authority coupled with an interest. Authority given to an agent for valuable consideration. ● This authority cannot be unilaterally terminated by the principal.

express authority. Authority given to the agent by explicit agreement, either orally or in writing.

implied authority. Authority given to the agent as a result of the principal's conduct, such as the principal's earlier acquiescence to the agent's actions.

incidental authority. Authority needed to carry out actual or apparent authority. ● For example, the actual authority to borrow money includes the incidental authority to sign commercial paper to bring about the loan.

naked authority. Authority delegated solely for the principal's benefit, no consideration being given to the agent. ● This authority can be revoked by the principal at any time.

authorized committee. See SPECIAL LITIGATION COMMITTEE.

51

authorized shares. See *authorized stock* under STOCK.

authorized stock. See STOCK.

automatic stay. See STAY.

average daily balance. See DAILY BALANCE.

average tax rate. See TAX RATE.

B

baby bond. See BOND (1).

Baby FTC Act. A state statute that, like the Federal Trade Commission Act, outlaws deceptive and unfair practices.

backdate, *vb.* **1.** To put a date earlier than the actual date on (something, as an instrument). ● Under the UCC, backdating does not affect an instrument's negotiability. Cf. POST-DATE. **2.** To make (something) retroactively valid.

back-to-back loan. See LOAN.

backwardation. In securities transactions, a fee paid by the seller so that the buyer will allow delivery of the securities after their original delivery date.—Also termed *backadation*.

bad-boy disqualification. An issuer's disqualification from certain SEC-registration exemptions as a result of the issuer's securities-law violations.

bad check. See CHECK.

bad debt. See DEBT.

bad-debt reserve. See RESERVE.

bad faith, *n*. **1.** Dishonesty of belief or purpose <the lawyer filed the pleading in bad faith>. **2.** An insurance company's unreasonable and unfounded (though not necessarily fraudulent) refusal to provide coverage <the insurer's decision not to pay for the roof damage was bad faith>. **3.** An insured's claim against an insurance company for an unreasonable and unfounded refusal to provide coverage <Cox sued the insurer for bad faith and breach of contract>. Cf. GOOD FAITH.

badge of fraud. An act or fact that the courts generally interpret as a reliable indicator that a party to a transaction was trying to hinder or defraud the other party, such as a transfer in anticipation of litigation, a transaction outside the usual course of business, or lying to the other party. See FRAUD.

bad title. See TITLE.

bailment. 1. A delivery of personal property by one person (the *bailor*) to another (the *bailee*) who holds the property under an express or implied-in-fact contract. • Unlike a sale or gift of personal property, a bailment involves a change in possession but not in title. **2.** The personal property delivered by the bailor to the bailee.

actual bailment. A bailment that arises from an actual or constructive delivery of property to the bailee.

bailment for hire. A bailment for which the bailee is compensated, as when one leaves a car with a parking attendant.

bailment for mutual benefit. A bailment for which the bailee is compensated and from which the bailor receives some additional benefit, as when one leaves a car with a parking attendant who will also wash the car while it is parked.

constructive bailment. A bailment that arises when the law imposes an obligation on a possessor of personal property to return the property to its rightful owner, as with an involuntary bailment.

gratuitous bailment. A bailment for which the bailee receives no compensation, as when one borrows a friend's car. • A gratuitous bailee is liable for loss of the property only if the loss is caused by the bailee's gross negligence.

involuntary bailment. A bailment that arises when a person accidentally, but without any negligence, leaves personal property in another's possession. • An involuntary bailee who refuses to return the property to the owner may be liable for conversion.

55

bailout, *n.* **1.** A rescue of an entity, usu. a corporation, from financial trouble. **2.** An attempt by a business owner to receive favorable tax treatment of its profits, such as by withdrawing profits at capital-gain rates rather than distributing stock dividends that would be taxed at higher ordinary-income rates.

bait and switch. A sales practice whereby a store advertises a low-priced product to lure customers into the store only to induce them to buy a higher-priced product. ● Most states prohibit the bait and switch when the original product is not actually available as advertised.

balance, *vb.* **1.** To calculate the difference between the debits and credits of (an account) <the accountant balanced the company's books>. **2.** To equalize in number, force, or effect; to bring into proportion <the company tried to balance the ratio of mid-level managers to assembly-line workers>.

balanced economy. See ECONOMY.

balanced fund. See MUTUAL FUND.

balance sheet. A statement of an entity's current financial position, disclosing the value of the entity's assets, liabilities, and owners' equity.—Also termed *statement of financial position*. Cf. INCOME STATEMENT.

balance-sheet insolvency. See INSOLVENCY.

balloon note. See NOTE.

balloon payment. See PAYMENT.

balloon-payment mortgage. See MORTGAGE.

bank. A financial establishment for the deposit, loan, exchange, or issue of money and for the transmission of funds; esp., a member of the Federal Reserve System.

advising bank. A bank that gives notice that another bank has issued a letter of credit.

collecting bank. In the check-collection process, any bank handling an item for collection except the payor bank or the depository bank.

commercial bank. A bank authorized to receive both demand and time deposits, to engage in trust services, to issue letters of credit, to rent time-deposit boxes, and to supply similar services.

confirming bank. A bank that declares either that it will honor a letter of credit issued by another bank or that such a credit will be honored by the issuer or a third bank.

correspondent bank. A bank that acts as an agent for another bank, or engages in an exchange of services with that bank, in a geographical area to which the other bank does not have direct access.

custodian bank. A bank or trust company that (1) is supervised and examined by state or federal authority having supervision over banks and (2) acts as custodian for a clearing corporation.

depositary bank. The first bank to which an item is transferred for collection.

drawee bank. See *payor bank.*

intermediary bank. A bank to which an item is transferred in the course of collection, even though the bank is not the depositary or payor bank.

investment bank. A bank whose primary purpose is to acquire financing for businesses, esp. through the sale of securities. ● An investment bank does not accept deposits and, apart from selling securities, does not deal with the public at large. Cf. INVESTMENT BANKER.

member bank. A bank that is a member of the Federal Reserve System.—Also termed *reserve bank.* See FEDERAL RESERVE SYSTEM.

mutual savings bank. A bank that has no capital stock and in which the depositors are the owners. See SAVINGS-AND-LOAN ASSOCIATION.

national bank. A bank incorporated under federal law and governed by a federally approved charter.

payor bank. A bank that is requested to pay the amount of a negotiable instrument and, on the bank's acceptance, is obliged to pay that amount; a bank by which an item is payable as drawn or accepted.—Also termed *drawee bank.*

presenting bank. A nonpayor bank that presents a negotiable instrument for payment.

respondent bank. A bank, association, or other entity that exercises fiduciary powers, that holds securities on behalf of beneficial owners, and that deposits the securities for safekeeping with another bank, association, or other entity exercising fiduciary powers.

savings bank. A bank that receives deposits, pays interest on them, and makes certain types of loans, but does not provide checking services.

59

state bank. A bank chartered by a state and supervised by the state banking department and the FDIC. ● A state bank must follow Federal Reserve Board regulations even if it is not a member of the Federal Reserve System.

bankbook. See PASSBOOK.

bank charter. See CHARTER.

bank draft. See DRAFT.

banker's acceptance. See ACCEPTANCE.

bank examiner. A federal or state official who audits banks with respect to their financial condition, management, and policies.

bank note. See NOTE.

bank rate. See INTEREST RATE.

bankrupt, *n.* **1.** A person who cannot meet his or her financial obligations; an insolvent person. **2.** DEBTOR (2).

bankruptcy. 1. The statutory procedure, usu. triggered by insolvency, by which a person is relieved of most debts and undergoes a judicially supervised reorganization or liquidation for the benefit of that person's creditors. ● For various types of bankruptcy under federal law, see the entries at CHAPTER. **2.** Loosely, the fact of being financially unable to pay one's debts and meet one's obligations; insolvency.

> ***involuntary bankruptcy.*** Bankruptcy proceedings initiated by creditors (usu. three or more) to force the debtor to declare bankruptcy or be legally declared bankrupt.

> ***voluntary bankruptcy.*** Bankruptcy proceedings initiated by the debtor.

Bankruptcy Code. The Bankruptcy Reform Act of 1978 (as amended and codified in 11 USCA), which governs bankruptcy cases filed on or after October 1, 1979.

bankruptcy court. (*often cap.*) A federal court that is a unit of a district court and that is exclusively concerned with administering bankruptcy proceedings.

bankruptcy estate. A debtor's legal and equitable interests in property as of the commencement of a bankruptcy case.

bankruptcy plan. A detailed program of action formulated by a debtor or its creditors to govern the debtor's rehabilitation, continued operation or liquidation, and payment of debts.
• The bankruptcy court and creditors must

approve the plan before it is implemented.—
Often shortened to *plan*.—Also termed *plan of reorganization* (for Chapter 11); *plan of rehabilitation* (for Chapter 13). See ARRANGEMENT WITH CREDITORS.

bankruptcy proceeding. 1. See BANKRUPTCY (1). **2.** Any judicial or procedural action—usu. in bankruptcy court—related to a bankruptcy, such as a hearing.

bankruptcy-remote entity. A business, usu. a special-purpose entity, established to perform limited functions and to have one or a few primary creditors. • This type of entity is sometimes established to protect lenders on large, complex projects, when the lender is to be paid solely or almost exclusively out of the money generated when the project becomes operational. This business is established to have no function other than to develop, own, and operate the project, and to have no principal creditors other than the project lenders. In this way, the lenders have additional protection in that there are fewer creditors to compete for the money generated by the project, and there is less likelihood that the project will be forced into bankruptcy. A bankruptcy-remote entity will sometimes issue securities instead of just receiving a direct loan. See SPECIAL-PURPOSE ENTITY; *project financing* under FINANCING.

bankruptcy trustee. See TRUSTEE (2).

Bank Secrecy Act of 1970. A federal law requiring banks to maintain records of all transactions with depositors and to report deposits of more than $10,000 to the U.S. Treasury.

bargain, *n.* An agreement between parties for the exchange of promises or performances. ● A bargain is not necessarily a contract because the consideration may be insufficient or the transaction may be illegal.

bargain-and-sale deed. See DEED.

bargaining agent. See AGENT.

bargaining unit. A group of employees authorized to engage in collective bargaining on behalf of all the employees of one company.

barter, *n.* The exchange of one commodity for another without the use of money.

basic-form policy. See INSURANCE POLICY.

basis. The value assigned to a taxpayer's investment in property and used primarily for computing gain or loss from a transfer of the property. ● When the assigned value represents the cost of acquiring the property, it is also called *cost basis*.—Also termed *tax basis*.

>   *adjusted basis.* Basis increased by capital improvements and decreased by depreciation deductions.

>   *carryover basis.* A basis used for property transferred by gift or in trust, equaling the transferor's basis.—Also termed *substituted basis*.

>   *stepped-up basis.* The basis of property transferred by inheritance. ● Stepped-up basis equals the fair market value of property on the date of the decedent's death (or on the alternate valuation date).

>   *substituted basis.* **a.** The basis of property transferred in a tax-free exchange or other specified transactions. **b.** See *carryover basis*.

basis point. One-hundredth of one percent (.01%). ● Basis points are used in computing investment yields, apportioning costs, and figuring interest rates in real-estate transactions.

battle of the forms. The conflict between the terms of standard forms exchanged between a buyer and a seller during contract negotiations. ● The UCC attempts to resolve battles of the forms by abandoning the common-law requirement of mirror-image acceptance and providing that an acceptance with additional terms is normally valid. See MIRROR-IMAGE RULE.

bearer. One who possesses a negotiable instrument marked "payable to bearer" or indorsed in blank.

bearer bond. See BOND (1).

bearer paper. See PAPER.

bear market. See MARKET.

bear raid. *Slang*. High-volume stock selling by a large trader in an effort to drive down a stock price in a short time. • Bear raids are prohibited by federal law.

below-market loan. See *interest-free loan* under LOAN.

below-the-line, *adj*. (Of a deduction) taken after calculating adjusted gross income and before calculating taxable income. • Examples of below-the-line deductions are medical payments and local taxes. Cf. ABOVE-THE-LINE.

beneficial interest. A right or expectancy in something (such as a trust or an estate), as opposed to legal title to that thing. • For example, a person with a beneficial interest in a trust receives income from the trust but does not hold legal title to the trust property.

beneficial owner. See OWNER.

beneficiary. A person who is designated to benefit from an appointment, disposition, or assignment (as in a will, insurance policy, etc.); one designated to receive something as a result of a legal arrangement or instrument.

> *creditor beneficiary.* A third-party beneficiary who is owed a debt that is to be satisfied by performance of the contract.

> *incidental beneficiary.* A third-party beneficiary who is not intended to benefit from a contract and thus does not acquire rights under the contract.

> *third-party beneficiary.* A person who is not a party to a contract but who may benefit from the contract's performance. ● For example, if Ann and Bob agree to a contract under which Bob will render some performance to Chris, then Chris is a third-party beneficiary.

benefit, *n.* **1.** Profit or gain <a benefit received from the sale>.

> *fringe benefit.* A benefit received by an employee from an employer, other than di-

rect salary or compensation, such as insurance, a company car, or a tuition allowance.

general benefit. In the law of eminent domain, the whole community's benefit as a result of the taking. • It cannot be considered to reduce the compensation that is due the condemnee.

pecuniary benefit. A benefit capable of monetary valuation.

2. Financial assistance that is received from an employer, insurance, or a public program (such as social security) in time of sickness, disability, or unemployment <welfare benefits>.

benefit-of-the-bargain rule. The principle that a party who breaches a contract must provide the aggrieved party everything the aggrieved party would have received, including profits, had the contract been fully performed.

best efforts. Diligent attempts to carry out an obligation. • As a standard, a best-efforts obligation is stronger than a good-faith obligation <the contractor must use best efforts to complete its work within the stated time>. Cf. DUE DILIGENCE (1); GOOD FAITH.

best-efforts underwriting. See UNDERWRITING.

BFOQ. *abbr.* BONA FIDE OCCUPATIONAL QUALIFICA-
TION.

BFP. See *bona fide purchaser* under PURCHAS-
ER.

bid, *n.* **1.** A buyer's offer to pay a specified
price for something that may or may not be for
sale <a bid at an auction> <a takeover bid>.
2. A submitted price at which one will perform
work or supply goods <the subcontractor's
bid>.

  open bid. A bid that the bidder may reduce
  after submission in order to meet competing
  bids.

  sealed bid. A bid that is not disclosed until
  all submitted bids are opened and considered simultaneously.

bid and asked. In securities transactions, a
notation describing the range of prices quoted
in an over-the-counter stock exchange. ● *Bid*
denotes the buying price, and *asked* denotes
the selling price. See SPREAD (2).

bid price. See PRICE.

bifactoral obligation. See OBLIGATION.

bilateral contract. See CONTRACT.

bilateral monopoly. See MONOPOLY.

bill. 1. An itemized list of charges; an invoice <hospital bill>. **2.** A bill of exchange; a draft <the bank would not honor the unsigned bill>. See DRAFT.

> *finance bill.* A bill of exchange drawn by a bank in one country on a bank in another country for the purpose of raising short-term credit. ● Finance bills are often issued in tight money periods, and usu. have maturity dates of more than 60 days.

3. A formal document or note; an instrument <bill of sale>.

bill of exchange. See DRAFT.

bill of lading. A document of title acknowledging the receipt of goods by a carrier or by the shipper's agent; a document that indicates the receipt of goods for shipment and that is issued by a person engaged in the business of transporting or forwarding goods. ● An airbill is usu. included within the definition of the term.—Also termed *waybill*.

> *order bill of lading.* A negotiable bill of lading stating that the goods are consigned to the order of the person named in the bill.

straight bill of lading. A nonnegotiable bill of lading that specifies a consignee to whom the carrier is contractually obligated to deliver the goods.

bill of sale. An instrument for the conveyance of title to personal property. Cf. DEED.

binder. 1. A document in which the buyer and the seller of real property declare their common intention to bring about a transfer of ownership, usu. accompanied by the buyer's initial payment. **2.** Loosely, the buyer's initial payment in the sale of real property. Cf. EARNEST MONEY. **3.** An insurer's memorandum giving the insured temporary coverage while the application for an insurance policy is being processed.

blackmail suit. See SUIT.

black market. See MARKET.

blanket bond. See BOND (2).

blanket mortgage. See MORTGAGE.

blanket policy. See INSURANCE POLICY.

blank indorsement. See INDORSEMENT.

block, *n.* A quantity of things bought or sold as a unit <a block of preferred shares>.

blockage rule. The principle allowing a large block of stock shares to be valued for tax purposes at less than the sum of the values of the individual shares because such a large block may be difficult to sell at full price.

blocked income. See INCOME.

blue chip, *n.* A corporate stock that is considered a safe investment because the corporation has a history of stability, consistent growth, and reliable earnings.—Also termed *blue-chip stock*.

blue law. A statute regulating or prohibiting commercial activity on Sundays. • Formerly common, blue laws have been on the decline since the 1980s, when many courts held them invalid because of their origin in religion (i.e., Sunday being the Christian Sabbath). Blue laws usu. pass constitutional challenge if they are enacted to support a nonreligious purpose, such as a day of rest for workers.

blue-sky law. A state statute establishing standards for offering and selling securities, the purpose being to protect citizens from investing in fraudulent or otherwise unsuitable companies.

board of directors. The governing body of a corporation, elected by the shareholders to establish corporate policy, appoint executive officers, and make major business and financial decisions. See DIRECTOR.

> *staggered board of directors.* A board of directors in which a fraction of the board is elected every year to serve for two or three years.

Board of Governors. The group of persons who oversee the Federal Reserve System.

board of zoning appeals. See ADJUSTMENT BOARD.

boilerplate, *n*. **1.** Ready-made or all-purpose language that will fit in a variety of documents. **2.** Fixed or standardized contractual language that, in the view of the party whose forms contain it, is rarely subject to modification.

bona fide occupational qualification. An employment qualification that discriminates against a protected class (such as sex, religion, or national origin) but that also relates to an essential job duty and is reasonably necessary to the operations of the particular business. • This type of qualification is not illegal under federal employment-discrimination laws.— Abbr. BFOQ.

bona fide purchaser. See PURCHASER.

bond. 1. A long-term interest-bearing debt instrument that is issued by a corporation or governmental entity usu. to provide for a particular financial need; esp., such an instrument in which the debt is secured by a lien on the issuer's property. Cf. DEBENTURE (2).

   accrual bond. A bond—usu. the last collateralized-mortgage-obligation issue—from which no principal or interest payments will be made until the earlier issues have been fully paid.—Also termed *Z-bond.*

   adjustment bond. A bond issued when a corporation is reorganized.—Also termed *reorganization bond.*

   annuity bond. A bond that lacks a maturity date and that perpetually pays interest.

   arbitrage bond. A municipal bond the proceeds of which are invested in bonds paying a higher yield than that paid by the municipality on its own bonds. • Under the Internal Revenue Code, the tax-free aspect of municipal-bond income may be lost if the bonds are classified as arbitrage bonds. Cf. ARBITRAGE.

73

assessment bond. A municipal bond repaid by property-assessment taxes.

baby bond. A bond usu. having a face value of $1,000 or less.

bearer bond. A bond payable to the person holding it. • The transfer of the bond's possession transfers its ownership. Cf. *registered bond.*

closed-end mortgage bond. A mortgage bond with provisions prohibiting the debtor from issuing additional bonds against the bond's collateral.

collateral trust bond. **a.** A bond representing a debt secured by the deposit of another security with a trustee. **b.** A long-term corporate bond that is secured by other companies' mortgage bonds held by the corporation, which pledges and deposits the mortgage bonds in trust.

commodity-backed bond. A bond with interest payments or principal repayment tied to the price of a specific commodity, such as gold.

convertible bond. A bond that can be exchanged for shares in the corporation that issued the bond.

coupon bond. A bond with attached interest coupons that the holder may present to receive interest payments.

deferred-interest bond. A bond whose interest payments are postponed for a time.

discount bond. A bond sold at its current market value, which is less than its face value.—Also termed *non-interest-bearing bond.*

first-mortgage bond. A long-term bond that has first claim on specified assets.

flat bond. A bond that trades without accrued interest.

floating-interest bond. A bond with an interest rate that moves up and down with changing economic conditions.

flower bond. A treasury bond that is redeemable before maturity if it is used to settle federal estate taxes. ● Flower bonds were issued before April 1971 and reached final maturity in 1998.

foreign bond. A bond issued in a currency different from that used where the issuer is located, such as a Canadian-government bond that is denominated in U.S. dollars and issued in the United States.

general-mortgage bond. A corporate bond secured by a blanket mortgage on property. • The general-mortgage bond, however, is often less valuable because it is subordinate to prior mortgages.

general-obligation bond. A municipal bond payable from general revenue rather than from a special fund. • It has no collateral to back it other than the issuer's taxing power.—Also termed *full-faith-and-credit bond*.

gold bond. **a.** Formerly, a bond payable in gold coin or U.S. currency. • This type of bond existed until 1933, when the U.S. monetary system abandoned the gold standard. **b.** A commodity-backed bond that is secured by gold and issued by a gold-mining company.

guaranteed bond. **a.** A bond issued by a corporation and guaranteed by a third party. • This type of bond is common among railroads. **b.** A bond issued by a subsidiary corporation whose parent corporation guarantees the principal and interest payments.

income bond. A corporate bond secured by a pledge of or lien on the corporation's net income, after payment of interest on senior mortgages. • Sometimes this type of bond is a *cumulative-income bond*, in which case, if the net surplus income of any year is insufficient to pay full interest on the income bond, the deficit is carried forward as a lien on any surplus income in future years, until paid in full.

indeterminate bond. A callable bond with no set maturity date.

industrial-development bond. **a.** A type of revenue bond in which interest and principal payments are backed by a corporation rather than a municipality. ● These bonds usu. finance private business facilities. **b.** A tax-exempt municipal bond that finances a usu. local industry.—Also termed *industrial-revenue bond.*

interchangeable bond. A bond that can be exchanged for a different type of bond, such as a coupon bond that may be exchanged for a registered bond.

interest bond. A bond paid in lieu of interest due on other bonds.

investment-grade bond. A bond with a rating of BBB or better by the leading bond rating services. Cf. INVESTMENT-GRADE RATING.

joint and several bond. A bond in which the principal and interest are guaranteed by two or more persons.

joint bond. A bond signed by two or more obligors. • In contrast to a joint and several bond, all the obligors must be joined if an action is brought on the bond.

junior bond. A bond subordinate in priority to another bond.

junk bond. A high-risk, high-yield, highly subordinated bond issued by a corporation with a below-standard industry rating.

leasehold-mortgage bond. A bond issued by a lessee and secured by the lessee's leasehold interest.

mortgage bond. A bond secured by a pledge of the issuer's property.

municipal bond. A bond issued by a nonfederal government or governmental unit, such as a state bond to finance local improvements. • The interest received from a municipal bond is generally exempt from federal, state, and local taxes.—Often shortened (in plural) to *municipals; munies.*

open-end mortgage bond. A mortgage bond that can be used as security for another bond issue.

optional bond. A bond that the holder may redeem before its maturity date if the issuer agrees.

participating bond. A bond that entitles the holder to a share of corporate profits but that does not have a fixed interest rate.

passive bond. A bond bearing no interest. See *passive debt* under DEBT.

premium bond. A bond with a selling price above face or redemption value.

put bond. A bond that gives the holder the right to redeem for full value at specified times before maturity. Cf. *put option* under OPTION.

redeemable bond. A bond that the issuer may call for payment.—Also termed *callable bond*.

re-funding bond. A bond designed to help the issuer raise enough funds to retire a mature outstanding bond.

registered bond. A bond that only the recorded holder may redeem, enjoy benefits from, or transfer to another. Cf. *bearer bond*.

revenue bond. A government bond repayable by the income from a public project.

savings bond. A nontransferable bond issued by the U.S. Government.

secured bond. A bond backed by some type of security. Cf. DEBENTURE (2).

serial bond. A bond issued concurrently with other bonds that have different maturity dates.

series bonds. A group of bonds issued under the authority of the same indenture, but offered publicly at different times and with distinct maturity dates and interest rates.

sinking-fund bond. A bond issue that requires the establishment of a sinking fund for bond redemption. See SINKING FUND.

special-tax bond. A municipal bond secured by taxes levied for a specific governmental purpose, usu. improvements.

tax-exempt bond. A bond that pays tax-free interest.

term bond. A bond issue in which all bonds mature concurrently unless previously redeemed.

zero-coupon bond. A bond without interest coupons. ● It is sold for a discount price and later redeemed at face value, the profit being the difference.

2. A written promise to pay money or do some act if certain circumstances occur; a promise that is defeasible upon a condition subsequent.

blanket bond. **a.** A bond covering several projects that require performance bonds. **b.** See *fidelity bond*.

fidelity bond. A bond that covers an employer or business for loss due to embezzlement, larceny, or gross negligence by an employee or other person holding a position of trust.—Also termed *blanket bond*.

payment bond. A bond given by a surety to cover any fees that, because of the general contractor's default, are not paid to subcontractors or materialmen.

performance bond. **a.** A bond given by a surety to ensure the timely performance of a contract. **b.** A third party's agreement to guarantee the completion of a construction contract upon the default of the general contractor.—Also termed *surety bond*.

bond coupon. See COUPON.

bonded debt. See DEBT.

bond fund. See MUTUAL FUND.

bonus stock. See STOCK.

book account. See ACCOUNT.

book entry. 1. A notation made in an accounting journal. **2.** The method of reflecting ownership of publicly traded securities whereby customers of brokerage firms receive confirmations of transactions and monthly statements, but not stock certificates. See CENTRAL CLEARING SYSTEM.

bookkeeping, *n*. The mechanical recording of debits and credits or the summarizing of financial information, usu. about a business enterprise. Cf. ACCOUNTING.

book value. The value at which an asset is carried on a company's balance sheet.

book-value stock. See STOCK.

boot, *n*. **1.** In tax accounting, supplemental money or property that is subject to tax and is used to equalize an otherwise tax-free exchange. **2.** In a corporate reorganization, anything received other than the stock or securities of a controlled corporation. **3.** Cash or other consideration used to balance an otherwise unequal exchange.

bootleg, *vb*. To manufacture, reproduce, or distribute (something) illegally or without authorization <he was bootlegging copyrighted videotapes>.

bootstrap sale. See SALE.

borrowed employee. See EMPLOYEE.

box-top license. See *shrink-wrap license* under LICENSE.

boycott, *n.* **1.** Any number of possible measures designed to achieve the social or economic isolation of an adversary. **2.** A concerted refusal to do business with a party in order to express disapproval of that party's practices. **3.** A refusal to deal with another in unrelated transactions in order to achieve terms desired in a targeted transaction. • Under the Sherman Antitrust Act, even peaceful persuasion of a person to refrain from dealing with another can amount to a boycott. Cf. PICKETING; STRIKE.

> *consumer boycott.* A boycott by consumers of products or services to show displeasure with the manufacturer, seller, or provider.

> *group boycott.* A type of secondary boycott among two or more competitors in which they all agree to refuse to do business with one firm unless it refrains from doing business with an actual or potential competitor of the boycotters. • Such boycotts can violate the Sherman Antitrust Act and are analyzed under either the per se rule or the rule of reason, depending on the nature of the boycott. Cf. PER SE RULE; RULE OF REASON.

primary boycott. A boycott by union members who stop dealing with a former employer.

secondary boycott. A boycott of the customers or suppliers of a given business so that they will withhold their patronage from that business. ● For example, a group might boycott a manufacturer's goods if that manufacturer advertises on a radio station that broadcasts messages that the group finds objectionable.

breach of contract. Violation of a contractual obligation, either by failing to perform one's own promise or by interfering with the other party's performance.

anticipatory breach. A breach of contract caused by a party's anticipatory repudiation, i.e., unequivocally indicating that the party will not perform when performance is due. ● Under these circumstances, the nonbreaching party may treat the repudiation as an immediate breach and sue for damages.— Also termed *constructive breach*. See REPUDIATION.

continuing breach. A breach of contract that endures for a considerable amount of time, or that is repeated at short intervals.

efficient breach. An intentional breach of contract and payment of damages by a party who would incur greater economic liability in performing under the contract. See EFFICIENT-BREACH THEORY.

material breach. A substantial breach of contract, usu. excusing the aggrieved party from further performance and affording it the right to sue for damages.

partial breach. A breach of contract that is less significant than a material breach and that gives the aggrieved party a right to damages but does not generally excuse that party from performance.

total breach. A material breach of contract that gives rise to a claim for damages based on all the injured party's remaining rights to performance under the contract.

breaking bulk. 1. The act of dividing a large shipment into smaller units. **2.** Larceny by a bailee, esp. a carrier, who opens or reduces items delivered in bulk and then converts some of them to his or her own use.

bribery. The corrupt payment, receipt, or solicitation of a private favor for official action. • Bribery is a felony in most jurisdictions.

> ***commercial bribery.*** Corrupt dealing with the agents or employees of prospective buyers in order to secure an advantage over business competitors.

bridge loan. See LOAN.

broad-form policy. See INSURANCE POLICY.

broker, *n*. **1.** An agent who acts as an intermediary or negotiator, esp. between prospective buyers and sellers; a person employed to make bargains and contracts between other persons in matters of trade, commerce, and navigation. ● A broker differs from a factor because the broker usu. does not have possession of the property. **2.** In securities law, a person engaged in the business of effecting transactions in securities for the account of others.

brokerage. 1. The business or office of a broker <a profitable stock brokerage>. **2.** A broker's fee <collect the brokerage after the house sells>.

building-and-loan association. A quasi-public corporation that accumulates funds through member contributions and lends money to the members for the purpose of purchasing or building homes. Cf. SAVINGS-AND-LOAN ASSOCIATION.

bulk transfer. A sale of a large quantity of inventory outside the ordinary course of the seller's business. • Bulk transfers are regulated by UCC art. 6, which is designed to prevent sellers from defrauding unsecured creditors by making such transfers and dissipating the sale proceeds.—Also termed *bulk sale*.

bull market. See MARKET.

business cycle. The recurrent expansion and contraction of economic activity.

business expense. See *operating expense* under EXPENSE.

business-interruption insurance. See INSURANCE.

business-judgment rule. The presumption that in making business decisions not involving direct self-interest or self-dealing, corporate directors act on an informed basis, in good faith, and in the honest belief that their actions are in the corporation's best interest. • The rule shields directors and officers from liability for unprofitable or harmful corporate transactions if the transactions were made in good faith, with due care, and within the directors' or officers' authority.

business trust. See TRUST.

bust-up merger. See MERGER.

buyer's market. See MARKET.

buying in, *n.* The purchasing of property by the original owner or an interested party at an auction or mortgage foreclosure sale.

buying on margin. See MARGIN TRANSACTION.

buyout, *n.* The purchase of all or a controlling percentage of the assets or shares of a business. Cf. MERGER (3).

　leveraged buyout. The purchase of a publicly held corporation's outstanding stock by its management or outside investors, financed mainly with funds borrowed from investment bankers or brokers and usu. secured by the corporation's assets.—Abbr. LBO.

　management buyout. **a.** A buyout of a corporation by its own directors and officers. **b.** A leveraged buyout of a corporation by an outside entity in which the corporation's management has a material financial interest.—Abbr. MBO.

buy-sell agreement. 1. An arrangement between owners of a business by which the surviving owners agree to purchase the interest of a withdrawing or deceased owner. **2.** In corporate law, a share-transfer restriction that commits the shareholder to sell, and the corporation or other shareholders to buy, the shareholder's shares at a fixed price when a specified event occurs. Cf. OPTION AGREEMENT.

by-bidding. The illegal practice of employing a person to bid at an auction for the sole purpose of stimulating bidding on the seller's property.—Also termed *puffing*.

bylaw. A rule or administrative provision adopted by an association or corporation for its internal governance. • Corporate bylaws are enacted apart from the articles of incorporation.

C

cafeteria plan. An employee fringe-benefit plan allowing a choice of basic benefits up to a certain dollar amount.

call, *n.* **1.** A demand for payment of money.

> **_maintenance call._** A securities broker's demand that an investor increase the money or securities put up as collateral for stock that is owned on margin and that has gone down or is likely to go down in value, so that the minimum required margin may be met.

> **_margin call._** A securities broker's demand that a customer put up money or stock as collateral when the broker finances the purchase of securities. ● A margin call usu. occurs when the market prices of the securities are falling.

2. See *call option* under OPTION. **3.** A demand for the presentation of a security (esp. a bond) for redemption before the maturity date.

callable, *adj.* (Of a security) redeemable before maturity by the issuing corporation. See REDEMPTION.

callable bond. See *redeemable bond* under BOND (1).

callable security. See *redeemable security* under SECURITY.

call loan. See LOAN.

call option. See OPTION.

call price. See PRICE.

canceled check. See CHECK.

C & F. *abbr.* COST AND FREIGHT.

capacity. 1. The role in which one performs an act <in her corporate capacity>. **2.** A legal qualification, such as legal age, that determines one's ability to sue or be sued, to enter into a binding contract, and the like <she had full capacity to bind the corporation with her signature>.

capital. 1. The total assets of a business, esp. those that help generate profits; net worth <the manufacturer bought more equipment to increase its capital>. **2.** Money or assets invested, or available for investment, in a business <the capital needed to start a new company>. **3.** The total amount or value of a corporation's stock; corporate equity <Zytech's stated capital>. See *capital stock* under STOCK.

debt capital. Funds raised by issuing bonds.

equity capital. Funds provided by a company's owners in exchange for evidence of ownership, such as stock.

fixed capital. **a.** The amount of money that is permanently invested in the business. **b.** The amount of money invested in fixed assets, such as land and machinery.

floating capital. Capital not presently invested or committed; esp., capital retained for the purpose of meeting current expenditures.—Also termed *circulating capital.*

impaired capital. Capital that is worth less than the par value of the issued stock.

legal capital. The amount of contributed capital that must, by law, stay in the firm as protection against creditors. • Legal capital is usu. equal to the par or stated value of issued capital stock.—Also termed *stated capital.*

moneyed capital. Capital consisting of money used or invested for profit-making purposes, such as money invested by a bank.—Also spelled *monied capital.*

paid-in capital. The amount paid for the capital stock of a corporation.

risk capital. **a.** Money or property invested and exchanged for common stock in a business venture, esp. one in which the investor has no managerial control. **b.** See *venture capital.*

stated capital. **a.** See *legal capital.* **b.** The total equity of a corporation as it appears on the balance sheet.

subscribed capital. The total amount of stock or capital for which there are subscriptions (contracts of purchase).

venture capital. Funds invested in a new company or enterprise that has high risk and the potential for a high return.—Also termed *risk capital.* See SEED MONEY.

working capital. A firm's investment in current assets such as cash, inventory, or accounts receivable. • Working capital measures liquidity and the ability to discharge short-term liabilities.

capital account. See ACCOUNT.

capital asset. See ASSET.

capital contribution. 1. Cash, property, or services contributed by partners to a partnership. **2.** Funds made available by a shareholder without increasing his or her stock holdings.

capital expenditure. An outlay of funds for acquiring or improving a fixed asset.—Also termed *capital outlay*.

capital gain. The profit realized on selling or exchanging a capital asset.—Also termed *capital gains*. Cf. *ordinary gain* under GAIN.

capital-gain dividend. See DIVIDEND.

capital-gains tax. See TAX.

capital goods. See GOODS.

capitalism. An economic system that depends on the private ownership of the means of production and on competitive forces to determine what is produced.

capitalization. 1. The total amount of a corporation's long-term financing, including stock, bonds, and retained earnings. **2.** In accounting, the recording of an expenditure with long-term benefits as an asset instead of as a current expense. **3.** A process for determining the value of property by dividing its income by a predetermined annual rate.

thin capitalization. The financial condition of a company that is indebted to its shareholders beyond the value of shareholder equity.

undercapitalization. The financial condition of a business that does not have enough cash or patronage to carry on its business.

capitalization accounting method. See AC-COUNTING METHOD.

capitalization rate. The interest rate used in calculating the present value of future periodic payments. • It is determined by dividing the net operating income for the first year by the total investment.—Also termed *income yield*.

capitalization ratio. The ratio between the amount of capital raised from a particular source and the total capitalization of the firm.—Also termed *capital ratio*.

capitalized expense. See EXPENSE.

capital lease. See LEASE-PURCHASE AGREEMENT.

capital loss. See LOSS.

capital market. See MARKET.

capital outlay. 1. See CAPITAL EXPENDITURE. **2.** Money expended in acquiring, equipping, and promoting an enterprise.

capital ratio. See CAPITALIZATION RATIO.

capital stock. See STOCK.

capital-stock tax. See TAX.

capital structure. The mix of debt and equity by which a corporation finances its operations; the relative proportions of short-term debt, long-term debt, and capital stock.

capital surplus. See *paid-in surplus* under SURPLUS.

carrier. 1. An individual or organization that transports passengers or goods for hire, such as a railroad or airline.

> *common carrier.* A carrier that is required by law to convey passengers or freight, without refusal, if the approved fare or charge is paid.—Also termed *public carrier*.

> *private carrier.* A carrier that does not accept business from the general public and is therefore not considered a common carrier.—Also termed *contract carrier*.

2. See INSURER.

carryback. An income-tax deduction, esp. for a net operating loss, that cannot be taken entirely in a given period and that therefore may be taken in an earlier period (usu. the past three years). Cf. CARRYOVER.

carryover. An income-tax deduction, esp. for a net operating loss, that cannot be taken entirely in a given period and that therefore may be taken in a later period (usu. the next five years).—Also termed *carryforward*. Cf. CARRYBACK.

carryover basis. See BASIS.

cartel (kahr-**tel**). **1.** A combination of producers who join together to control the production and price of a product. **2.** An association of companies or sections of companies with common interests, seeking to prevent extreme or unfair competition, allocate markets, or share knowledge.

carveout, *n.* The separation, for tax purposes, of the income derived from a property from the property itself.

caselaw. The collection of reported cases that form the body of jurisprudence within a given jurisdiction.

cash, *n.* **1.** Money or its equivalent. **2.** Currency or coins, negotiable checks, and balances in bank accounts.

cash-basis accounting method. See AC-COUNTING METHOD.

cash dividend. See DIVIDEND.

cash equivalent. A short-term security that is liquid enough to be considered financially equivalent to cash.

cash-equivalent doctrine. The tax-law doctrine requiring income to be reported even if it is not cash, as when the taxpayer barters to receive in-kind payments.

cash flow. 1. The movement of cash through a business, as a measure of profitability or liquidity. **2.** The cash generated from a business or transaction. **3.** Cash receipts minus cash disbursements for a given period.

  cash flow per common share. The difference between cash flow from operations and preferred stock dividends, divided by the number of outstanding common shares.

  discounted cash flow. A method of evaluating a capital investment by comparing its future income and costs with its equivalent current value.

  incremental cash flow. The net increase in a firm's cash flow attributable to a particular capital investment.

negative cash flow. A financial situation in which one's cash needs exceed cash intake. See INSOLVENCY.

net cash flow. Cash inflow minus cash out-flow.

cashier's check. See CHECK.

cash merger. See MERGER.

cashout, *n.* An arrangement by a seller to receive the entire amount of equity in cash rather than retaining an interest in the property.

cash sale. See SALE.

cash surrender value. The amount of money that an insurance policy having cash value, such as a whole-life policy, would yield if cashed in with the insurance company.—Also termed *surrender value.*

cash tender offer. See TENDER OFFER.

cash-value option. See OPTION.

casualty insurance. See INSURANCE.

casualty loss. See LOSS.

cause of action. 1. A group of operative facts, such as a harmful act, giving rise to one or more bases for suing <the surgeon's conduct gave rise to the family's cause of action>. **2.** A legal theory of a lawsuit <a fraud cause of action>. **3.** Loosely, a lawsuit <there are four defendants in the pending cause of action>. Cf. RIGHT OF ACTION.

caveat emptor (**em[p]**-tər *or* -tor). [Latin "let the buyer beware"] A doctrine holding that purchasers buy at their own risk. • Modern statutes and cases have greatly limited the importance of this doctrine.

CBOE. *abbr*. CHICAGO BOARD OPTIONS EXCHANGE.

CBOT. *abbr*. CHICAGO BOARD OF TRADE.

CBT. *abbr*. CHICAGO BOARD OF TRADE.

C corporation. See CORPORATION.

CD. *abbr*. CERTIFICATE OF DEPOSIT.

ceiling price. See PRICE.

central clearing system. A method of facilitating securities transactions in which an agent or subsidiary of an exchange acts as a clearinghouse for member brokerage firms by clearing their checks, settling their accounts, and delivering their payments. • Most transactions are reflected solely by computerized book entries, and clearinghouse statements are submitted showing the net balance to be paid or received to reconcile the member firm's accounts.

CEO. *abbr.* CHIEF EXECUTIVE OFFICER.

CERCLA (sər-klə). *abbr.* Comprehensive Environmental Response, Compensation, and Liability Act of 1980. • This statute holds responsible parties liable for the cost of cleaning up hazardous-waste sites. 42 USCA §§ 9601 et seq. See SUPERFUND.

certificated security. See SECURITY.

certificate of deposit. 1. A banker's certificate acknowledging the receipt of money with a promise to pay to the depositor. **2.** A bank document showing the existence of a time deposit, usu. one that pays interest.—Abbr. CD.

certificate of incorporation. 1. A document issued by a state authority (usu. the secretary of state) granting a corporation its legal existence and the right to function as a corporation.—Also termed *corporate charter*. **2.** See ARTICLES OF INCORPORATION.

certificate of title. A document indicating ownership of real or personal property and identifying any liens or other encumbrances.

certification mark. A trademark or service-mark used to indicate that a product or service meets certain standards of quality or regional origin, such as the mark "Made in the USA." Cf. COLLECTIVE MARK.

certified check. See CHECK.

certified public accountant. See ACCOUN-TANT.

CF. *abbr.* COST AND FREIGHT.

CFO. *abbr.* CHIEF FINANCIAL OFFICER.

CFR. *abbr.* CODE OF FEDERAL REGULATIONS.

CGL policy. See *comprehensive general liability policy* under INSURANCE POLICY.

chain of title. 1. The ownership history of a piece of land, from its first owner to the present one. **2.** The ownership history of a negotiable instrument, traceable through its indorsements. • For the holder to have good title, every prior negotiation must have been proper. If a necessary indorsement is missing or forged, the chain of title is broken and no later transferee can become a holder.

chamber of commerce. An association of businesspeople and merchants who organize to promote the commercial interests of a given area and whose group is generally affiliated with the national organization of the same name.

Chapter 7. 1. The chapter of the Bankruptcy Code calling for a trustee to collect and liquidate a debtor's property, either voluntarily or by court order, to satisfy creditors. **2.** A bankruptcy proceeding filed under this chapter. • An individual debtor who undergoes this type of liquidation (the most common type of bankruptcy) usu. gets a fresh financial start by receiving a discharge of all debts.—Also termed (in sense 2) *straight bankruptcy*.

Chapter 9. 1. The chapter of the Bankruptcy Code governing the adjustment of a municipality's debts. **2.** A bankruptcy proceeding filed under this chapter.

Chapter 11. 1. The chapter of the Bankruptcy Code allowing an insolvent business, or one that is threatened with insolvency, to reorganize itself under court supervision while continuing its normal operations and restructuring its debt. • Although the Code does not expressly prohibit the use of Chapter 11 by an individual nonbusiness debtor, the vast majority of Chapter 11 cases involve business debtors. **2.** A business reorganization conducted under this chapter; REORGANIZATION (2).

Chapter 12. 1. The chapter of the Bankruptcy Code providing for a court-approved debt-payment relief plan for family farmers with a regular income. **2.** A bankruptcy proceeding filed under this chapter.—Also termed (in sense 2) *family-farmer bankruptcy*.

Chapter 13. 1. The chapter of the Bankruptcy Code calling for a person's future earnings to be placed under the supervision of a trustee until all unsecured creditors are satisfied. ● A plan filed under Chapter 13 is sometimes called a *wage-earner's plan* or an *income-based plan*. A Chapter 13 debtor does not receive a discharge of debts; rather, Chapter 13 allows the debtor to propose a plan of rehabilitation to extend or reduce the balance of his or her obligations. **2.** A bankruptcy proceeding filed under this chapter.

charge, *vb.* **1.** To impose a lien or claim; to encumber <charge the land with a tax lien>. **2.** To demand a fee; to bill <the clerk charged a small filing fee>.

chargee. 1. The holder of a charge on property or of a security on a loan. **2.** One charged with a crime.

charging order. In partnership law, a statutory procedure whereby an individual partner's creditor can satisfy its claim from the partner's interest in the partnership.

charitable contribution. 1. A contribution of money or property to an organization that is engaged in charitable activities. **2.** A contribution to a qualified nonprofit charitable organization—deductible for certain tax purposes.

charitable corporation. See CORPORATION.

charitable deduction. See DEDUCTION.

charitable organization. A tax-exempt organization that (1) is created and operated exclusively for religious, scientific, literary, athletic, public-safety, or community-service purposes, (2) does not distribute net earnings for the benefit of a private shareholder or individual, and (3) does not interfere in any way with political campaigns and decision-making processes. IRC § 501(c)(3).—Also termed *charity*. See *charitable corporation* under CORPORATION.

charter, *n.* **1.** A legislative act that creates a business or defines a corporate franchise. Cf. ARTICLES OF INCORPORATION.

bank charter. A document that a governmental authority issues to permit a bank to conduct business.

corporate charter. **a.** See CERTIFICATE OF INCORPORATION (1). **b.** See ARTICLES OF INCORPORATION.

2. The leasing or hiring of an airplane, ship, or other vessel.

charterparty. A contract by which a ship, or some principal part of it, is leased to a merchant for the conveyance of goods on a predetermined voyage to one or more places; a special contract between the shipowner and the freighter for the carriage of goods at sea.— Also spelled *charter-party*; *charter party*.

chattel (**chat**-[ə]l). (*usu. pl.*) Movable or transferable property; any property other than freehold land, esp. personal property.

chattel personal. Tangible goods or intangible rights (as in patents, stocks, or shares).

chattel real. A real-property interest that is less than a freehold or fee, such as a leasehold estate. ● The most important chattel real is an estate for years in land, which is considered a chattel because it lacks the indefiniteness of time essential to real property.

chattel mortgage. See MORTGAGE.

chattel paper. See PAPER.

check, *n*. A draft that is signed by the maker or drawer, drawn on a bank, payable on demand, and unlimited in negotiability. See DRAFT.

> *bad check.* A check that is not honored upon proper presentation because there are insufficient funds in the account or because the account does not exist.

> *canceled check.* A check bearing a notation indicating that it has been paid by the bank it was drawn on. ● A canceled check is often useful as evidence of payment.

> *cashier's check.* A check drawn by a bank on itself, directed to another person, and showing that the payee is authorized to receive from the bank the amount of money represented by the check.

> *certified check.* A check drawn on a bank that guarantees the check's signature and amount by noting the word *certified* or *accepted* on its face.

depository-transfer check. An unsigned, nonnegotiable check that is used by banks to transfer funds from the branch bank to the collection bank.

memorandum check. A check that a borrower gives to a lender for the amount of a short loan, with the understanding that it is not to be presented at the bank but will be redeemed by the maker when the loan falls due.

postdated check. A check bearing a date later than the date of its issue, so that it is payable on or after the stated date.

raised check. A check whose face amount has been increased, usu. without the knowledge of the issuer—an act that under the UCC is considered a material alteration. See RAISING AN INSTRUMENT.

registered check. A check purchased at a bank and drawn on bank funds that have been set aside for that check.

stale check. A check that has been outstanding for an unreasonable time—more than six months under the UCC. • Banks in jurisdictions adopting the UCC may choose not to honor stale checks.

check-kiting. The illegal practice of writing a check against a bank account with insufficient funds to cover the check, in the hope that the funds from a previously deposited check will reach the account before the bank debits the amount of the outstanding check.—Also termed *kiting*.

check-off system. The procedure by which an employer deducts union dues directly from the employees' wages and forwards those dues to the union.

Chicago Board of Trade. The commodities exchange where futures contracts in a large number of agricultural products are transacted.—Abbr. CBT; CBOT.

Chicago Board Options Exchange. The predominant organized marketplace in the U.S. for trading options. ● This exchange was established in 1973.—Abbr. CBOE.

chief executive officer. A corporation's highest-ranking administrator who manages the firm on a daily basis and reports to the board of directors.—Abbr. CEO.

chief financial officer. An executive in charge of making a company's fiscal decisions.—Abbr. CFO.

chief operating officer. A manager who supervises a company's day-to-day operations and usu. reports to the chief executive officer.—Abbr. COO.

child-and-dependent-care tax credit. See TAX CREDIT.

child-labor law. A state or federal statute that protects children by prescribing the necessary working conditions for children in a workplace.

chilling a sale. The act or practice of bidders' or others' combining or conspiring to discourage others from attempting to buy an item so that they might buy the item themselves for a lower price.

chit. A signed voucher for money received or owed, usu. for food, drink, or the like.

churning. A stockbroker's excessive trading of customers' accounts in order to earn more commissions rather than to further the customers' interests. ● Churning is illegal under federal securities laws.

C.I.F. *abbr.* COST, INSURANCE, AND FREIGHT.

circular note. See LETTER OF CREDIT.

circulating capital. See *floating capital* under CAPITAL.

civil conspiracy. See CONSPIRACY.

civil law. 1. The law of civil or private rights, as opposed to criminal law or administrative law. **2.** (*usu. cap.*) One of the two prominent legal systems in the Western World, originally administered in the Roman Empire and still in effect in continental Europe, Latin America, Scotland, and Louisiana, among other parts of the world. Cf. COMMON LAW (2).

claim, *n.* **1.** The assertion of an existing right; any right to payment or to an equitable remedy, even if contingent or provisional <the spouse's claim to half of the lottery winnings>. **2.** A demand for money or property to which one asserts a right <an insurance claim>.

> *liquidated claim.* A claim concerning an amount that has been agreed on by the parties or that can be precisely determined by operation of law or by the terms of the parties' agreement.

> *matured claim.* A claim based on a debt that is due for payment.

> *unliquidated claim.* A claim in which the liability of the party or the amount of the claim is in dispute.

3. A cause of action; an interest or remedy recognized at law; the means by which a person can obtain a privilege, possession, or enjoyment of a right or thing <claim against the employer for wrongful termination>. **4.** Under the Bankruptcy Code, the right to payment or performance, whether or not the right is fixed, matured, disputed, or secured <the lender's priority claim>.

secured claim. A claim held by a creditor who has a lien or a right of setoff against the debtor's property.

unsecured claim. **a.** A claim held by a creditor who does not have a lien or a right of setoff against the debtor's property. **b.** A claim held by a creditor who has a lien on, or right of setoff against, the debtor's property worth less than the amount of the debt.

claim dilution. In bankruptcy law, the reduction in the likelihood that a debtor's claimants will be fully repaid, including considerations of the time value of money.

claim-of-right doctrine. In tax law, the rule that any income constructively received must be reported as income, whether or not the taxpayer has an unrestricted claim to it.

claims-made policy. See INSURANCE POLICY.

class action. A lawsuit in which a single person or a small group of people represent by their litigation the interests of a larger group. • Federal procedure has several requirements for maintaining a class action: (1) the class must be so large that individual suits would be impracticable, (2) there must be legal or factual questions common to the class, (3) the claims or defenses of the representative parties must be typical of those of the class, and (4) the representative parties must adequately protect the interests of the class.—Also termed *representative action*.

class representative. See REPRESENTATIVE.

class voting. See VOTING.

clawback, *n.* A tax abatement used to attract a business to a region served by the government granting the abatement, returnable (often with interest) if the business leaves the region or fails to fulfill promised economic development.

Clayton Act. A federal statute—enacted in 1914 to amend the Sherman Act—that prohibits price discrimination, tying arrangements, and exclusive-dealing contracts, as well as mergers and interlocking directorates if their effect might substantially lessen competition or create a monopoly in any line of commerce.

Clean Air Act. A federal law establishing standards for air-pollution control, esp. for automobile emissions. • Enacted in 1970, the Clean Air Act is enforced by the EPA, but it also gives citizens' groups the right to sue alleged violators.

cleanup clause. A provision in an ongoing loan agreement requiring the borrower to periodically pay off all outstanding loans before more credit will be extended in order to demonstrate to the lender that the loans meet seasonal demands rather than operate as permanent working capital.

clearing corporation. See CORPORATION.

clearinghouse. 1. A place where banks exchange checks and drafts and settle their daily balances. **2.** A stock-and-commodity exchange where the daily transactions of the brokers are cleared. **3.** Any place for the exchange of specialized information.

clear title. See TITLE.

clog on the equity of redemption. An agreement or condition that prevents a mortgagor who defaults from getting back the property free from encumbrance upon paying the debt or performing the obligation for which the security was given. See REDEMPTION.

close, *n.* The final price of a stock at the end of the exchange's trading day.

close-connectedness doctrine. A doctrine used by some courts to deny holder-in-due-course status to an assignee of a negotiable note if the assignee is too closely connected to the original holder-mortgagee.—Also termed *close-connection doctrine.*

close corporation. See CORPORATION.

closed account. See ACCOUNT.

closed-end fund. See MUTUAL FUND.

closed-end mortgage. See MORTGAGE.

closed-end mortgage bond. See BOND (1).

closed mortgage. See MORTGAGE.

closed shop. A workplace in which the employees must be members of a particular union to work there. ● In most cases, closed shops are illegal under the Taft–Hartley Act.—Also termed *union shop.* See RIGHT-TO-WORK LAW. Cf. OPEN SHOP.

closed transaction. See TRANSACTION.

closing, *n.* In the sale of real estate, the final transaction between the buyer and seller, during which the conveyancing documents are concluded and the money and property transferred.—Also termed *settlement*.

closing costs. In a real-estate transaction, the expenses that must be paid in addition to the purchase price.

closing price. See PRICE.

closing statement. A written breakdown of the costs involved in a particular real-estate transaction, usu. prepared by a lender or an escrow agent.—Also termed *settlement sheet*; *settlement statement*.

cloud on title. A defect or potential defect in the owner's title to a piece of land arising from some claim or encumbrance, such as a lien, an easement, or a court order.

CMO. *abbr.* COLLATERALIZED MORTGAGE OBLIGATION.

co-agent. See AGENT.

Coase Theorem. An economic proposition describing the relationship between legal rules about entitlements and economic efficiency and holding that if there are no transaction costs—such as the costs of bargaining or acquiring information—then any legal rule will produce an efficient result.

C.O.D. *abbr.* **1.** Cash on delivery; collect on delivery. **2.** Costs on delivery. **3.** Cash on demand.—Sometimes written *c.o.d.*

code. A complete system of positive law, carefully arranged and officially promulgated; a systematic collection or revision of laws, rules, or regulations <the Uniform Commercial Code>. ● Strictly, a code is a compilation not just of existing statutes, but also of much of the unwritten law on a subject, which is newly enacted as a complete system of law.

Code of Federal Regulations. The annual collection of executive-agency regulations published in the daily Federal Register, combined with previously issued regulations that are still in effect.—Abbr. CFR.

cognovit clause. A clause, outlawed or restricted in most states, by which the debtor agrees to jurisdiction in certain courts, waives notice requirements, and authorizes the entry of an adverse judgment in the event of a default or breach.

coinsurance. See INSURANCE.

collateral, *n.* Property pledged by a borrower as security against a debt.

> **_cross-collateral._ a.** Security given by all parties to a contract. **b.** In bankruptcy, bargained-for security that protects a creditor's postpetition extension of credit in addition to the creditor's prepetition unsecured claims that, as a result of the security, have priority over other creditors' prepetition unsecured claims. ● The process by which a creditor obtains this security is called *cross-collateralization.* Only some bankruptcy courts allow it.

collateralize, *vb.* **1.** To serve as collateral for <the purchased property collateralized the loan agreement>. **2.** To make (a loan) secure with collateral <the creditor insisted that the loan be collateralized>.

collateralized mortgage obligation. A bond secured by a group of mortgage obligations or pass-through securities and paid according to the payment schedule of its class (or *tranche*).—Abbr. CMO. See *pass-through security* under SECURITY; TRANCHE (1).

collateral security. See SECURITY.

collateral trust bond. See BOND (1).

collateral use. The legal use of a trademark by someone other than the trademark owner, whereby the other party must clearly identify itself, the use of the trademark, and the absence of affiliation with the trademark owner.

collecting bank. See BANK.

collective bargaining. Negotiations between an employer and the representatives of organized employees for the purpose of determining the conditions of the employment, such as wages, hours, and fringe benefits.

collective mark. A trademark or servicemark used by an association, union, or other group either to indicate the group's products or services or to signify membership in the group. ● Collective marks—such as "Realtor" or "American Peanut Farmers"—can be federally registered under the Lanham Act. Cf. CERTIFICATION MARK.

collusion. An agreement between two or more persons to defraud another or to obtain something forbidden by law.

colorable transaction. See TRANSACTION.

comaker. One who participates jointly in borrowing money on a promissory note; esp., one who acts as surety under a note if the maker defaults.—Also termed *cosigner*. Cf. MAKER.

comment period. See NOTICE-AND-COMMENT PERIOD.

commerce. The exchange of goods and services, esp. on a large scale involving transportation between cities, states, and nations.

> *interstate commerce.* Trade and other business activities between persons located in different states; esp., traffic in goods and travel of persons between states. ● For purposes of this phrase, most statutory definitions include a territory of the United States as a state. Some statutory definitions of *interstate commerce* include commerce between a foreign country and a state.

> *intrastate commerce.* Commerce that begins and ends entirely within the borders of a single state.

Commerce Clause. The constitutional provision giving Congress the exclusive power to regulate commerce between the states, with foreign nations, and with Indian tribes. U.S. Const. art. I, § 8, cl. 3.

commercial bank. See BANK.

commercial bribery. See BRIBERY.

commercial domicile. See DOMICILE.

commercial frustration. See FRUSTRATION.

commercial general liability policy. See *comprehensive general liability policy* under INSURANCE POLICY.

commercial impracticability. See IMPRACTICABILITY.

commercial insurance. See INSURANCE.

commercial law. The substantive law dealing with the sale and distribution of goods, the financing of credit transactions on the security of the goods sold, and negotiable instruments. ● Most American commercial law is governed by the Uniform Commercial Code.

commercial letter of credit. See LETTER OF CREDIT.

commercial loan. See LOAN.

commercial paper. See PAPER.

commercial speech. Communication (such as advertising and marketing) that involves only the commercial interests of the speaker and the audience, and is therefore afforded lesser First Amendment protection than social, political, or religious speech.

commingle, *vb.* To put together in one mass, as when one mixes separate funds or properties into a common fund.

commingling. A fiduciary's mixing of his or her own funds with those of a beneficiary or client. • Commingling is usu. considered a breach of the fiduciary relationship.

commission. 1. The authority under which a person transacts business for another <the client gave her attorney express commission to sign the contract>. **2.** A fee paid to an agent or employee for a particular transaction, usu. as a percentage of the money received from the transaction <a real-estate agent's commission>.

commission del credere (del-**krayd**-ə-ray). The guaranty of a buyer's debt by the seller's agent. See *del credere agent* under AGENT.

commission merchant. See FACTOR (1).

commitment. An agreement to do something in the future, esp. to assume a financial obligation <the builders relied on the bank's loan commitments>.

commodity. 1. An article of trade or commerce. • The term embraces only tangible articles of commerce, such as products, merchandise, or other tangible goods, as distinguished from services. **2.** An economic good, esp. a raw material or an agricultural product.

commodity-backed bond. See BOND (1).

commodity option. See OPTION.

common carrier. See CARRIER.

common law. 1. The body of law derived from judicial decisions and opinions, rather than from statutes or constitutions. See CASE-LAW. **2.** The body of law based on the English legal system, as distinct from a civil-law system. • All states except Louisiana have the common law as their legal system. Cf. CIVIL LAW (2).

common market. See MARKET.

common-situs picketing. See PICKETING.

common stock. See STOCK.

common-stock equivalent. A security that is exchangeable for common stock and thus is considered to be the same as common stock for calculating earnings per share. • Common-stock equivalents include certain types of convertible securities, stock options, and stock warrants.

common-stock fund. See MUTUAL FUND.

common-stock ratio. The ratio between a corporation's outstanding common stock and its total capitalization. • The common-stock ratio measures the relative claims of stockholders to earnings (earnings per share and payout ratio), cash flow (cash flow per share), and equity (book value per share).

commuted value. 1. The present value of a future interest in property. **2.** The value of future payments when discounted to present value.

company. A corporation—or, less commonly, an association, partnership, or union—that carries on a commercial or industrial enterprise.

> *controlled company.* A company that is under the control of an individual, group, or corporation that owns most of the company's voting stock. Cf. *subsidiary corporation* under CORPORATION.

> *development-stage company.* In securities law, a company that is devoting substantial-

ly all its efforts to establishing a new business in which the principal operations either have not yet begun or have begun but without significant revenue.

diversified investment company. An investment company that by law must invest 75% of its assets but may not invest more than 5% of its assets in any one company or hold more than 10% of the voting shares in any one company.

growth company. A company whose earnings have increased at a rapid pace usu. by directing a high proportion of income back into the business.

holding company. A company formed to control other companies, usu. confining its role to owning stock and supervising management.

investment company. A company formed to acquire and manage a portfolio of diverse assets by investing money collected from different sources.—Also termed *investment trust*. See REAL-ESTATE INVESTMENT TRUST; MUTUAL FUND.

joint-stock company. **a.** An unincorporated association of individuals possessing common capital, the capital being contributed by the members and divided into shares, of which each member possesses a number of shares proportionate to his or her invest-ment. **b.** A partnership in which the capital is divided into shares that are transferable without the express consent of the partners.

limited company. A company, such as a corporation, in which the liability of each shareholder is limited to the amount individ-ually invested.

limited-liability company. A company—statutorily authorized in many states—that is characterized by limited liability, manage-ment by members or managers, and limita-tions on ownership transfer.—Abbr. L.L.C.

mutual company. A company that is owned by its customers rather than by a separate group of stockholders. ● Many in-surance companies are mutual companies.

personal holding company. A holding company subject to special taxes and having five or fewer shareholders, with most of its revenue deriving from passive income such as dividends, interest, rent, and royalties.

title company. A company that examines real-estate titles for any encumbrances, claims, or other flaws. See TITLE SEARCH.

trust company. A company that acts as a trustee for individuals and entities and that sometimes also operates as a commercial bank.

company union. See UNION.

compensable injury. See INJURY.

compensating balance. The amount of money a borrower from a bank is required to keep on deposit as a condition for a loan or a line of credit.

compensation. 1. Remuneration for services rendered; salary or wages. **2.** Payment of damages, or any other act that a court orders to be done by a person who has caused injury to another and must therefore make the other whole.

accrued compensation. Remuneration that has been earned but not yet paid.

deferred compensation. **a.** Payment for work performed, paid in the future or when some future event occurs. **b.** An employee's earnings that are taxed when received or distributed and not when earned, such as contributions to a qualified pension or profit-sharing plan.

unreasonable compensation. Under the Internal Revenue Code, pay that is out of proportion with the actual services rendered and therefore not deductible.

compensatory damages. See *actual damages* under DAMAGES.

completed-contract accounting method. See ACCOUNTING METHOD.

compound, *vb.* **1.** To compute (interest) on the principal and the accrued interest. **2.** To settle (a matter, esp. a debt) by a money payment, in lieu of other liability; to adjust by agreement.

compound interest. See INTEREST.

comprehensive general liability policy. See INSURANCE POLICY.

comprehensive insurance. See INSURANCE.

compromise, *n.* **1.** An agreement between two or more persons to settle matters in dispute between them. **2.** A debtor's partial payment coupled with the creditor's promise not to claim the rest of the amount due or claimed.

comptroller (kən-**trohl**-ər). An officer of a business, private, state, or municipal corporation, who is charged with duties usu. relating to fiscal affairs, including auditing and examining accounts and reporting the financial status periodically.—Also spelled *controller*.

compulsory insurance. See INSURANCE.

concerted action. An action that has been planned, arranged, and agreed on by parties acting together to further some scheme or cause, so that all involved are responsible for the actions of one.—Also termed *concert of action*.

concerted refusal to deal. In antitrust law, an agreement between two or more persons or firms to not do business with a third party. ● The parties to the agreement may or may not be competitors. Concerted refusals to deal can violate section 1 of the Sherman Act and are analyzed under either the per se rule or the rule of reason, depending on the nature of the agreement. See BOYCOTT. Cf. PER SE RULE; RULE OF REASON.

concession. A rebate or abatement.

concurrent condition. See CONDITION.

concurrent covenant. See COVENANT (1).

concurrent insurance. See INSURANCE.

condition. 1. A future and uncertain event on which the existence or extent of an obligation or liability depends; an uncertain act or event that triggers or negates a duty to render a promised performance. ● For example, if Jones promises to pay Smith $500 for repairing a car, Smith's failure to repair the car (a condition) relieves Jones of the promise to pay. **2.** A stipulation or prerequisite in a contract or other legal instrument. ● A condition is of the essence of the instrument. If a court construes a contractual term to be a condition, then its untruth or breach will entitle the party to whom it is made to be discharged from all liabilities under the contract. **3.** Loosely, a term, provision, or clause in a contract.

> *concurrent condition.* A condition that must occur or be performed at the same time as another condition, the performance by each party being separately operative as a condition precedent; a condition that is mutually dependent on another, arising when the parties to a contract agree to exchange performances simultaneously.—Also termed *condition concurrent.*

> *condition precedent.* An act or event, other than a lapse of time, that must exist or occur before a duty to perform a promised performance arises.

condition subsequent. A condition that, if it occurs, will bring something else to an end; an event the existence of which, by agreement of the parties, discharges a duty of performance that has arisen.

conditional delivery. See DELIVERY.

conditional indorsement. See INDORSEMENT.

conditional sale. See SALE.

confidential relationship. See FIDUCIARY RELATIONSHIP.

confirming bank. See BANK.

conflict of interest. 1. A real or seeming incompatibility between one's private interests and one's public or fiduciary duties. **2.** A real or seeming incompatibility between the interests of two of a lawyer's clients, the result being that the lawyer is disqualified from representing both clients if the dual representation adversely affects either client or if the clients do not consent.

confusion of goods. Mixture of similar things belonging to different owners so that the owners can no longer identify their own property. ● If this occurs with the consent of both owners, they become owners in common of the goods. But if the mixture is done willfully by one person alone, that person loses all right to the property unless (1) the goods can be distinguished and separated, or (2) that person's goods are equal in value to the goods they were mixed with.

conglomerate, *n.* A corporation that owns unrelated enterprises in a wide variety of industries.

conglomerate merger. See MERGER.

conscionable, *adj.* Conforming with good conscience; just and reasonable <a conscionable bargain>. Cf. UNCONSCIONABLE.

consciously parallel. In antitrust law, of, relating to, or characterizing the conduct of a party who has knowledge of a competitor's course of action and who makes an independent decision to take the same actions. ● In some cases this is viewed as evidence of a conspiracy.

consent decree. An agreed order between a government agency and a defendant in which the defendant agrees to refrain from certain prohibited business practices without admitting culpability.

consent dividend. See DIVIDEND.

consequential loss. See LOSS.

consideration. Something of value (such as an act, a forbearance, or a return promise) received by one party to a contract from the other party. • Consideration, or a substitute such as promissory estoppel, is necessary for a contract to be enforceable.

> *fair consideration.* **a.** Consideration that is a reasonable equivalent of the thing being exchanged and given in good faith. **b.** Consideration that is honest, reasonable, and free from suspicion, but not strictly adequate or full.

> *good consideration.* **a.** Consideration based on natural love, affection, or moral duty. • Such consideration is usu. not valid for the enforcement of a contract. **b.** Loosely, valuable consideration.

> *illegal consideration.* Consideration that is contrary to the law or prejudicial to the public interest. • Such consideration is invalid for the enforcement of a contract.

> *nominal consideration.* Consideration that is so low as to bear no relationship to the value of what is being conveyed (e.g., conveying a piece of real estate for $1 or for no money at all). • Such consideration can be valid, since courts do not ordinarily ex-

amine the adequacy of consideration (although they do often inquire into such issues as fraud and duress).

past consideration. An act done or a promise given by a promisee before the making of a promise sought to be enforced. • Past consideration is not consideration for the new promise, since it has not been given in exchange for this promise (although exceptions exist for new promises to pay debts barred by limitations or debts discharged in bankruptcy). Cf. PREEXISTING-DUTY RULE.

consignment (kən-**sin**-mənt). **1.** The transfer of goods to the custody of another (the *consignee*) for future delivery or sale. **2.** The goods so transferred. • When a merchant takes goods on consignment, the usual agreement is that the owner (the *consignor*) will be paid only for goods that are sold, and that any unsold goods will be returned to the owner.

consignment sale. See SALE.

consolidated financial statement. See FINANCIAL STATEMENT.

consolidated return. See TAX RETURN.

consolidation. The unification of two or more corporations by dissolving the existing ones and creating a single new corporation. Cf. MERGER (3).

consolidation loan. See LOAN.

consortium (kən-**sor**-sh[ee]əm). A group of companies that agree to join or associate for an enterprise beyond their individual capabilities or resources <several high-tech businesses formed a consortium to create a new super-computer>. Pl. **consortiums, consortia.**

conspiracy. An agreement by two or more persons to commit an unlawful act; a combination for an unlawful purpose. ● Conspiracy is a separate offense from the crime that is the object of the conspiracy.

   civil conspiracy. A tortious conspiracy to defraud or cause damage to a person or property.

construction lien. See *mechanic's lien* under LIEN.

constructive bailment. See BAILMENT.

constructive breach. See *anticipatory breach* under BREACH OF CONTRACT.

constructive delivery. See DELIVERY.

constructive dividend. See DIVIDEND.

constructive eviction. See EVICTION.

constructive fraud. See FRAUD.

constructive knowledge. Knowledge that one using reasonable care or diligence should have, and therefore that is attributed by law to a given person <the court held that the partners had constructive knowledge of the partnership agreement even though none of them had read it>. Cf. ACTUAL KNOWLEDGE.

constructive notice. See NOTICE.

constructive payment. See PAYMENT.

constructive-receipt doctrine. The rule that taxable income under a taxpayer's control before it is actually received (such as accumulated interest income that has not been withdrawn) must be included by the taxpayer in gross income, unless the actual receipt is subject to significant constraints.

constructive total loss. See LOSS.

constructive trust. See TRUST.

consumer. One who buys goods or services for personal, family, or household use, with no intention of resale; a user of a commodity.

consumer boycott. See BOYCOTT.

Consumer Credit Protection Act. A federal statute that safeguards the consumer in connection with the use of credit by (1) requiring full disclosure of the terms of the loan agreement, including finance charges, (2) restricting the garnishment of wages, and (3) regulating the use of credit cards (15 USCA §§ 1601 et seq.). • Many states have adopted their own consumer-credit-protection acts.—Also termed *Truth in Lending Act.* Cf. UNIFORM CONSUMER CREDIT CODE.

consumer debt. See DEBT.

consumer goods. See GOODS.

consumer loan. See LOAN.

consumer price index. An index that tracks the price level of goods and services purchased by the average consumer and that is published monthly by the Bureau of Labor Statistics.— Abbr. CPI.—Also termed *cost-of-living index.*

consumer-protection law. A state or federal statute designed to protect consumers against unfair trade and credit practices involving consumer goods, as well as to protect consumers against faulty and dangerous goods.

contingent annuity. See ANNUITY.

contingent debt. See DEBT.

contingent fund. See FUND (1).

contingent-interest mortgage. See MORT-GAGE.

continuing breach. See BREACH OF CONTRACT.

continuity of business enterprise. A judicial requirement for acquisitive reorganizations whereby the acquiring corporation must continue the target corporation's historical business or must use a significant portion of the target's business assets in a new business.

continuity of interest. 1. A judicial requirement for acquisitive reorganizations whereby a target corporation's shareholders must retain a share in the acquiring corporation. **2.** A judicial requirement for divisive reorganizations whereby a target corporation's shareholders must retain an interest in both the distributing and the controlled corporations.

contort (**kon**-tort), *n.* (*usu. pl.*) The overlapping domain of contract law and tort law.

contraband, *n.* **1.** Illegal or prohibited trade; smuggling. **2.** Goods that are unlawful to import, export, or possess.

contract, *n.* **1.** An agreement between two or more parties creating obligations that are enforceable or otherwise recognizable at law <a contract for the sale of a house>. **2.** The writing that sets forth such an agreement <Follett misplaced the signed contract>. **3.** The body of law dealing with agreements and exchange <the plaintiff sued in contract and in tort>.

adhesion contract. A standard-form contract prepared by one party, to be signed by the party in a weaker position (usu. a consumer) who has little choice about the terms.

aleatory contract. A contract in which either party's performance depends on some uncertain event that is beyond the parties' control. ● Most insurance contracts are of this type.—Also termed *hazardous contract*.

alternative contract. A contract in which the performing party may elect to perform one of two or more specified acts to satisfy the obligation.

bilateral contract. A contract in which each party promises a performance, so that each party is an obligor on his or her own promise and an obligee on the other's promise.—Also termed *mutual contract*.

contract for deed. A conditional sales contract for the sale of real property.

contract for sale. **a.** A contract for the present transfer of property for a price. **b.** A contract to sell goods at a future time.—Also termed (in sense b) *contract to sell.*

contract under seal. A formal contract that requires no consideration and has the seal of the signer attached. ● Modern statutes have mostly eliminated the special effects of a sealed contract. It must be in writing or printed on paper or parchment and is conclusive between the parties when signed, sealed, and delivered.—Also termed *sealed contract.*

cost-plus contract. A contract in which payment is on the basis of a fixed fee or a percentage added to the actual cost incurred.

destination contract. A contract between a buyer and seller providing that the risk of loss passes to the buyer once the seller delivers the goods to their destination.

executory contract. A contract that remains wholly unperformed or for which there remains something still to be done on both sides.

gratuitous contract. A contract made for the benefit of a promisee who does not give or promise consideration to the promisor.

hot-cargo contract. A labor contract between an employer and a union in which the employer agrees not to handle or deal in non-union-produced goods. • Hot-cargo contracts are prohibited by federal law.

implied contract. **a.** An implied-in-law contract. **b.** An implied-in-fact contract.

implied-in-fact contract. A contract that the parties presumably intended, either by tacit understanding or by the assumption that it existed.

implied-in-law contract. An obligation imposed by law because of the conduct of the parties, because of some special relationship between them, or because one of them would otherwise be unjustly enriched. • An implied-in-law contract is not actually a contract, but a remedy that allows the plaintiff to sue to recover a benefit conferred on the defendant.—Also termed *quasi-contract*. See UNJUST ENRICHMENT.

integrated contract. One or more writings constituting a final expression of one or more terms of an agreement. See INTEGRATION (1).

naked contract. See NUDUM PACTUM.

output contract. A contract in which a buyer promises to buy all the goods or services that a seller can supply during a specified period and at a set price; the quantity term is measured by the seller's output. Cf. *requirements contract*.

parol contract. **a.** A contract or modification of a contract that is not in writing or is only partially in writing.—Also termed *oral contract*. **b.** At common law, a contract not under seal, although it could be in writing.— Also termed *simple contract*. See PAROL-EVIDENCE RULE.

precontract. A contract that precludes a party from entering into a comparable agreement with someone else. Cf. LETTER OF INTENT.

procurement contract. A contract in which a government agency receives goods or services. • A procurement contract, including the bidding process, is subject to government regulation.—Also termed *government contract*.

requirements contract. A contract in which a seller promises to supply all the goods or services that a buyer needs during a specific period and at a set price, and in which the buyer promises (explicitly or implicitly) to obtain those goods or services exclusively from the seller. • The quantity term is measured by the buyer's requirements. Cf. *output contract*; EXCLUSIVE-DEALING ARRANGEMENT.

retail installment contract. A contract for the sale of goods under which the buyer makes periodic payments and the seller retains title to or a security interest in the goods. Cf. *chattel mortgage* under MORTGAGE.

severable contract. A contract that includes two or more promises each of which can be enforced separately, so that failure to perform one of the promises does not necessarily put the promisor in breach of the entire contract. See SEVERABILITY CLAUSE.

special contract. **a.** See *contract under seal*. **b.** A contract with peculiar provisions that are not ordinarily found in contracts relating to the same subject matter.

subcontract. A contract made by a party to another contract for carrying the other contract, or a part of it, out.

take-or-pay contract. A contract requiring the buyer to either purchase and receive a minimum amount of product at a set price ("take") or pay for this minimum without taking immediate delivery ("pay"). ● Take-or-pay contracts are most often used in the energy and oil-and-gas business.

143

unilateral contract. A contract in which only one party makes a promise or undertakes a performance.

contract carrier. See *private carrier* under CARRIER.

contractor. 1. A party to a contract. **2.** More specifically, one who contracts to do work or provide supplies for another.

general contractor. One who contracts for the completion of an entire project, including hiring and paying subcontractors and coordinating all the work.

independent contractor. One who is hired to complete a specific project but who is left free to do the assigned work and to choose the method for accomplishing it. ● Someone who hires an independent contractor is usu. not vicariously liable for the contractor's wrongful acts. Cf. EMPLOYEE.

subcontractor. One who is awarded a portion of an existing contract by a contractor, esp. a general contractor. ● For example, a contractor who builds homes typically retains subcontractors to perform specialty work such as installing plumbing, laying carpet, making cabinetry, and landscaping.

contract rate. See INTEREST RATE.

Contracts Clause. U.S. Const. art. I, § 10, cl. 1, which prohibits states from impairing private contractual obligations. • The Supreme Court generally has interpreted this clause so that states can in fact regulate contractual obligations if such regulation is reasonable and necessary.

contribution. The right that gives one of several persons who are liable on a common debt the ability to recover from each of the others in proportion when that one person discharges the debt for the benefit of all; the right to demand that another who is jointly responsible for a third party's injury pay part of what one is required to compensate the third party. Cf. INDEMNITY.

contributory infringement. See INFRINGE-MENT.

controlled company. See COMPANY.

controller. See COMPTROLLER.

controlling shareholder. See SHAREHOLDER.

control person. A person who has actual control or significant influence over the issuer of securities, as by directing corporate policy. • The control person is subject to the same liability as the controlled person unless the

145

control person proves that it acted in good faith.—Also termed *controlling person*.

conventional mortgage. See MORTGAGE.

conversion. The wrongful possession or disposition of another's tangible property as if it were one's own; an act or series of acts of willful interference, without lawful justification, with any chattel in a manner inconsistent with another's right, whereby that other person is deprived of the use and possession of the chattel.

conversion price. The contractually specified price per share at which a convertible security can be converted into shares of common stock.

conversion ratio. 1. The number of common shares into which a convertible security may be converted. **2.** The ratio of the face amount of the convertible security to the conversion price.

conversion security. See SECURITY.

convertible arbitrage. See *kind arbitrage* under ARBITRAGE.

convertible bond. See BOND (1).

convertible debenture. See DEBENTURE.

convertible debt. See DEBT.

convertible security. See SECURITY.

conveyance. 1. The voluntary transfer of a right. **2.** The transfer of a property right that does not pass by delivery of a thing or merely by agreement. **3.** The transfer of an interest in real property from one living person to another, by means of an instrument such as a deed. See FRAUDULENT CONVEYANCE.

COO. *abbr.* CHIEF OPERATING OFFICER.

cooling-off period. 1. A period during which a buyer may cancel a purchase. **2.** In securities law, a period (usu. at least 20 days) between the filing of a registration statement and the effective date of the registration statement.

cooperative, *n.* An organization or enterprise (as a store) owned by those who use its services.—Often shortened to *coop*; *co-op*.

co-owner. A person who is in concurrent ownership, possession, and enjoyment of property with one or more others; a tenant in common or a joint tenant.

copyright. 1. A property right in an original work of authorship fixed in any tangible medium of expression (such as a literary, musical, artistic, photographic, or film work), giving the holder the exclusive right to reproduce, adapt, distribute, perform, and display the work. **2.** The body of law relating to such works. • Federal copyright law is governed by the Copyright Act of 1976.

copyright infringement. See INFRINGEMENT.

copyright notice. A notice that a work is copyright-protected, usu. placed in each published copy of the work. • Since 1989, such notice is not required for a copyright to be valid, although it continues to provide certain procedural advantages.

core proceeding. In bankruptcy law, a proceeding involving claims that substantially affect the debtor-creditor relationship (such as an action to recover a preferential transfer). Cf. RELATED PROCEEDING.

cornering the market. The act or process of acquiring ownership or control of a large portion of the available supply of a commodity or security, permitting manipulation of the commodity's or security's price.

corporate acquisition. The purchase of a controlling interest in one corporation by another if both parties retain their legal existence after the transaction. Cf. MERGER (3).

corporate agent. See AGENT.

corporate charter. See CHARTER.

corporate citizenship. Corporate status in the state of incorporation, though a foreign corporation is not a citizen for the purposes of the Privileges and Immunities Clause of the U.S. Constitution.

corporate domicile. See DOMICILE.

corporate franchise. See FRANCHISE (1).

corporate indenture. See INDENTURE.

corporate name. A corporation's official name; the name that a corporation files with a state authority (usu. the secretary of state) as the name under which the corporation will conduct its legal affairs, such as suing, being sued, and paying taxes. ● Many states require the corporate name to include the word "corporation," "incorporated," or "company," or an abbreviation of one of those words. Cf. ASSUMED NAME.

corporate-opportunity doctrine. The rule that a corporation's directors, officers, employees, and controlling shareholders are precluded from taking personal advantage of any business opportunities that the corporation has an

149

expectancy right or property interest in, or that in fairness should otherwise belong to the corporation. • In a partnership, the analogous principle is the *firm-opportunity doctrine*.

corporate purpose. The general scope of the business or other objective for which a corporation was created. • A statement of this purpose is commonly required in the articles of incorporation.

corporate raider. A person or business that attempts to take control of a corporation, against its wishes, by seeking to buy a controlling percentage of its stock and replacing its management.—Often shortened to *raider*. Cf. WHITE KNIGHT.

corporate seal. See SEAL.

corporate stock. See STOCK.

corporate veil. The legal assumption that the actions of a corporation are not the actions of its owners, so that the owners are exempt from liability for the corporation's actions. See ALTER EGO; PIERCING THE CORPORATE VEIL.

corporation. A statutory entity (usu. a business) having authority under law to act as a single person distinct from the shareholders who make it up and having rights to issue stock and exist indefinitely. See COMPANY.

aggressor corporation. A corporation seeking to gain control of another corporation, usu. by merger or direct cash offer to shareholders. See TAKEOVER.

C corporation. A corporation whose income is taxed at the corporate level rather than at the shareholder level. • Any corporation not electing S-corporation tax status under the Internal Revenue Code is a C corporation by default. Cf. *S corporation*.

charitable corporation. A nonprofit corporation that is dedicated to benevolent purposes and thus entitled to special tax status under the Internal Revenue Code.—Also termed *eleemosynary corporation*. See CHARITABLE ORGANIZATION.

clearing corporation. A corporation that acts as a clearinghouse by facilitating the confirmation, delivery, and settlement of securities transactions. • Most clearing corporations are affiliated with a national securities exchange and registered under federal law.

close corporation. A corporation whose stock is not freely traded and is held by only a few shareholders, often within the same family.—Also termed *closely held corporation*.

corporation by estoppel. A partnership or sole proprietorship that is deemed, by operation of law, to be a corporation in a given case because a third party dealt with the business as if it were a corporation, thus preventing the third party from holding an owner or officer of the business individually liable.

de facto corporation. An incompletely formed corporation whose existence operates as a defense to personal liability of the owners who in good faith thought they were operating the business as a duly formed corporation. ● To assert this status, the corporation must file its articles of incorporation with the appropriate state official. Modern corporation statutes have largely eliminated the de facto corporation.

de jure corporation. A corporation formed in accordance with all applicable laws and recognized as a corporation for liability purposes.

dummy corporation. A corporation whose only function is to protect the principal from liability and (sometimes) to hide the principal's identity.

foreign corporation. A corporation that was created or organized under the laws of another state, government, or country <in Arizona, a California corporation is said to be a foreign corporation>.

nonprofit corporation. A corporation organized under special statutes for some purpose other than making a profit (such as charitable or educational purposes), and therefore afforded special tax treatment.— Also termed *not-for-profit corporation.*

nonstock corporation. A corporation that does not issue shares of stock as evidence of ownership but instead is owned by its members in accordance with a charter or agreement. ● Examples are mutual insurance companies, charitable organizations, and private clubs.

parent corporation. A corporation that owns more than 50% of the voting shares of, or has an otherwise controlling interest in, another corporation (called a *subsidiary corporation*).—Also termed *parent company.*

professional corporation. A corporation that renders a personal service to the public of a type that requires a license or legal authorization, such as architects, accountants, physicians, veterinarians, and the like.—Abbr. P.C.

public corporation. **a.** A corporation whose shares are traded to and among the general public.—Also termed *publicly held corporation*. **b.** A corporation that is created by the state for political purposes and to act as an agency in the administration of civil government. **c.** A government-owned corporation that engages in a specific governmental activity, usu. while remaining financially independent. • Such a corporation is managed by a publicly appointed board.—Also termed (in sense c) *government corporation*.

quasi-corporation. An entity that exercises some of the functions of a corporation but that has not been granted corporate status by statute; esp., a public corporation with limited authority and powers (such as a county or school district).

registered corporation. A publicly held corporation that has registered under section 12 of the Securities Exchange Act of 1934 and is therefore subject to the Act's periodic disclosure requirements and proxy regulations.

S corporation. A corporation whose income is taxed at the shareholder level (similar to a partnership's income) rather than at the corporate level. • Only corporations with a limited number of shareholders can elect S-corporation tax status under Subchapter S of the Internal Revenue Code. Cf. *C corporation*.

shell corporation. A corporation that has no active business and usu. exists only in name as a vehicle for another company's or person's business maneuvers.

sister corporation. One of two or more corporations having the same, or substantially the same, owners.

stock corporation. A corporation in which the capital is contributed by the shareholders and divided into shares represented by certificates.

subsidiary corporation. A corporation in which a parent corporation has a controlling interest.—Often shortened to *subsidiary*. Cf. *controlled company* under COMPANY.

target corporation. A corporation over which control is being sought by another party. See TAKEOVER.

thin corporation. A corporation with an excessive amount of debt in its capitalization. See *thin capitalization* under CAPITALIZATION.

corpus (**kor**-pəs). [Latin "body"] Principal (as of a fund or estate), as opposed to interest or income. Pl. **corpora.**

correction. A decrease in business activity or market price following and counteracting an increase in such activity or price <the broker advised investors to sell before the inevitable stock-market correction>.

corrective advertising. Advertising that informs consumers that earlier advertisements contained a deceptive claim, and that provides consumers with corrected information. ● This type of advertising is usu. ordered by the Federal Trade Commission.

correspondence audit. See AUDIT.

correspondent, *n.* A securities firm or financial institution that performs services for another in a place or market that the other does not have direct access to.

correspondent bank. See BANK.

cosign, *vb.* To sign a document along with another person, usu. to assume obligations and to supply credit support to the main obligor.

cosigner. See COMAKER.

cost, *n.* The amount paid or charged for something; price or expenditure. Cf. EXPENSE.

direct cost. The amount of money for material and labor and variable overhead to produce a product.

distribution cost. Any cost incurred in marketing a product or service, such as advertising, storage, and shipping.

fixed cost. A cost whose value does not fluctuate according to changes in output or business activity; esp., overhead expenses such as rent, salaries, and depreciation.

indirect cost. A cost that is not specific to the production of any specific good or service, but that arises from any production activity in general, such as overhead allocations for general and administrative activities.

marginal cost. The additional cost incurred in producing one more unit of output.

net cost. The cost of an item, arrived at by subtracting any financial gain from the total cost.

opportunity cost. The cost of acquiring an asset measured by the value of an alternative investment that is forgone <her opportunity cost of $1,000 in equipment was her consequent inability to invest that money in bonds>.

replacement cost. The cost of acquiring an asset that is as equally useful or productive as an asset currently held.

sunk cost. A cost that has already been incurred and that cannot be recovered.

transaction cost. (*usu. pl.*) A cost connected with the making of a transaction, such as a commission to a broker or the time and effort expended to arrange a deal.

unit cost. The cost of a single unit of a product or service; the total cost divided by the number of units.

variable cost. The cost that varies in the short run in close relationship with changes in output.

cost accounting method. See ACCOUNTING METHOD.

cost and freight. A term in a quoted sales price indicating that the quoted price includes the cost of the goods and freight charges, but not insurance or other special charges. • During shipment, the risk of loss is on the buyer.—Abbr. C.F.; C & F.

cost basis. See BASIS.

cost-benefit analysis. An analytical technique that weighs the expense of a proposed decision, holding, or project against the expected advantages, economic or otherwise.

cost, insurance, and freight. A term in a quoted sales price indicating that the quoted price includes the cost of the goods as well as freight and insurance charges. ● During shipment, the risk of loss is on the buyer. But the seller must provide insurance at a specified amount (usu. at a minimum of 110%).—Abbr. C.I.F. Cf. FREE ON BOARD.

cost justification. Under the Robinson–Patman Act, an affirmative defense against a charge of price discrimination dependent on the seller's showing that it incurs lower costs in serving those customers who are paying less.

cost-of-living clause. A provision (as in a contract or lease) that gives an automatic wage, rent, or benefit increase tied in some way to cost-of-living rises in the economy. See INFLATION.

cost-of-living index. See CONSUMER PRICE INDEX.

cost-plus contract. See CONTRACT.

cosurety. One of two or more sureties to the same obligation. See SURETY.

counsel, *n.* One or more lawyers who represent a client <the client acted on advice of counsel>.—In the singular, also termed *counselor*. Cf. ATTORNEY (2).

> *general counsel.* **a.** A lawyer or law firm that represents a client in all or most of the client's legal matters, but that sometimes refers extraordinary matters—such as intellectual-property cases—to a specialist. **b.** The most senior lawyer in a corporation's legal department, usu. also a corporate officer.

> *in-house counsel.* One or more lawyers employed full-time by a company.

counteroffer. In contract law, an offeree's new offer that varies the terms of the original offer. ● By varying the terms, the offeree rejects the original offer. See MIRROR-IMAGE RULE.

countersign, *vb.* To write one's own name next to someone else's in order to verify the other signer's identity.

coupon (**koo**-pon). An interest or dividend certificate that is attached to another instrument, such as a bond, and that may be detached and separately presented for payment of a definite sum at a specified time.

bond coupon. The part of a coupon bond that is clipped by the holder and surrendered for an interest payment. Cf. *coupon bond* under BOND (1).

coupon bond. See BOND (1).

coupon note. See NOTE.

coupon security. See SECURITY.

coupon yield. See YIELD.

course of business. That which is normally done in managing a trade or business.—Also termed *ordinary course of business*; *regular course of business*.

course of dealing. An established pattern of conduct between the parties to a transaction. • If a dispute arises, the parties' course of dealing can be used as evidence of how they intended to carry out the transaction.

course of employment. Events that occur or circumstances that exist as a part of one's employment; esp., the time during which an employee furthers an employer's goals through employer-mandated directives.

Court of International Trade. A court with jurisdiction over any civil action against the

United States arising from federal laws governing import transactions or the eligibility of workers, firms, and communities for adjustment assistance under the Trade Act of 1974.
• Its exclusive jurisdiction also includes actions to recover customs duties, to recover on a customs bond, and to impose certain civil penalties for fraud or negligence.

covenant. **1.** A formal agreement or promise, usu. in a contract.

 concurrent covenant. A covenant that requires performance by one party at the same time as another's performance.

 covenant not to sue. A covenant in which a party having a right of action agrees not to assert that right in litigation.

 independent covenant. A covenant that makes each party independently liable for its promises, regardless of the other party's actions.

 negative covenant. A covenant that requires a party to refrain from doing something; esp., in a real-estate financing transaction, the borrower's promise to the lender not to encumber or transfer the real estate as long as the loan remains unpaid.

noncompetition covenant. A contractual provision—typically found in employment, partnership, or sale-of-business agreements—in which one party agrees to refrain from conducting business similar to that of the other party. ● Courts generally uphold these clauses for the duration of the original business relationship, but clauses extending beyond termination must usu. be reasonable as to scope, time, and territory.—Also termed *restrictive covenant*.

2. A promise made in a deed or implied by law; esp., an obligation in a deed burdening or favoring a landowner.

covenant running with the land. A covenant whose benefit or liability concerns the land itself, so that every consecutive grantee is tied to it, neither the land nor the covenant being transferable without the other.— Also termed *real covenant*.

restrictive covenant. **a.** A private agreement, usu. in a deed or lease, that restricts the use and occupancy of real property, esp. by specifying lot size, building lines, architectural styles, and the uses to which the property may be put. **b.** See *noncompetition covenant* under COVENANT (1).

cover, *n.* The purchase on the open market, by the buyer in a breach-of-contract dispute, of goods to substitute for those promised but never delivered by the seller. ● Under the UCC, the buyer can recover from the seller the difference between the cost of the substituted goods and the original contract price.

coverage. 1. Inclusion of a risk under an insurance policy; the risks within the scope of an insurance policy.

> *full coverage.* Insurance protection that pays for the full amount of a loss with no subtraction for the amount of a deductible.

2. The ratio between corporate pretax income and corporate liability for bond interest payments. ● The coverage ratio is an important measure of a corporation's ability to meet its obligations.

CPA. See *certified public accountant* under AC-COUNTANT.

CPI. *abbr.* CONSUMER PRICE INDEX.

craft union. See UNION.

cramdown. Court confirmation of a Chapter 11 bankruptcy plan despite the opposition of certain creditors. ● Under the Bankruptcy

Code, a court may confirm a plan—even if it has not been accepted by all classes of creditors—if the plan (1) has been accepted by at least one impaired class, (2) does not discriminate unfairly, and (3) is fair and equitable.

credit, *n.* **1.** One's ability to borrow money; the faith in one's ability to pay debts <a customer with good credit>. **2.** The time that a seller gives the buyer to make the payment that is due <30 days' credit>. **3.** The availability of funds either from a financial institution or under a letter of credit <the bank extended a line of credit to the customer>. **4.** See LETTER OF CREDIT <the bank issued a credit in favor of the exporter>. **5.** A deduction from an amount due; an accounting entry reflecting an addition to revenue or net worth <confirm that the credit was properly applied to my account>. Cf. DEBIT. **6.** See TAX CREDIT <the $500 credit reduced his income-tax liability by $500>.

> *installment credit.* Consumer credit scheduled to be repaid in two or more payments, usu. at regular intervals. • The seller ordinarily imposes finance charges.

> *revolving credit.* A consumer-credit arrangement that allows the borrower to buy goods or secure loans on a continuing basis as long as the outstanding loans do not exceed a specified limit.

credit balance. In accounting, the status of an account when the sum of the credit entries exceeds the sum of the debit entries.

credit insurance. See INSURANCE.

credit line. See LINE OF CREDIT.

creditor. 1. One to whom a debt (esp. money) is owed. **2.** A person or entity with a definite claim against another, esp. one that is capable of adjustment and liquidation at trial.

> *hypothetical creditor.* In bankruptcy law, an actual or code-created judicial-lien creditor or bona fide purchaser who claims property through the debtor at the time of the bankruptcy filing, and whose rights and powers the trustee assumes in the Bankruptcy Code's priority scheme.

> *judgment creditor.* See JUDGMENT CREDITOR.

> *junior creditor.* A creditor whose claim accrued at a later date than that of another creditor; a creditor who holds a debt that is subordinate to another's.

> *known creditor.* A creditor whose identity or claim is either known or reasonably ascertainable by the debtor. • Known creditors are entitled to notice of the debtor's bank-

ruptcy or corporate dissolution, as well as notice of any deadline for filing proofs of claim.

lien creditor. A creditor whose claim is secured by a lien on a particular piece of the debtor's property.

secured creditor. A creditor who has the right, on the debtor's default, to proceed against collateral and apply it to the payment of the debt.

unsecured creditor. A creditor who, upon giving credit, takes no rights against specific property of the debtor.—Also termed *general creditor*.

creditor beneficiary. See BENEFICIARY.

creditors' committee. In bankruptcy law, a committee comprising representatives of the creditors in a Chapter 11 proceeding, formed to negotiate the debtor's plan of reorganization.

creditors' meeting. See MEETING.

credit sale. See SALE.

credit union. A cooperative association that offers low-interest loans and other consumer banking services to persons sharing a common bond—often fellow employees and their family members.

creditworthy, *adj.* (Of a borrower) financially sound enough that a lender will extend credit in the belief that the chances of default are slight; fiscally healthy.

creeping tender offer. See TENDER OFFER.

criminal law. The body of law defining offenses against the community at large, regulating how suspects are investigated, charged, and tried, and establishing punishments for convicted offenders.

cross-collateral. See COLLATERAL.

cross-offer, *n.* In contract law, an offer made to another in ignorance that the offeree has made the same offer to the offeror.

crown jewel. A company's most valuable asset, esp. as valued at a time when the company is the subject of a hostile takeover. • A possible antitakeover device, if judicially allowed, is for the target company to sell its crown jewel to a third party so that the company will be less attractive to an unfriendly suitor. See SCORCHED-EARTH DEFENSE.

cum dividend. With dividend. • Stocks purchased cum dividend entitle the buyer to any pending declared dividends. Cf. EX DIVIDEND.

cumulative dividend. See DIVIDEND.

cumulative-effects doctrine. The rule that a transaction affecting interstate commerce in a trivial way may be taken together with other transactions of a similar nature to establish that the combined effect on interstate commerce is far from trivial and can therefore be regulated under the Commerce Clause.

cumulative preferred stock. See STOCK.

cumulative–to–the–extent–earned dividend.
See DIVIDEND.

cumulative voting. See VOTING.

cure. The right of a seller under the UCC to correct a nonconforming delivery of goods within the contract period.

currency swap. See SWAP.

current asset. See ASSET.

current funds. See FUND (2).

current income. See INCOME.

current yield. See YIELD.

cushion. See EQUITY (1).

custodian bank. See BANK.

custom, *n.* **1.** A practice that by its common adoption and long, unvarying habit has attained force of law with respect to the place or subject matter to which it relates. See USAGE. **2.** (*pl.*) Duties imposed on imports or exports.

D

daily balance. The final daily accounting for a day on which interest is to be accrued or paid.

> *average daily balance.* The average amount of money in an account (such as a bank account or credit-card account) during a given period. ● This amount serves as the basis for computing interest or a finance charge for the period.

daisy chain. A series of purchases and sales of the same stock issue by a small group of securities dealers attempting to drive the stock's price up in order to attract unsuspecting buyers' interest. ● Once the buyers have invested (i.e., are caught up in the chain), the traders sell for a quick profit, leaving the buyers with overpriced stock. This practice is illegal.

damage, *n.* Loss or injury to person or property <actionable damage resulting from the defendant's negligence>.

damages, *n. pl.* Money claimed by, or ordered to be paid to, a person as compensation for loss or injury caused by a wrongdoer <the plaintiff seeks $8,000 in damages from the defendant>.

actual damages. An amount awarded to a complainant to compensate for a proven injury or loss; damages that repay actual losses.—Also termed *compensatory damages*.

liquidated damages. An amount contractually stipulated as a reasonable estimation of actual damages to be recovered by one party if the other party breaches. ● If the parties to a contract have agreed on liquidated damages, the sum fixed is the measure of damages for a breach, whether it exceeds or falls short of the actual damages. See LIQUIDATED-DAMAGES CLAUSE. Cf. PENALTY (2).

punitive damages. Damages awarded in addition to actual damages when the defendant acted with recklessness, malice, or deceit. ● Punitive damages, which are intended to punish and thereby deter blameworthy conduct, are generally not recoverable for breach of contract.—Also termed *exemplary damages*; *vindictive damages*.

treble damages. Damages that, by statute, are three times the amount that the factfinder determines is owed.

D & O liability insurance. See *directors' and officers' liability insurance* under INSURANCE.

date of issue. 1. An arbitrary date fixed as the beginning of a term. **2.** In an insurance policy, the date set forth in the policy itself, rather than the date of actual signing or the delivery date.

date of maturity. The date when a debt falls due, such as a debt on a promissory note or bond.

day order. See ORDER.

d/b/a. *abbr.* Doing business as. • The abbreviation usu. precedes a person's or business's assumed name <Paul Smith d/b/a Paul's Dry Cleaners>.

dead asset. See ASSET.

deadlock. In corporate law, the blocking of corporate action by one or more factions of shareholders or directors who disagree about a significant aspect of corporate policy.

dealer. 1. A person who purchases goods or property for sale to others; a retailer. **2.** A person or firm that buys and sells securities for its own account as a principal, and then sells to a customer. Cf. BROKER.

> *registered dealer.* A dealer registered or required to be registered under the Securities Exchange Act.

debenture. 1. A debt secured only by the debtor's earning power, not by any specific asset. **2.** An instrument acknowledging such a debt. **3.** A bond that is backed only by the general credit and financial reputation of the corporate issuer, not by a lien on the corporation's assets. Cf. BOND (1).

> *convertible debenture.* A debenture that the holder may change or convert into some other security, such as stock.

> *sinking-fund debenture.* A debenture that is secured by periodic payments into a fund established to retire long-term debt.

> *subordinate debenture.* A debenture that is subject to the prior payment of ordinary debentures and other indebtedness.

debit. 1. A sum charged as due or owing. **2.** In bookkeeping, an entry made on the left side of a ledger or account, noting an increase in assets or a decrease in liabilities. **3.** An account balance showing that something remains owing to the holder of the account. Cf. CREDIT (5).

debt. 1. Liability on a claim; a specific sum of money due by agreement or otherwise <the debt amounted to $2,500>. **2.** The aggregate of all existing claims against a person, entity, or state <the bank denied the loan application after analyzing the applicant's outstanding debt>. **3.** A nonmonetary thing that one person owes another, such as goods or services <her debt was to supply him with 20 international first-class tickets on the airline of his choice>.

antecedent debt. a. In contract law, an old debt that may serve as consideration for a new promise if the statute of limitations has run on the old debt. See PREEXISTING-DUTY RULE. **b.** In bankruptcy law, a debtor's prepetition obligation that existed before a debtor's transfer of an interest in property. ● For a transfer to be preferential, it must be for or on account of an antecedent debt. See PREFERENTIAL TRANSFER.

bad debt. A debt that is uncollectible and that may be deductible for tax purposes.

bonded debt. A debt secured by a bond; a business or government debt represented by issued bonds.

consumer debt. A debt incurred by someone primarily for a personal, family, or household purpose.

contingent debt. A debt that is not presently fixed but that may become fixed in the future with the occurrence of some event.

convertible debt. A debt whose security may be changed by a creditor into another form of security.

floating debt. Short-term debt that is continuously renewed to finance the ongoing operations of a business or government.

funded debt. **a.** A state or municipal debt to be paid out of an accumulation of money or by future taxation. **b.** Secured long-term corporate debt meant to replace short-term, floating, or unsecured debt.

installment debt. A debt that is to be paid at regular times over a specified period.

judgment debt. A debt that is evidenced by a legal judgment or brought about by successful lawsuit against the debtor.

liquidated debt. A debt whose amount has been predetermined by agreement of the parties or by operation of law.

liquid debt. A debt that is due immediately and unconditionally.

long-term debt. Generally, a debt that will not come due within the next year.

passive debt. A debt that, by agreement between the debtor and creditor, is interest-free.

public debt. A debt owed by a municipal, state, or national government.

secured debt. A debt backed by collateral.

short-term debt. Debts and other liabilities payable within one year.

unliquidated debt. A debt that has not been reduced to a specific amount, and about which there may be a dispute.

unsecured debt. A debt not supported by collateral or other security.

debt capital. See CAPITAL.

debt-equity ratio. See DEBT-TO-EQUITY RATIO.

debt financing. See FINANCING.

debt instrument. A written promise to repay a debt, such as a promissory note, bill, bond, or commercial paper.

debtor. **1.** One who owes an obligation to another, esp. an obligation to pay money. **2.** In bankruptcy, a person who files a voluntary petition or against whom an involuntary petition is filed.—Also termed (in sense 2) *bankrupt.*

debtor-in-possession. In bankruptcy law, a Chapter 11 or 12 debtor that continues to operate its business as a fiduciary to the bankruptcy estate. • With certain exceptions, the debtor-in-possession has all the rights, powers, and duties of a Chapter 11 trustee.

debt pooling. An arrangement by which a person's debts are consolidated and adjustments are made with creditors to accept lower monthly payments or to take less money.

debt ratio. A corporation's total long-term and short-term liabilities divided by the firm's total assets. • A low debt ratio indicates conservative financing and thus usu. an enhanced ability to borrow in the future.—Also termed *debt-to-total-assets ratio*.

debt security. See SECURITY.

debt service. 1. The funds needed to meet a long-term debt's annual interest expenses, principal payments, and sinking-fund contributions. **2.** Payments due on a debt, including interest and principal.

debt-to-equity ratio. A corporation's long-term debt divided by its owners' equity, calculated to assess a firm's capitalization.—Also termed *debt-equity ratio*.

debt-to-total-assets ratio. See DEBT RATIO.

deceptive act. As defined by the Federal Trade Commission and most state statutes, conduct that is likely to deceive a consumer acting reasonably in the circumstances.—Also termed *deceptive practice*.

declaration of dividend. A corporation's setting aside of a portion of its net or surplus income for distribution to its shareholders.

declining-balance depreciation method. See DEPRECIATION METHOD.

deductible, *adj.* Capable of being subtracted, esp. from taxable income. See DEDUCTION.

deductible, *n.* **1.** Under an insurance policy, the portion of the loss to be borne by the insured before the insurer becomes responsible for payment. **2.** The insurance-policy clause specifying the amount of this portion.

deduction. In tax law, an amount subtracted from gross income when calculating adjusted gross income, or from adjusted gross income when calculating taxable income. Cf. EXEMPTION; TAX CREDIT.

    additional standard deduction. The sum of the additional amounts that a taxpayer is entitled to deduct if he or she turns 65 or becomes blind before the close of the taxable year.

charitable deduction. A deduction for a contribution to a qualified charity or other tax-exempt institution. See CHARITABLE CONTRIBUTION (2); CHARITABLE ORGANIZATION.

itemized deduction. An expense—such as medical payments, home-mortgage interest, or charitable contributions—that can be subtracted from adjusted gross income to determine taxable income.

miscellaneous itemized deduction. Generally, an itemized deduction of job or investment expenses; a deduction other than those allowable in computing adjusted gross income, those enumerated in IRC § 67(b), and personal exemptions. ● Such a deduction is allowed only to an itemizing taxpayer whose total miscellaneous itemized deductions exceed a statutory percentage of adjusted gross income.

standard deduction. A specified dollar amount that a taxpayer can deduct from adjusted gross income, instead of itemizing deductions, to determine taxable income.

deed. A written instrument by which land is conveyed. Cf. BILL OF SALE; CONVEYANCE.

bargain-and-sale deed. A deed that conveys property to a buyer for valuable consideration but that lacks any guarantee from the seller about the validity of the title.

deed in lieu of foreclosure. A deed by which a borrower conveys fee-simple title to a lender in satisfaction of a mortgage debt and as a substitute for foreclosure.

deed of trust. A deed conveying title to real property to a trustee as security until the grantor repays a loan. • This type of deed resembles a mortgage.

deed poll. A deed made by and binding on only one party, or on two or more parties having similar interests. • It is so called because traditionally the parchment was "polled" (that is, shaved) so that it would be even at the top (unlike an indenture). Cf. IN-DENTURE.

quitclaim deed. A deed that conveys a grantor's complete interest or claim in real property but that neither warrants nor professes that the title is valid.—Often shortened to *quitclaim.*

special warranty deed. **a.** A deed in which the grantor covenants to warrant and defend the title against claims and demands of only the grantor and all persons claiming by and under him or her. **b.** In a few jurisdictions, a quitclaim deed.

warranty deed. A deed that expressly guarantees the grantor's good, clear title and that contains covenants concerning the quality of title, including a covenant of quiet enjoyment and a defense of title against all claims.

deep pocket. 1. (*pl.*) Substantial wealth and resources <the plaintiff nonsuited the individuals and targeted the corporation with deep pockets>. **2.** A person or entity with substantial wealth and resources against which a claim may be made or a judgment may be taken <that national insurance company is a favorite deep pocket among plaintiff's lawyers>.

Deep Rock doctrine. In bankruptcy law, the principle by which unfair or inequitable claims presented by controlling shareholders of bankrupt corporations may be subordinated to claims of general or trade creditors. • The doctrine is named for a corporation used to make fraudulent transfers to its parent corporation in *Taylor v. Standard Gas & Elec. Co.*, 306 U.S. 307 (1939).

de facto corporation. See CORPORATION.

de facto dissolution. See DISSOLUTION.

de facto merger. See MERGER.

defamation. 1. The act of harming the reputation of another by making a false statement to a third person. **2.** A false written or oral statement that damages another's reputation. See LIBEL; SLANDER. Cf. DISPARAGEMENT.

default, *n.* The failure to perform a legal or contractual duty; esp., the failure to pay a debt when due.

defeasance clause. A mortgage provision stating that the conveyance to the mortgagee will be ineffective if the mortgagor pays the debt on time.

defect, *n.* An imperfection or shortcoming, esp. in a part that is essential to the operation or safety of a product. See PRODUCTS LIABILITY.

   design defect. A product imperfection occurring when the seller or distributor could have reduced or avoided the foreseeable risks of harm by adopting a reasonable alternative design, and when, as a result of not using that alternative, the product is not reasonably safe.

183

hidden defect. A product imperfection that is not discoverable by reasonable inspection and for which a seller or lessor is generally liable if the flaw causes harm.—Also termed *latent defect*.

manufacturing defect. An imperfection in a product that departs from its intended design even though all possible care was exercised in its assembly and marketing.

product defect. An imperfection in a product that has a manufacturing defect or design defect, or is faulty because of inadequate instructions or warnings.

defective title. See TITLE.

defense. 1. A defendant's statement of a reason why the plaintiff or prosecutor has no valid case against the defendant; esp., a defendant's answer, denial, or plea. **2.** A basis for avoiding liability on a negotiable instrument.

personal defense. An ordinary defense in a contract action—such as failure of consideration or nonperformance of conditions—that the maker or drawer of a negotiable instrument is precluded from raising against one who has the rights of a holder in due course. ● A personal defense can be asserted only against those transferees of an instrument who are not holders in due course.

real defense. One of the limited number of defenses that are good against every possible claimant, so that the maker or drawer of a negotiable instrument can raise it even against a holder in due course. • The ten real defenses are (1) fraud in the factum, (2) forgery of a necessary signature, (3) adjudicated insanity that, under state law, renders the contract void from its inception, (4) material alteration of the instrument, (5) infancy, which renders the contract voidable under state law, (6) illegality that renders the underlying contract void, (7) duress, (8) discharge in bankruptcy, or any discharge known to the holder in due course, (9) suretyship defenses (for example, if the holder knew that one indorser was signing as a surety or accommodation party), and (10) statute of limitations (generally three years after dishonor or acceptance on a draft and six years after demand or other due date on a note).—Also termed *absolute defense*.

deferred annuity. See ANNUITY.

deferred compensation. See COMPENSATION.

deferred expense. See EXPENSE.

deferred income. See INCOME.

deferred-interest bond. See BOND (1).

deferred stock. See STOCK.

deficiency, *n.* **1.** A shortfall in paying taxes; the amount by which the tax properly due exceeds the sum of the amount of tax shown on a taxpayer's return plus amounts previously assessed or collected as a deficiency, minus any credits, refunds, or other payments due the taxpayer. **2.** The amount still owed on a secured debt (such as a mortgage) after the sale of the secured property fails to yield sufficient proceeds to cover the debt's full amount; esp., the shortfall between the proceeds of a foreclosure sale and the principal debt plus interest together with the foreclosure costs.

deficiency assessment. See ASSESSMENT.

deficiency dividend. See DIVIDEND.

deficiency judgment. A judgment against a debtor for the unpaid balance of the debt if a foreclosure sale or a sale of repossessed personal property fails to yield the full amount due.

deficiency letter. An SEC letter to a registrant of a securities offering, detailing the ways in which the registration statement fails to meet SEC requirements.—Also termed *letter of comment*; *letter of comments*.

deficit. **1.** A deficiency or disadvantage; a deficiency in the amount or quality of something.

  trade deficit. In economics, the excess of merchandise imports over merchandise exports during a specific period.—Also termed *trade gap.*

2. An excess of expenditures or liabilities over revenues or assets.

deflation, *n.* A decline in the price of goods and services. Cf. INFLATION.

deforce, *vb.* To detain (a creditor's money) unjustly and forcibly.

de jure corporation. See CORPORATION.

del credere agent. See AGENT.

delegable duty. See DUTY.

delegation. The act of entrusting another with authority or empowering another to act as an agent or representative <delegation of contractual duties>.

delisting. The suspension of the privileges of having a security listed on an exchange for failure to meet the exchange's listing requirements, such as a failure to meet the minimum net-asset requirement. Cf. DEREGISTRATION.

delivery. **1.** The formal act of transferring or conveying something, such as a deed; the giving or yielding possession or control of something to another. **2.** The thing so transferred or conveyed.

> *absolute delivery.* A delivery that is complete upon the actual transfer of the instrument from the grantor's possession.

> *actual delivery.* The act of giving real and immediate possession to the buyer or the buyer's agent.

> *conditional delivery.* A delivery that passes the thing subject to delivery from the grantor's possession upon the happening of a specified event.

> *constructive delivery.* An act that amounts to a transfer of title by operation of law when the actual transfer is impractical or impossible. ● For example, the delivery of a deposit-box key by someone who is ill and immobile amounts to a constructive delivery of the box's contents even though the box may be miles away.

> *symbolic delivery.* The constructive delivery of the subject matter of a sale by the

actual delivery of an article that represents the item, that renders access to it possible, or that is the evidence of the purchaser's title to it, such as the key to a warehouse or a bill of lading for goods on shipboard.

delivery in escrow. The physical transfer of something to an escrow agent to be held until some condition is met, at which time the agent will release it. ● An example of such a delivery is a stock buyer's transfer of cash to a bank that will give the seller the cash upon receiving the stock certificates. See ESCROW.

demand, *n.* **1.** The assertion of a legal right. **2.** A request for payment of a debt or an amount due. **3.** In economics, the intensity of buyer pressure on the availability and cost of a commodity or service.

demand clause. A provision in a note allowing the holder to compel full payment if the maker fails to meet an installment.

demand deposit. See DEPOSIT.

demand draft. See *sight draft* under DRAFT.

demand instrument. An instrument payable on demand, at sight, or on presentation, as opposed to an instrument that is payable at a set future date.

demand letter. A letter by which one party explains its legal position in a dispute and requests that the recipient take some action, such as paying money owed, or else risk being sued. • Under some statutes (esp. consumer-protection laws), a demand letter is a prerequisite for filing a lawsuit.

demand loan. See *call loan* under LOAN.

demand note. See NOTE.

demutualization. The process of converting a mutual insurance company (which is owned by its policyholders) to a stock insurance company (which is owned by outside shareholders), usu. as a means of increasing the insurer's capital by allowing the insurer to issue shares.

denationalization. The act of returning government ownership and control of an industry or function to private ownership and control.

dependency exemption. See EXEMPTION.

dependent, *n.* A relative, such as a child or parent, for which a taxpayer may claim an exemption if the taxpayer provides more than half the person's financial support during the taxable year.

depletion. An emptying, exhausting, or wasting of an asset, esp. of a finite natural resource such as oil.

deposit, *n.* **1.** The act of giving money or other property to another who promises to preserve it or to use it and return it in kind; esp., the act of placing money in a bank for safety and convenience. **2.** The money or property so given.

> *demand deposit.* A bank deposit that the depositor may withdraw at any time without prior notice to the bank.

> *direct deposit.* An automatic deposit of money (esp. wages) into a bank account by electronic transfer.

> *frozen deposit.* A bank deposit that cannot be withdrawn, as because the financial institution is insolvent.

> *general deposit.* **a.** A bank deposit of money that is commingled with other depositors' money. **b.** A bank deposit that is to the depositor's credit, thus giving the depositor a right to the money and creating a debtor-creditor relationship between the bank and the depositor. • A bank is not required to return the actual money deposited as a general deposit, as it must with a general depos-

191

it; the bank need return only an equivalent sum.

special deposit. A bank deposit that is made for a specific purpose, that is kept separately, and that is to be returned to the depositor. ● The bank serves as a bailee or trustee for a special deposit.

time deposit. A bank deposit that is to remain for a specified period or on which notice must be given to the bank before withdrawal.

3. Money placed with a person as earnest money or security for the performance of a contract. ● The money will be forfeited if the depositor fails to perform.

depositary. 1. A person or institution that one leaves money or valuables with for safekeeping <a title-insurance officer is the depositary of the funds>. Cf. DEPOSITORY. **2.** A gratuitous bailee.

depositary bank. See BANK.

deposit insurance. See INSURANCE.

depository. A place where one leaves money or valuables for safekeeping <the grade school's depository for used books>. Cf. DEPOSITARY.

depository bank. See BANK.

depository-transfer check. See CHECK.

Depository Trust Corporation. The principal central clearing agency for securities transactions on the public markets.—Abbr. DTC.

depreciation. A decline in an asset's value because of use, wear, or obsolescence. Cf. APPRECIATION; AMORTIZATION (2).

depreciation method. A formula used in estimating an asset's use, wear, or obsolescence over its useful life. ● Depreciation methods are used to calculate the allowable annual tax deduction for depreciation.

accelerated-depreciation method. A depreciation method that yields larger deductions in the earlier years of an asset's life and smaller deductions in the later years.

declining-balance depreciation method. A method of computing the annual depreciation allowance by multiplying the asset's undepreciated cost each year by a uniform rate that may not exceed double the straight-line rate or 150%.

double-declining depreciation method. A depreciation method that spreads over time the initial cost of a capital asset by

193

deducting in each period twice the percentage recognized by the straight-line method and applying that double percentage to the undepreciated balance existing at the start of each period.

replacement-cost depreciation method. A depreciation method that fixes an asset's value by the price of its substitute.

sinking-fund depreciation method. A depreciation method that accounts for the time value of money by setting up a depreciation-reserve account that earns interest, resulting in a gradual yearly increase in the depreciation deduction.

straight-line depreciation method. A depreciation method that writes off the cost or other basis of the asset by deducting the expected salvage value from the initial cost of the capital asset, and dividing the difference by the asset's estimated useful life.

sum-of-the-years'-digits depreciation method. A method of calculating the annual depreciation allowance by multiplying the depreciable cost basis (cost minus salvage value) by a constantly decreasing fraction, which is represented by the remaining years of useful life at the beginning of each year divided by the total number of years of useful life at the time of acquisition.

unit depreciation method. A depreciation method—directly related to the productivity of the asset—that divides the asset's value by the estimated total number of units to be produced, and then multiplies the unit cost by the number of units sold during the year, representing the depreciation expense for the year.

units-of-output depreciation method. A method by which the cost of a depreciable asset, minus salvage value, is allocated to the accounting periods benefited based on output (as miles, hours, number of times used, and the like).

depression. A period of economic stress that persists over an extended period, accompanied by poor business conditions and high unemployment. Cf. RECESSION.

deregistration. The point at which an issuer's registration under section 12 of the Securities Exchange Act of 1934 is no longer required because of the decline in the number of holders of the issuer's securities. Cf. DE-LISTING.

deregulation. The reduction of governmental control of business, esp. to permit free markets and competition.

derivative. A financial instrument whose value depends on or is derived from the performance of an underlying stock, bond, currency, or commodity. ● Derivatives are often used to hedge a market position. Examples of derivatives include options, warrants, and futures, as well as instruments not traded on stock or commodity exchanges.—Also termed *derivative instrument*.

derivative action. A lawsuit asserted by a shareholder on the corporation's behalf against a third party (usu. a corporate director or officer) because of the corporation's failure to take some action against the third party.— Also termed *derivative suit*; *shareholder derivative suit*; *representative action*. Cf. DIRECT ACTION (3).

derivative liability. See LIABILITY.

derivative title. See TITLE.

design defect. See DEFECT.

design patent. See PATENT.

destination contract. See CONTRACT.

determination letter. A document issued by the Internal Revenue Service, at a taxpayer's request, giving an opinion about the tax signif-icance of a transaction.

detriment. In contract law, the relinquish-ment of some legal right that a promisee would have otherwise been entitled to exercise.

detrimental reliance. See RELIANCE.

devaluation. The reduction in the value of one currency in relation to another currency. Cf. REVALUATION.

development-stage company. See COMPANY.

differential pricing. The setting of the price of the same product or service differently for different customers. See PRICE DISCRIMINATION.

dilution. **1.** In corporate law, the reduction in the monetary value or voting power of stock by increasing the total number of outstanding shares. Cf. ANTIDILUTION PROVISION. **2.** In trade-mark law, the use of a trademark by a party who is prohibited from using it—even when there is no competition or likelihood of confu-sion—because of the concern that the use will impair the trademark's effectiveness by blur-ring its distinctive character or tarnishing it through unsavory association.

197

diminution-in-value method. A way of calculating damages for breach of contract based on the reduced value in the market price caused by the breach.

direct action. 1. A lawsuit by an insured against his or her own insurance company rather than against the tortfeasor and the tortfeasor's insurer. **2.** A lawsuit by a person claiming against an insured but suing the insurer directly instead of pursuing compensation indirectly through the insured. **3.** A lawsuit to enforce a shareholder's own rights against a corporation. Cf. DERIVATIVE ACTION.

direct charge-off accounting method. See ACCOUNTING METHOD.

direct cost. See COST.

direct deposit. See DEPOSIT.

direct loss. See LOSS.

director. 1. One who manages, guides, or orders; a chief administrator. **2.** A person appointed or elected to sit on a board that manages the affairs of a corporation or company by electing and exercising control over its officers. See BOARD OF DIRECTORS. Cf. OFFICER.

dummy director. A board member who is a mere figurehead and exercises no real control over the corporation's business.

inside director. A director who is also an employee, officer, or major shareholder of the corporation.

interlocking director. A director who simultaneously serves on the boards of two or more corporations that deal with each other or have allied interests.

outside director. A nonemployee director with little or no direct interest in the corporation.

provisional director. A director appointed by a court to serve on a close corporation's deadlocked board of directors.

direct order of alienation. In real-property law, the principle that a grantee who assumes the debt on a portion of mortgaged property is required to pay the mortgage debt if the original mortgagor defaults.

directors' and officers' liability insurance. See INSURANCE.

direct placement. The offering by a company, such as an industrial or utility company, of an entire issue of securities directly to a lender, such as an insurance company or group of investors, instead of involving an underwriter. ● Direct placements are exempt from SEC filing.

direct-reduction mortgage. See MORTGAGE.

disability. The lack of ability to perform some function; an objectively measurable condition of impairment, physical or mental <his disability entitled him to workers'-compensation benefits>.

disability compensation. Payments from public or private funds to a person during a period of disability and incapacity from work, such as social-security or workers'-compensation benefits.—Also termed *disability benefits*.

disability insurance. See INSURANCE.

disaster loss. See LOSS.

disbursement. The act of paying out money, commonly from a fund or in settlement of a debt or account payable <dividend disbursement>.

discharge. 1. To pay a debt or satisfy some other obligation <Thompson discharged all the debts>. **2.** To release (a debtor) from monetary obligations upon adjudication of bankruptcy <Thompson was discharged from those debts>. **3.** To fire (an employee) <the company discharged the whole department>.

discharge in bankruptcy. 1. The release of a debtor from any further personal liability for prebankruptcy debts. **2.** A bankruptcy court's decree releasing a debtor from that liability.

disclaimer. 1. A renunciation of one's own legal right or claim. **2.** A repudiation of another's legal right or claim. **3.** A writing that contains such a renunciation or repudiation.

disclaimer of warranty. An oral or written statement intended to limit a seller's liability for defects in the goods sold. ● In some circumstances, printed words must be specific and conspicuous to be effective.

disclosed principal. See PRINCIPAL (1).

disclosure. The act or process of making known something that was previously unknown; a revelation of facts <a lawyer's disclosure of a conflict of interest>.

discount, *n.* **1.** A reduction from the full amount or value of something, esp. a price. **2.** A deduction of interest in advance when one lends money on a note, bill of exchange, or other commercial paper, resulting in its present value. See PRESENT VALUE. **3.** The amount by which a security's market value is below its face value. Cf. PREMIUM (3).

discount bond. See BOND (1).

discounted cash flow. See CASH FLOW.

discount market. See MARKET.

discount rate. See INTEREST RATE.

discount share. See *discount stock* under STOCK.

discount stock. See STOCK.

discovery policy. See *claims-made policy* under INSURANCE POLICY.

discretionary account. An account that allows a broker access to a customer's money to purchase and sell securities or commodities for the customer based on the broker's judgment and without first having to obtain the customer's consent to the purchase or sale.

discretionary order. See ORDER.

discrimination. 1. The effect of a statute or established practice that confers privileges on a certain class or that denies privileges to another class because of race, age, sex, nationality, religion, or handicap. **2.** Differential treatment; esp., a failure to treat all persons equally when no reasonable distinction can be found between those favored and those not favored.

invidious discrimination. Discrimination that is offensive or objectionable, esp. because it involves prejudice or stereotyping.

reverse discrimination. Preferential treatment of minorities, usu. through affirmative-action programs, in a way that adversely affects members of a majority group. See AFFIRMATIVE ACTION.

sex discrimination. Discrimination based on gender, esp. against women, and sometimes based on sexual orientation. ● Sex discrimination is illegal under Title VII of the U.S. Code, other federal statutes, and many state and local laws.—Also termed *gender discrimination.*

disenfranchisement. The act of depriving a member of a corporation of a right, as by expulsion.

disguised dividend. See *informal dividend* under DIVIDEND.

dishonor, *vb.* To refuse to accept or pay (a negotiable instrument) when properly presented. See NOTICE OF DISHONOR.

disintermediation. The process of bank depositors' withdrawing their funds to put them into investments that pay higher returns when the free-market interest rates exceed the regulated interest ceiling for time deposits.

disinvestment. 1. The consumption of capital. **2.** The withdrawal of investments, esp. on political grounds.—Also termed (in sense 2) *divestment.*

dismissal. A release or discharge from employment.

disparagement (di-**spar**-ij-mənt). A false statement that discredits or detracts from the reputation of another's property, product, or business.—More narrowly termed *trade libel.* Cf. DEFAMATION.

disparate impact (**dis**-pə-rət). The adverse effect of a facially neutral practice (esp. an employment practice) that nonetheless discriminates against persons because of their race, sex, national origin, age, or disability and that is not justified by business necessity. • Discriminatory intent is irrelevant in a disparate-impact claim.

disparate treatment. The practice, esp. in employment decisions, of intentionally dealing with persons differently because of their race, sex, national origin, age, or disability. ● To succeed on a disparate-treatment claim, the plaintiff must prove that the defendant acted with discriminatory intent or motive.

display right. A copyright holder's exclusive right to show or exhibit a copy of the protected work publicly, whether directly or by technological means. ● For example, this right makes it illegal for a copyrighted work to be transmitted without permission over the Internet.

disposable income. See INCOME.

dissenters' right. See APPRAISAL REMEDY.

dissolution. 1. The act of bringing to an end; termination. **2.** The cancellation or abrogation of a contract by the parties, with the effect of annulling the contract's binding force and restoring the parties to their original rights. See RESCISSION. **3.** The termination of a corporation's legal existence by expiration of its charter, by legislative act, by bankruptcy, or by other means; the event immediately preceding the liquidation or winding-up process.

de facto dissolution. The termination and liquidation of a corporation's business, esp. because of an inability to pay its debts.

involuntary dissolution. The termination of a corporation administratively (as by the state for failure to file reports or pay taxes), judicially (as by the attorney general for abuse of corporate authority, management deadlock, or failure to pay creditors), or by filing bankruptcy.

voluntary dissolution. A corporation's termination initiated by the board of directors and approved by the shareholders.

distinctiveness. The quality of a trademarked word, symbol, or device that identifies the goods of a particular merchant and distinguishes them from the goods of others.

distressed goods. See GOODS.

distressed property. See PROPERTY.

distress sale. See SALE.

distribution. The apportionment and disbursement of money or property that a number of people are entitled to share; specif., a corporation's or mutual fund's transfer of money or property to its shareholders, esp. in the form of dividends.

distribution cost. See COST.

distribution right. A copyright holder's exclusive right to sell, lease, or otherwise transfer copies of the protected work to the public.

distributive share. 1. The portion (as determined in the partnership agreement) of a partnership's income, gain, loss, or deduction that is passed through to a partner and reported on the partner's tax return. **2.** The share of assets or liabilities that a partner or partner's estate acquires after the partnership is dissolved.

distributor. A wholesaler, jobber, or other manufacturer or supplier that sells chiefly to retailers and commercial users.

diversification. 1. A company's movement into a broader range of products, usu. by buying firms already serving the market or by expanding existing operations <the soft-drink company's diversification into the potato-chip market has increased its profits>. **2.** The act of investing in a wide range of companies to reduce the risk if one sector of the market suffers losses <the prudent investor's diversification of the portfolio among 12 companies>.

diversified investment company. See COMPANY.

divestiture (dɪ-**ves**-tə-chuur). **1.** The loss or surrender of an asset or interest. **2.** In antitrust law, a court order to a defendant to rid itself of property, securities, or other assets to prevent a monopoly or restraint of trade.

divestment. 1. The complete or partial loss of an interest in an asset, such as land or stock. **2.** DISINVESTMENT (2).

dividend. A portion of a company's earnings or profits distributed pro rata to its shareholders.

asset dividend. A dividend paid in the form of property, usu. the company's product, rather than in cash or stock.

capital-gain dividend. A payment made to a mutual-fund shareholder. ● The payment is the shareholder's proportional share of the net capital gain realized by securities sales from the mutual fund's portfolio.

cash dividend. A dividend paid to shareholders in the form of money.

consent dividend. A dividend that is not actually paid to the shareholders, but that is taxed to the shareholders and increases the basis in their stock investment. ● A corporation declares a consent dividend to avoid or reduce an accumulated-earnings or personal-holding-company penalty tax.

constructive dividend. A taxable benefit derived by a shareholder from the corporation even though the benefit was not designated a dividend. • The IRS may consider excessive compensation, bargain purchases of corporate property, or shareholder use of corporate property to be constructive dividends.

cumulative dividend. A dividend—usu. on preferred shares—that must be paid in full before common shareholders may receive any dividend. • If the corporation passes a dividend in a particular year or period, it is carried over to the next year or period and must be paid before the common shareholders receive any payment. Cf. *noncumulative dividend.*

cumulative-to-the-extent-earned dividend. A cumulative dividend that supplies the holder with priority in that year only.

deficiency dividend. A dividend paid to reduce or avoid personal-holding-company tax in a prior year.

extraordinary dividend. An irregular dividend that is not derived from profits arising out of the ordinary course of business but that is declared because of unusually large income or an unexpected increment in capital assets due to fortuitous conditions.

fixed-return dividend. A dividend that is constant throughout the investment's life.

informal dividend. A payment of salary, rent, interest, or the like to a shareholder as a substitute for a dividend.—Also termed *disguised dividend.*

liquidation dividend. A dividend paid to a dissolving corporation's shareholders, usu. from the capital of the corporation, upon the decision to suspend all or part of its business operations.—Also termed *liquidating dividend.*

nimble dividend. A dividend paid out of current earnings when there is a deficit in the account from which dividends may be paid. • Some state statutes prohibit nimble dividends.

noncumulative dividend. A dividend that does not accrue for the benefit of a preferred shareholder if there is a passed dividend in a particular year or period. Cf. *cumulative dividend.*

passed dividend. A dividend not paid when due by a company that usu. pays regular dividends.

preferred dividend. A dividend paid to preferred shareholders who are generally paid a fixed amount and who take priority over common shareholders.

scrip dividend. A dividend paid in certificates entitling the holder to ownership of capital stock to be issued in the future. • This type of dividend usu. signals that the corporation's cash flow is poor.

stock dividend. A dividend paid in stock expressed as a percentage of the number of shares already held by a shareholder.

year-end dividend. An extra dividend paid at the end of the fiscal year depending on the amount of the profits.

dividend date. The date on which a corporation distributes dividends to record owners of stock shares. Cf. EX-DIVIDEND DATE; RECORD DATE.

dividend-payout ratio. A profitability ratio based on annual dividends per share divided by earnings per share.

dividend preference. The right of a holder of preferred shares to receive a dividend before the company pays dividends to holders of common shares. See *preferred stock* under STOCK.

dividend-reinvestment plan. A company-sponsored program that enables common shareholders to reinvest their dividends plus supplementary cash into shares of the firm's common stock.

dividend yield. The current annual dividend divided by the market price per share.

DJIA. *abbr*. DOW JONES INDUSTRIAL AVERAGE.

dock receipt. An interim certificate issued by a maritime shipping company for the delivery of goods at the dock and entitling the designated person to receive a bill of lading.—Also termed *dock warrant*. See DOCUMENT OF TITLE.

documentary draft. See DRAFT.

documentary sale. See SALE.

document of title. A written description, identification, or declaration of goods authorizing the holder (usu. a bailee) to receive, hold, and dispose of the document and the goods it covers. • Documents of title, such as bills of lading, warehouse receipts, and delivery orders, are governed by Article 7 of the UCC. See BAILMENT.

　　negotiable document of title. A document of title that actually stands for the goods it covers, so that any transfer of the goods requires a surrender of the document.

nonnegotiable document of title. A document of title that merely serves as evidence of the goods it covers.

***D'Oench Duhme* doctrine.** The rule that estops a borrower from asserting claims or defenses against a federal successor to a failed financial institution—if those claims or defenses are based on side or secret agreements or representations—unless the agreements or representations have been (1) put into writing, (2) executed by the financial institution and borrower when the loan was issued, (3) approved by the financial institution's board of directors or loan committee, and (4) made a permanent part of the financial institution's records. *D'Oench, Duhme & Co. v. FDIC*, 315 U.S. 447 (1942) (now partially codified at 12 USCA § 1823(e), and otherwise of questionable standing in light of *O'Melveny & Myers v. FDIC*, 512 U.S. 79 (1994)).

dollar-averaging. The investment practice of purchasing a fixed dollar amount of a given security at regular intervals.

domicile. The residence of a person or corporation for legal purposes.

***commercial domicile.* a.** A domicile acquired by a nonresident corporation conducting enough managerial activities to permit taxation of the corporation's property or activities located outside the bounds of the taxing state. **b.** A domicile acquired by a person or company freely residing or carrying on business in enemy territory or enemy-occupied territory.

corporate domicile. The place considered by law as the center of corporate affairs and as the place where the corporation's functions are discharged; the legal home of a corporation, usu. its state of incorporation.

double-declining depreciation method. See DEPRECIATION METHOD.

double taxation. See TAXATION.

doubtful title. See TITLE.

Dow Jones Industrial Average. A stock-market-performance indicator that consists of the price movements in the stocks of 30 leading industrial companies in the United States.—Abbr. DJIA.—Often shortened to *Dow*.

down payment. See PAYMENT.

downstream merger. See MERGER.

draft, *n.* An unconditional written order signed by one person (the *drawer*) directing another person (the *drawee* or *payor*) to pay a certain sum of money on demand or at a definite time to a third person (the *payee*) or to bearer. ● A check is the most common example of a draft <a draft in the amount of $500>.— Also termed *bill of exchange.* Cf. NOTE.

bank draft. A draft drawn by one financial institution on another.

documentary draft. A payment demand conditioned on the presentation of a document, such as a document of title, invoice, certificate, or notice of default.

export draft. A draft drawn by a domestic seller on a foreign buyer, directing the buyer to pay the trade amount to the seller or the seller's bank.

foreign draft. A draft drawn in one country or state but payable in another.

share draft. An instrument used to withdraw funds from a credit union.

sight draft. A draft that is payable on the bearer's demand or on proper presentment to the drawer.—Also termed *demand draft.*

time draft. A draft that contains a specified payment date.

215

dram-shop liability. 1. A statutory claim to recover limited damages from a commercial seller of alcoholic beverages for a person's injuries caused by a customer's intoxication. **2.** Any common-law claim recognized against a commercial seller of alcoholic beverages.

draw, *vb.* **1.** To create and sign (a draft) <draw a check to purchase goods>. **2.** To prepare or frame (a legal document) <draw up a contract>. **3.** To take out (money) from a bank, treasury, or depository <she then drew $6,000 from her account>.

drawee. The person or entity that a draft is directed to and that is requested to pay the amount stated on it. ● The drawee is usu. a bank that is directed to pay a sum of money on an instrument.—Also termed *payor*.

drawee bank. See *payor bank* under BANK.

drawer. One who directs a person or entity, usu. a bank, to pay a sum of money stated in an instrument—for example, a person who writes a check; the maker of a note or draft. See MAKER.

DTC. *abbr.* DEPOSITORY TRUST CORPORATION.

dual distributor. A firm that sells goods simultaneously to buyers on two different levels of the distribution chain; esp., a manufacturer who sells directly to both wholesalers and retailers.

dual fund. See MUTUAL FUND.

dual listing. See LISTING (2).

due bill. See IOU.

due diligence. 1. The care and attention, continuous directed effort, and timeliness as may reasonably be expected from, and are ordinarily exercised by, a person who seeks to satisfy a legal requirement or to discharge an obligation. Cf. BEST EFFORTS. **2.** In corporate and securities law, a prospective buyer's, broker's, dealer's, or underwriter's investigation and analysis of a target company or of newly issued securities. • A failure to exercise due diligence may sometimes result in liability, as when a broker recommends a security without first investigating it adequately.

due-on-encumbrance clause. A mortgage provision giving the lender the option to accelerate the debt if the borrower further mortgages the real estate without the lender's consent.

due-on-sale clause. A mortgage provision that gives the lender the option to accelerate the debt if the borrower transfers or conveys any part of the mortgaged real estate to someone without the lender's consent.

due process. The conduct of legal proceedings according to the rules and principles established in the systems of jurisprudence for the protection and enforcement of private rights, including notice and the right to a fair hearing before a tribunal with the power to decide the case.—Also termed *due process of law*.

dummy. 1. A party who participates in a transaction only to help achieve a legal goal but who really has no interest in the transaction. **2.** One who purchases property and holds legal title for another.

dummy corporation. See CORPORATION.

dummy director. See DIRECTOR.

dummy shareholder. See SHAREHOLDER.

dumping. 1. The act of selling a large quantity of goods at less than fair value. **2.** Selling goods abroad at less than the market price at home. See ANTIDUMPING LAW.

dun, *vb.* To demand payment from (a delinquent debtor) <his creditors are dunning him daily>.

durable goods. See GOODS.

durable power of attorney. See POWER OF ATTORNEY.

duty. 1. A legal disadvantage that is owed or due to another and that needs to be satisfied; an obligation for which somebody else has a corresponding right.

delegable duty. A duty that may be transferred to another to perform. See ASSIGNMENT.

legal duty. A duty arising by contract or by operation of law; an obligation the breach of which would be a legal wrong <the legal duty of parents to support their children>.

nondelegable duty. A duty that cannot be delegated by a contracting party to a third party. ● If the duty is transferred, the other party's refusal to accept performance by the third party is not a breach of contract.

preexisting duty. A duty that one is already legally bound to perform. See PREEXISTING-DUTY RULE.

2. Any action, performance, task, or observance required by a person in an official or fiduciary capacity. **3.** A tax imposed on a commodity or transaction, esp. on imports; IMPOST. • A duty in this sense is imposed on things, not persons.

duty-to-defend clause. A liability-insurance provision obligating the insurer to take over the defense of any lawsuit brought by a third party against the insured on a claim that falls within the policy's coverage.

E

E & O insurance. See *errors-and-omissions insurance* under INSURANCE.

earned income. See INCOME.

earned-income credit. See TAX CREDIT.

earned premium. See PREMIUM (1).

earned surplus. See *retained earnings* under EARNINGS.

earnest money. A deposit paid by a buyer both to hold a seller to a deal and to show good faith, and ordinarily forfeited if the buyer defaults. ● Although an *earnest* has traditionally been a nominal sum (such as a nickel or a dollar) used in the sale of goods, *earnest money* is not a mere token in the real-estate context: it may amount to many thousands of dollars, or more. Cf. BINDER (2).

earnings. Revenue gained from one's labor or services or from the investment of capital. See EARNINGS PER SHARE; INCOME. Cf. PROFIT.

   appropriated retained earnings. Retained earnings that a company's board designates for a distinct use and that thus are not available to pay dividends or for other uses.—Also termed *surplus revenue.*

retained earnings. A corporation's accumulated income after dividends have been distributed.—Also termed *earned surplus*; *undistributed profit.*

surplus earnings. The excess of corporate assets over liabilities.

earnings per share. The value of a common-stock share, determined by dividing a corporation's annual net income by the number of common-stock shares outstanding throughout the year.—Abbr. EPS.

fully diluted earnings per share. The value of a common-stock share if all convertible securities had been transferred to common equity and all stock options had been exercised.

earnings yield. See YIELD.

earnout agreement. An agreement for the sale of a business whereby the buyer first pays an amount up front, and the final purchase price is later determined by the business's future profits. • Usu. the seller helps manage the business for a period after the sale.— Sometimes shortened to *earnout.*

easement. A legal or equitable right acquired by the owner of one piece of land (the *domi-*

nant estate) to use another's land (the *servient estate*) for a special purpose, such as to drive through it to reach a road.

economic duress. An unlawful coercion to perform by threatening financial injury at a time when one cannot exercise free will.

economic frustration. See *commercial frustration* under FRUSTRATION.

economic indicator. A statistical measure of a market area used to describe the state of the economy or predict its direction.

   lagging economic indicator. An economic indicator that tends to respond to the direction of the economy, such as new-home sales.

   leading economic indicator. An economic indicator that tends to predict the future direction of the economy, such as interest rates.

economic life. The duration of an asset's profitability, usu. shorter than its physical life.

economic-realities test. A method by which a court determines the nature of a business transaction or situation. ● This test is used most often by courts in determining whether a person is an employee or an independent contractor. Factors include who controls the details of the work and whether taxes are withheld from payments made to the worker.

economic rent. 1. The return gained from an economic resource (such as a worker or land) above the minimum cost of keeping the resource in service. **2.** Rent that yields a fair return on capital and expenses.

economy. 1. The management or administration of the wealth and resources of a community (e.g., a city, state, or country). **2.** The sociopolitical organization of a community's wealth and resources.

 balanced economy. An economy in which the monetary values of imports and exports are equal.

 overheated economy. An economy that, although it has a high level of economic activity, has the capacity to increase interest rates and inflation.

economy of scale. (*usu. pl.*) A decline in the per-unit cost of a product resulting from increased output, usu. due to increased production facilities; savings resulting from the greater efficiency of large-scale processes.

ECU. *abbr.* EUROPEAN CURRENCY UNIT.

educational expense. See EXPENSE.

EEOC. *abbr.* EQUAL EMPLOYMENT OPPORTUNITY COMMISSION.

effective rate. See INTEREST RATE.

efficient breach. See BREACH OF CONTRACT.

efficient-breach theory. The view that a party should be allowed to breach a contract and pay damages, if that would be economically efficient, rather than be forced to perform under the contract. • This relatively modern theory stems from the law-and-economics movement. See BREACH OF CONTRACT.

8–K. An SEC form that a registered corporation is required to file if a material event affecting the corporation's financial condition occurs between the due dates for regular SEC filings.

eleemosynary (el-ə-**mos**-ə-ner-ee), *adj.* Of, relating to, or assisted by charity; not-for-profit <an eleemosynary institution>.

eleemosynary corporation. See *charitable corporation* under CORPORATION.

embargo. 1. A government's wartime or peacetime detention of an offending nation's private ships found in the ports of the aggrieved nation <the President called off the embargo of Iraq's ships after the war ended>. **2.** The unilateral or collective restrictions on the import or export of goods, materials, capital, or services into or from a specific country or group of countries for political or security reasons <for a time, the industrialized nations placed an embargo on all goods from Libya>.

embezzlement. The fraudulent taking of personal property with which one has been entrusted, esp. as a fiduciary. ● The criminal intent for embezzlement—unlike larceny and false pretenses—arises after taking possession (not before or during the taking).

eminent domain. The power of a governmental entity to convert privately owned property, esp. land, to public use, subject to reasonable compensation for the taking.

employee. One who works for another under an express or implied contract. Cf. AGENT; *independent contractor* under CONTRACTOR.

borrowed employee. An employee whose services are, with the employee's consent, lent to another employer who temporarily assumes control over the employee's work. ●

The borrowing employer bears vicarious liability for the employee's acts under the doctrine of *respondeat superior*.

Employee Retirement Income Security Act. A federal statute that regulates private pensions and established the Pension Benefit Guaranty Corporation.—Abbr. ERISA.

employee stock option. See STOCK OPTION.

employers'-liability insurance. See INSURANCE.

employment. **1.** The act of employing; the state of being employed. **2.** Work for which one has been hired and is being paid by an employer.

> *employment at will.* An employee–employer relationship that usu. is undertaken without a contract and that may be severed at any time by either party without cause.

encumbrance. A claim or liability (such as a lien or mortgage) that is attached to property or some other interest and that may lessen its value; any property right that is not an ownership interest.

endorsee. See INDORSEE.

227

endorsement. **1.** See INDORSEMENT. **2.** An amendment to an insurance policy; a rider.

endorser. See INDORSER.

English rule. The requirement that a losing litigant must pay the winner's costs and attorney's fees. Cf. AMERICAN RULE.

enrolled agent. One who, though neither a certified public accountant nor an attorney, has been admitted to practice before the IRS either by passing an examination or by working for the IRS in a technical area for at least five years. ● The enrolled agent is one of four types of persons who are allowed to practice before the IRS, the other three being attorneys, certified public accountants, and persons who are admitted to represent either themselves or others in a particular case.

enterprise liability. See LIABILITY.

entity assumption. The presumption that a business is a unit separate from its owners or from other firms.

environmental-impact statement. A federally required report that accompanies a proposal for a program or law and details the likely effects on the environment.

228

Environmental Protection Agency. A federal agency created in 1970 to coordinate governmental action to protect the environment.—Abbr. EPA.

EPS. *abbr.* EARNINGS PER SHARE.

equal-dignities rule. In agency law, the doctrine that all acts requiring a writing signed by the principal can be performed by the agent only if there is a writing that sets forth the agent's authority. ● This rule is an adjunct to the statute of frauds in circumstances in which one or more of the signatories to a contract acted through an agent.

Equal Employment Opportunity Commission. A federal agency created under the Civil Rights Act of 1964 to end discriminatory employment practices and to promote nondiscriminatory employment programs.—Abbr. EEOC.

equalization. **1.** The raising or lowering of assessed values to achieve conformity. **2.** The adjustment of an assessment or tax to create a rate uniform with another.

equal-opportunity employment practice. An employer's method of hiring without regard to race, color, religion, sex, or national origin.

equal protection. 1. A constitutional requirement guaranteeing that similarly situated persons will receive the same constitutional rights.—Also termed *equal protection of the laws*. **2.** In tax law, a rule providing that persons will receive different classifications based only on actual and relevant differences, and that any disparate treatment will not be arbitrary.

equitable foreclosure. See FORECLOSURE.

equitable owner. See *beneficial owner* (a) under OWNER.

equitable remedy. See REMEDY.

equitable title. See TITLE.

equity, *n.* **1.** The amount by which the value of a property or an interest in property exceeds secured claims or liens; the difference between the value of the property and all encumbrances upon it <thanks to the real-estate boom, the mortgaged house still had high equity>.—Also termed *cushion*. **2.** An ownership interest in property, esp. in a business <the founders gave her equity in the business in return for all her help>. See OWNERS' EQUITY. **3.** A share in a publicly traded company <he did not want to cash in his equity>.

equity accounting method. See ACCOUNTING METHOD.

equity capital. See CAPITAL.

equity financing. See FINANCING.

equity insolvency. See INSOLVENCY.

equity loan. See *home equity loan* under LOAN.

equity of redemption. The right of a mortgagor in default to recover property before a foreclosure sale by paying the principal, interest, and other costs that are due and owing. ● A defaulting mortgagor with an equity of redemption has the right, until the foreclosure sale, to reimburse the mortgagee and erase the default. In many jurisdictions, the mortgagor also has a statutory right to redeem within six months after the foreclosure sale, and the mortgagor becomes entitled to any surplus from the sale proceeds above the amount of the outstanding mortgage.—Also termed *right of redemption*. See CLOG ON THE EQUITY OF REDEMPTION.

equity participation. The inclusion of a lender in the equity ownership of a project as a condition of the lender's granting a loan.

equity ratio. 1. The percentage relationship between a purchaser's equity value (esp. the amount of a down payment) and the property value. **2.** The measure of a shareholder's equity divided by total equity.

equity security. See SECURITY.

ERISA. *abbr*. EMPLOYEE RETIREMENT INCOME SECURITY ACT.

errors-and-omissions insurance. See INSURANCE.

escape clause. A contractual provision that allows a party to avoid performance under specified conditions; esp., an insurance-policy provision—usu. contained in the "other insurance" section of the policy—requiring the insurer to provide coverage only if there is no other coverage available. Cf. EXCESS CLAUSE; PRO RATA CLAUSE.

escrow, *n*. **1.** A legal document or property delivered by a promisor to a third party to be held by the third party for a given amount of time or until the occurrence of a condition, at which time the third party is to hand over the document or property to the promisee <the agent received the escrow two weeks before the closing date>. **2.** An account held in trust or as security <the earnest money is in es-

crow>.—Also termed *escrow account*. See *escrow account* under ACCOUNT. **3.** The holder of such a document, property, or deposit <the attorney performed the function of escrow>.— Also termed *escrow agent*. **4.** The general arrangement under which a legal document or property is delivered to a third person until the occurrence of a condition <creating an escrow>.

escrow account. See ACCOUNT.

escrow agent. The third-party depositary of an escrow. See ESCROW (3).

escrow agreement. The instructions given to the third-party depositary of an escrow.

espionage (**es**-pee-ə-nahzh). The practice of using spies to collect information about what another government or company is doing or plans to do.

   industrial espionage. One company's spying on another with the goal of stealing the other company's trade secrets or other proprietary information.

estimated tax. See TAX.

estoppel (e-**stop**-əl). **1.** A legally imposed bar resulting from one's own conduct and precluding any denial or assertion regarding a fact. **2.** A doctrine that prevents a person from adopting an inconsistent position, attitude, or action if it will result in injury to another. **3.** An affirmative defense alleging good-faith reliance on a misleading representation and an injury or detrimental change in position resulting from that reliance. Cf. WAIVER (1).

> ***promissory estoppel.*** The principle that a promise made without consideration becomes binding if (1) the promisor intends, or should reasonably expect, the promise to induce reliance, (2) a party actually relies on the promise, and (3) nonenforcement of the promise will cause detrimental injury or injustice.

EU. *abbr.* EUROPEAN UNION.

euro. The official currency of 11 countries in the European Union. ● On January 1, 1999, the euro became the single currency of the 11 participating countries—Austria, Belgium, Finland, France, Germany, Ireland, Italy, Luxembourg, Netherlands, Portugal, and Spain. Euro notes and coins will be issued on January 1, 2002.

Eurodollar. A U.S. dollar deposited in a foreign bank and used in the European money markets.

European Currency Unit. A monetary unit whose value is calculated as a weighted average of currencies from ten member-nations of the European Union. ● The European Currency Unit was created in 1979 to promote currency stability. The unit is a hypothetical currency; no actual bills or coins exist.—Abbr. ECU; ecu.

European Union. An association of European nations with the purpose of achieving full economic unity (and eventual political union) by agreeing to eliminate barriers to the free movement of capital, goods, and labor among the member-nations. ● The European Union was originally formed as the European Economic Community (EEC) by the Treaty of Rome in 1957, and was later renamed as the European Community (EC). The European Community became the European Union when the Maastricht Treaty on European Union took effect in November 1993. Austria, Belgium, Denmark, Finland, France, Germany, Great Britain, Greece, Ireland, Italy, Luxembourg, Netherlands, Portugal, Spain, and Sweden currently have full membership privileges.—Abbr. EU.

even lot. See *round lot* under LOT.

eviction. The act or process of legally dispossessing a person of land or rental property.

actual eviction. A physical expulsion of a person from land or rental property.

constructive eviction. **a.** A landlord's act of making premises unfit for occupancy, often with the result that the tenant is compelled to leave. **b.** The inability of a land purchaser to obtain possession because of paramount outstanding title. • Such an eviction usu. constitutes a breach of the covenants of warranty and quiet enjoyment.

retaliatory eviction. An eviction—often illegal—commenced in response to a tenant's complaints or involvement in activities with which the landlord does not agree.

excess clause. An insurance-policy provision—usu. contained in the "other insurance" section of the policy—that limits the insurer's liability to the amount exceeding other available coverage. • This clause essentially requires other insurers to pay first. Cf. ESCAPE CLAUSE; PRO RATA CLAUSE.

excess insurance. See INSURANCE.

exchange, *n.* **1.** The act of transferring interests, each in consideration for the other. **2.** The payment of a debt using a bill of exchange or credit rather than money. **3.** An organization that brings together buyers and sellers of securities, commodities, and the like to promote uniformity in the customs and usages of merchants, to facilitate the speedy adjustment of business disputes, to gather and disseminate valuable commercial and economic information, and to secure to its members the benefits of cooperation in the furtherance of their legitimate pursuits. • The best-known exchanges are stock, produce, livestock, cotton, and grain exchanges. **4.** The building or hall where members of an exchange meet every business day to buy and sell for themselves, or as brokers for their customers, for present and future delivery. See SECURITIES EXCHANGE.

exchange broker. One who negotiates money or merchandise transactions for others.

exchange rate. The price of converting one country's money into another country's money. See FOREIGN EXCHANGE.

exchange ratio. The number of shares that an acquiring company must give for each share of an acquired company.

excise tax. See TAX.

exclusion, *n.* **1.** In tax law, an item of income that the Internal Revenue Code excludes from gross income.—Also termed *income exclusion.*

237

annual exclusion. The amount, such as $10,000, allowed as nontaxable gift income during the calendar year.

2. An insurance-policy provision that excepts certain events or conditions from coverage.

exclusive agency. See AGENCY (1).

exclusive-agency listing. See LISTING (1).

exclusive-dealing arrangement. An agreement requiring a buyer to purchase all needed goods from one seller. Cf. *requirements contract* under CONTRACT.

exclusive license. See LICENSE.

exclusive use. 1. The right to use a specific trademark without exception, and to prevent another from using a confusingly similar mark. **2.** The right of an adverse user to a property, exercised independently of any similar rights held by others.

ex dividend. Without dividend. • Shares are traded ex dividend when the seller, not the purchaser, is entitled to the next dividend payment because it will be made before the stock transfer is completed. The first day shares are traded ex dividend, the stock price will drop by an amount usu. approximating the amount of the dividend.—Abbr. XD. Cf. CUM DIVIDEND.

ex-dividend date. The date on or after which the buyer of a security does not acquire the right to receive a recently declared dividend.— Also termed *ex-date*. Cf. DIVIDEND DATE.

execute, *vb*. To perform or complete (a contract or duty) <once the contract was fully executed, the parties owed no further contractual duties to each other>.

execution. 1. Validation of a written instrument, such as a contract or will, by fulfilling the necessary legal requirements <delivery of the goods completed the contract's execution>. **2.** Judicial enforcement of a money judgment, usu. by seizing and selling the judgment debtor's property <even if the plaintiff receives a judgment against the foreign debtor, execution is unlikely>. **3.** A court order directing a sheriff or other officer to enforce a judgment, usu. by seizing and selling the judgment debtor's property <the court issued the execution authorizing seizure of the car>.—Also termed (in sense 3) *writ of execution*.

execution sale. See SALE.

executive, *n*. A corporate officer at the upper levels of management.

239

executory contract. See CONTRACT.

exemplary damages. See *punitive damages* under DAMAGES.

exempt income. See INCOME.

exemption. An amount allowed as a deduction from adjusted gross income, used to determine taxable income. Cf. DEDUCTION.

> *dependency exemption.* An exemption granted to an individual taxpayer for each dependent whose gross income is less than the exemption amount and for each child who is younger than 19 or, if a student, younger than 24.

> *personal exemption.* An amount allowed as a deduction from an individual taxpayer's adjusted gross income.

exempt property. See PROPERTY.

exempt security. See SECURITY.

exercise value. The value to the optionholder of using an option.

Ex-Im Bank. See EXPORT-IMPORT BANK.

expense, *n.* An expenditure of money, time, labor, or resources to accomplish a result. Cf. COST.

accrued expense. An expense incurred but not yet paid.

capitalized expense. An amortized expense.

deferred expense. A cost incurred by a business when the business expects to benefit from that cost over a period of time beyond the current year. • An example is a prepaid subscription to a business periodical the cost of which will be recognized as an expense over a multiyear subscription period.

educational expense. For tax purposes, a deductible expense incurred either to maintain or improve an existing job skill or to meet a legally imposed job requirement.

general administrative expense. (*usu. pl.*) An expense incurred in running a business, in contrast to an expense incurred in manufacturing or selling; overhead. • Examples include executive and clerical salaries, rent, utilities, and legal and accounting services.

operating expense. An expense incurred in running a business and producing output.— Also termed *business expense.*

organizational expense. An expense incurred while setting up a corporation or other entity.

out-of-pocket expense. An expense that one has to pay from one's own funds.

expiration date. The date on which an offer, option, or the like ceases to exist.

export, *n.* **1.** A product or service created in one country and transported to another. **2.** The process of transporting products or services to another country.

export draft. See DRAFT.

Export-Import Bank. A federal agency, established in 1934, that encourages trade with foreign countries by financing exports and imports with funds borrowed from the U.S. Treasury.—Abbr. Ex-Im Bank.

export letter of credit. See LETTER OF CREDIT.

express authority. See AUTHORITY.

express trust. See TRUST.

express warranty. See WARRANTY.

ex rights. Without rights. ● A stock traded ex rights does not give the stockholder the privilege to purchase shares of a new stock issue at a discount.

ex-rights date. The date on which a share of common stock no longer offers privilege subscription rights.

ex ship. Of or referring to a shipment of goods for which the liability passes to the buyer once the goods leave the ship.

extension. The continuation of the same contract for a specified period.

externality. (*usu. pl.*) A social or monetary consequence or side effect of one's economic activity, causing another to benefit without paying or to suffer without compensation.— Also termed *neighborhood effect*.

   negative externality. An externality that is detrimental to another, such as water pollution created by a nearby factory.

   positive externality. An externality that benefits another, such as the advantage received by a neighborhood when a homeowner attractively landscapes the property.

extortion. 1. The offense committed by a public official who illegally obtains property under the color of office; esp., an official's collection of an unlawful fee. **2.** The act or practice of obtaining something or compelling some action by illegal means, such as by force or coercion.

extrajudicial remedy. See REMEDY.

extraordinary dividend. See DIVIDEND.

F

face value. See PAR VALUE.

facility-of-payment clause. An insurance-policy provision allowing the appointment of a person to receive payment from the insurer on the beneficiary's behalf.

factor. 1. An agent who is employed to sell property for the principal and who is vested with the possession or control of the property; a person who receives and sells goods for a commission <a factor was employed to sell goods for the company>. ● A factor differs from a broker because the factor has possession or control of the property.—Also termed *commission merchant.* **2.** One who buys discounted accounts receivable <the company sold its old receivables to a factor at only 5% of their stated value>. **3.** A garnishee <the factor held $400 of the debtor's property when the garnishment was served>.

factor's act. A statute protecting a buyer of goods from a factor or agent by creating the presumption that the agent was acting on the owner's behalf and with the owner's approval.

failure of consideration. A situation in which a contract's basis or inducement ceases to exist or becomes worthless. ● This term, unlike *consideration* per se, relates not to the formation of a contract but to its performance.

fair consideration. See CONSIDERATION.

fair-credit-reporting act. A federal or state law that regulates the keeping of credit reports and ensures the right of consumers to access and correct their credit reports. ● The federal Fair Credit Reporting Act was enacted in 1970.

Fair Labor Standards Act. A federal law, enacted in 1938, that regulates minimum wages, overtime pay, and the employment of minors.

fair market value. The price at which a seller is ready and willing to sell and a buyer is ready and willing to buy on the open market and in an arm's-length transaction; the point at which supply and demand intersect.—Abbr. FMV.—Also termed *market value*.

fair rate of return. See RATE OF RETURN.

fair-trade agreement. A commercial agreement providing that a seller will sell all of a producer's goods for at least a specified minimum price. ● Fair-trade agreements were valid until Congress in 1975 passed the Consumer Goods Pricing Act, which made the agreements illegal.

fair use. A reasonable and limited use of a copyrighted work without the author's permission, such as quoting from a book in a book review. ● Fair use is a defense to an infringement claim, depending on the following statutory factors: (1) the purpose and character of the use, (2) the nature of the copyrighted work, (3) the amount of the work used, and (4) the economic impact of the use.

fair-value accounting method. See AC-COUNTING METHOD.

fair-value legislation. A statute requiring a deficiency judgment to be measured by the difference between the mortgage debt and the fair value of the foreclosed real estate.

false imprisonment. A confinement or restraint of a person to a bounded area without justification or consent.

false return. See TAX RETURN.

family-farmer bankruptcy. See CHAPTER 12.

family-partnership rules. Laws designed to prevent the shifting of income among partners, esp. family members, who may not be dealing at arm's length.

Fannie Mae. See FEDERAL NATIONAL MORTGAGE ASSOCIATION.

Farmers Home Administration. A division of the U.S. Department of Agriculture that makes mortgage loans to farmers, provides home-mortgage insurance, and funds public-works programs ·in rural areas and small towns.—Abbr. FHA.

F.A.S. *abbr.* FREE ALONGSIDE SHIP.

FASB. *abbr.* FINANCIAL ACCOUNTING STANDARDS BOARD.

FASB statement. An official pronouncement from the Financial Accounting Standards Board establishing a given financial-accounting practice as an acceptable accounting principle.

FDIC. *abbr.* FEDERAL DEPOSIT INSURANCE CORPORATION.

featherbedding. A union practice designed to increase employment and guarantee job security by requiring employers to hire or retain more employees than are needed. ● Featherbedding is restricted by federal law but is an unfair labor practice only if, for example, a union exacts pay from an employer for services not performed or not to be performed.

Fed. *abbr.* FEDERAL RESERVE SYSTEM.

Federal Deposit Insurance Corporation. An independent governmental agency that insures bank deposits up to a statutory amount per depositor at each participating bank. • The insurance fund is financed by a small fee paid by the participating banks.—Abbr. FDIC.

Federal Home Loan Mortgage Corporation. A corporation that purchases both conventional and federally insured first mortgages from members of the Federal Reserve System and other approved banks. • It is under the Federal Home Loan Bank Board.—Abbr. FHLMC.—Also termed *Freddie Mac*.

Federal Insurance Contributions Act. A federal law that imposes the social-security tax on employers and employees.—Abbr. FICA.

Federal National Mortgage Association. A corporation that is chartered by the U.S. Government but privately owned and managed, and that provides a secondary mortgage market for the purchase and sale of mortgages guaranteed by the Veterans Administration and those insured under the Federal Housing Administration.—Abbr. FNMA.—Also termed *Fannie Mae*.

Federal Register. A daily publication in which U.S. administrative agencies publish their rules and regulations, including proposed rules and regulations for public comment.

Federal Reserve System. A network of 12 central banks supervised by the Board of Governors, who are appointed by the President and confirmed by the Senate and who set the reserve requirements for the member banks, review the discount-rate actions of the regional Federal Reserve banks, and set ceilings on the interest rates that member banks may pay.— Abbr. Fed.

Federal Savings and Loan Insurance Corporation. A federal agency created in 1934 to insure deposits in savings-and-loan associations and savings banks. ● When this agency became insolvent in 1989, its assets and liabilities were transferred to an insurance fund managed by the FDIC.—Abbr. FSLIC. Cf. RESOLUTION TRUST CORPORATION.

Federal Trade Commission. The independent regulatory agency created in 1914 to enforce the antitrust laws and other prohibitions against false, deceptive, and unfair advertising or trade practices.—Abbr. FTC.

fee. 1. A charge for labor or services, esp. professional services <attorney's fees>. **2.** An inheritable interest in land, constituting maximal legal ownership <a fee simple>.

FHA. *abbr.* FARMERS HOME ADMINISTRATION.

FHLMC. *abbr.* FEDERAL HOME LOAN MORTGAGE CORPORATION.

FICA. *abbr.* FEDERAL INSURANCE CONTRIBUTIONS ACT.

fictitious person. See ARTIFICIAL PERSON.

fidelity bond. See BOND (2).

fidelity insurance. See INSURANCE.

fiduciary (fi-**d[y]oo**-shee-er-ee), *n.* **1.** One who owes to another the duties of good faith, trust, confidence, and candor <the corporate officer is a fiduciary to the shareholders>. **2.** One who must exercise a high standard of care in managing another's money or property <the beneficiary sued the fiduciary for investing in speculative securities>.

fiduciary relationship. A relationship in which one person is under a duty to act for the benefit of the other on matters within the scope of the relationship. ● Fiduciary relationships—such as trustee-beneficiary, guardian-ward, agent-principal, and attorney-client—require the highest duty of care.—Also termed *confidential relationship*.

fiduciary-shield doctrine. In corporate law, the principle that a corporate officer's act cannot provide the basis for jurisdiction over the officer in his or her individual capacity.

field audit. See AUDIT.

FIFO. *abbr*. FIRST-IN, FIRST-OUT.

finance bill. See BILL (2).

finance charge. An additional payment, usu. in the form of interest, paid by a retail buyer for the privilege of purchasing goods or services in installments.

finance lease. See LEASE.

financial accounting. See ACCOUNTING (1).

Financial Accounting Standards Board. The independent body of accountants responsible for establishing and interpreting generally accepted accounting principles.—Abbr. FASB.

financial institution. A business, organization, or other entity that manages money, credit, or capital, such as a bank, credit union, savings-and-loan association, securities broker or dealer, pawnbroker, or investment company.

financial intermediary. A financial entity—usu. a commercial bank—that advances the transfer of funds between borrowers and lenders, buyers and sellers, and investors and savers.

financial statement. A balance sheet, income statement, or annual report that summarizes an individual's or organization's financial condition on a certain date or for a specified period by analyzing its assets and liabilities.—Also termed *financial report*. Cf. FINANCING STATEMENT.

> *consolidated financial statement.* The financial report of a company and all its subsidiaries combined, usu. without intercompany transactions.

financing. 1. The act or process of raising or providing funds. **2.** Funds that are raised or provided.

> *asset-based financing.* A method of funding in which lenders and investors look principally to the cash flow from a particular asset for the return on their investment.

> *debt financing.* Raising funds by issuing bonds or notes or by borrowing from a fi-

nancial institution to acquire working capital or to retire short-term indebtedness.

equity financing. **a.** The raising of corporate capital by issuing securities rather than taking out loans or selling bonds. **b.** The capital so raised.

floor-plan financing. A loan that is secured by merchandise and paid off as the goods are sold. • Usu. such a loan is given by a manufacturer to a retailer or other dealer (as a car dealer).—Also termed *floor planning*.

gap financing. Interim financing used to fund the difference between a current loan and a loan for a greater amount to be received in the future. See *bridge loan* under LOAN.

interim financing. A short-term loan secured to cover certain major expenditures, such as construction costs, until permanent financing is obtained.

internal financing. A method of funding a project or investment using funds generated through the company's operations rather than from stock issues or bank loans.

link financing. The process of depositing funds in another's bank account to aid in obtaining a loan.

outside financing. The raising of funds by selling stocks (equity financing) or bonds (debt financing).

permanent financing. A long-term loan obtained to repay an interim loan, such as a mortgage loan used to repay a construction loan.

project financing. A method of funding in which the lender looks primarily to the money generated by a single project as security for the loan. • This type of financing is usu. used for large, complex, and expensive single-purpose projects such as power plants, chemical processing plants, mines, and toll roads. The lender is usu. paid solely or almost exclusively out of the money generated by the contracts for the facility's output (sometimes paid by customers directly into an account maintained by the lender), such as the electricity sold by a power plant. The lender usu. requires the facility to be developed and owned by a special-purpose entity (sometimes called a bankruptcy-remote entity), which can be a corporation, limited partnership, or other legal entity, that is permitted to perform no function other than developing, owning, and operating the facility. See SPECIAL-PURPOSE ENTITY; BANKRUPTCY-REMOTE ENTITY.

financing statement. A document filed properly in the public records to notify third parties, usu. prospective buyers and lenders, of a secured party's security interest in goods. Cf. FINANCIAL STATEMENT.

finder. An intermediary who brings together parties for a business opportunity, such as two companies for a merger, a borrower and a financial institution, or an issuer and an underwriter of securities. ● A finder differs from a broker-dealer because a finder merely brings two parties together to make their own contract, while a broker-dealer may participate in the negotiations.

finder's fee. The amount charged by one who brings together parties for a business opportunity.

fire insurance. See INSURANCE.

firm, *n*. **1.** The title under which one or more persons carry on business jointly. **2.** The association by which persons are united for business purposes; esp., a partnership.

firm-commitment underwriting. See UNDERWRITING.

firm offer. See *irrevocable offer* under OFFER (1).

firm-opportunity doctrine. See CORPORATE OPPORTUNITY DOCTRINE.

first-in, first-out. An accounting method that assumes that goods are sold in the order in which they were purchased—that is, the oldest items are sold first.—Abbr. FIFO. Cf. LAST-IN, FIRST-OUT; NEXT-IN, FIRST-OUT.

first lien. See LIEN.

first mortgage. See MORTGAGE.

first-mortgage bond. See BOND (1).

first option to buy. See RIGHT OF PREEMPTION.

first-party insurance. See *self-insurance* under INSURANCE.

fiscal (**fis**-kəl), *adj.* **1.** Of or relating to financial matters <fiscal year>. **2.** Of or relating to public finances or taxation <the city's sound fiscal policy>.

fiscal year. An accounting period of 12 consecutive months. ● A fiscal year is often different from the calendar year, esp. for tax purposes <the company's fiscal year is October 1 to September 30>.—Also termed *fiscal period*.

fixed annuity. See ANNUITY.

fixed asset. See *capital asset* (a) under ASSET.

fixed capital. See CAPITAL.

fixed cost. See COST.

fixed income. See INCOME.

fixed price. See PRICE.

fixed-rate mortgage. See MORTGAGE.

fixed-return dividend. See DIVIDEND.

fixture. Personal property that is attached to land or a building and that is regarded as an irremovable part of the real property, such as a fireplace built into a home. Cf. IMPROVEMENT.

   trade fixture. Removable personal property that a tenant attaches to leased property for business purposes, such as a display counter. ● Despite its name, a trade fixture is not usu. treated as a fixture—that is, as irremovable.

flat bond. See BOND (1).

flat tax. See TAX.

flexible-rate mortgage. See *renegotiable mortgage* under MORTGAGE.

flip, *vb. Slang.* **1.** To buy and then immediately resell securities or real estate in an attempt to turn a profit. **2.** To refinance consumer loans.

flip mortgage. See MORTGAGE.

float, *n.* **1.** The sum of money represented by outstanding or uncollected checks. **2.** The delay between a transaction (as by check or on credit) and the withdrawal of funds to cover the transaction. **3.** The amount of a corporation's shares that are available for trading on the securities market.

float, *vb.* **1.** (Of a currency) to attain a value in the international exchange market solely on the basis of supply and demand <the IMF allowed the peso to float>. **2.** To issue (a security) for sale on the market <PDQ Corp. floated a new series of preferred shares>. **3.** To arrange or negotiate (a loan) <the bank floated a car loan to Alice despite her poor credit history>.

floater insurance. See INSURANCE.

floating capital. See CAPITAL.

floating debt. See DEBT.

floating-interest bond. See BOND (1).

floating lien. See LIEN.

floating rate. See INTEREST RATE.

floor. The trading area where stocks and commodities are bought and sold on exchanges <the broker placed his buy order with the trader on the floor of the NYSE>.

floor-plan financing. See FINANCING.

floor price. See PRICE.

flower bond. See BOND (1).

FMV. *abbr.* FAIR MARKET VALUE.

FNMA. *abbr.* FEDERAL NATIONAL MORTGAGE ASSOCIATION.

FOB. *abbr.* FREE ON BOARD.

FOB destination. See FREE ON BOARD.

FOB shipping. See FREE ON BOARD.

forced sale. See SALE.

force majeure (fors-mə-**zhoor** or-mah-**zhər**). [Law French "a superior force"] An event or effect that can be neither anticipated nor controlled. • The term includes both acts of nature (such as floods or hurricanes) and acts of people (such as riots, strikes, or wars). Cf. ACT OF GOD.

forcible entry and detainer. A quick and simple legal proceeding for regaining possession of real property from someone who has wrongfully taken, or refused to surrender, possession.—Also termed *forcible detainer*. See EVICTION.

foreclosure. A legal proceeding for the termination of a mortgagor's interest in property, instituted by the lender (the mortgagee) either to gain title or to force a sale in order to satisfy all or part of the unpaid debt secured by the property.

   equitable foreclosure. A foreclosure method in which the court orders the property sold, and the proceeds are applied first to the payment of the costs of the suit and sale and then to the mortgage debt. • Any surplus is paid to the borrower.

   judicial foreclosure. A costly and time-consuming foreclosure method by which the mortgaged property is sold through a court proceeding requiring many standard legal steps such as the filing of a complaint, service of process, notice, and a hearing. • Judicial foreclosure is available in all states

261

and is the exclusive or most common method of foreclosure in many of them.

nonjudicial foreclosure. **a.** See *power-of-sale foreclosure.* **b.** A foreclosure method that does not require court involvement.

power-of-sale foreclosure. A foreclosure process by which, according to the mortgage instrument and a state statute, the mortgaged property is sold at a nonjudicial public sale by a public official, the mortgagee, or a trustee, without the stringent notice requirements, protections, or delays of a judicial foreclosure. • Power-of-sale foreclosure is authorized and used in more than half the states.—Also termed *nonjudicial foreclosure.*

strict foreclosure. A rare procedure that gives the mortgagee title to the mortgaged property—without first conducting a sale—after a defaulting mortgagor fails to pay the mortgage debt within a court-specified period. • The use of strict foreclosure is limited to special situations except in those few states that permit this remedy in all foreclosure proceedings.

foreclosure sale. See SALE.

foreign bond. See BOND (1).

foreign corporation. See CORPORATION.

foreign draft. See DRAFT.

foreign-earned-income exclusion. The Internal Revenue Code provision that excludes from taxation up to $70,000 in income earned outside the United States. ● The taxpayer must elect between this exclusion and the foreign tax credit. See *foreign tax credit* under TAX CREDIT.

foreign exchange. 1. The process of making international monetary transactions; esp., the conversion of one currency to that of a different country. **2.** Foreign currency or negotiable instruments payable in foreign currency, such as traveler's checks.

foreign tax credit. See TAX CREDIT.

forgery. 1. The act of fraudulently making a false document or altering a real one so that it may be used as if it were genuine <the contract was void because of the seller's forgery>. ● Though forgery was a misdemeanor at common law, modern statutes typically make it a felony. **2.** A false or altered document made to look genuine by someone with the intent to deceive <he was not the true property owner because the deed of trust was a forgery>.

forum-selection clause. A contractual provision in which the parties establish the venue (such as the country, state, or court) for any litigation between them arising under the contract.

forward contract. An agreement, usu. between financial institutions or a financial institution and its client, to buy or sell a particular nonstandardized asset at a fixed price on a future date. ● Unlike a futures contract, a forward contract is not traded on a formal exchange. Cf. FUTURES CONTRACT.

four-corners rule. 1. The principle that a document's meaning is to be gathered from the entire document and not from its isolated parts. **2.** The principle that no extraneous evidence should be considered when interpreting the meaning of an unambiguous document. Cf. PAROL-EVIDENCE RULE.

franchise, *n.* **1.** The right conferred by the government to engage in a certain business or to exercise corporate powers.—Also termed *corporate franchise.* **2.** The sole right granted by the owner of a trademark or tradename to engage in business or to sell a good or service in a certain area. **3.** The business or territory controlled by the person or entity that has been granted such a right.

franchise tax. See TAX.

fraud. 1. A knowing misrepresentation of the truth or concealment of a material fact to induce another to act to his or her detriment. ● Fraud is usu. a tort, but in some cases (esp. when the conduct is willful) it may be a crime. **2.** Unconscionable dealing; esp., in contract law, the unconscientious use of the power arising out of the parties' relative positions and resulting in an unconscionable bargain.

   actual fraud. A concealment or false representation through a statement or conduct that causes injury to another.

   constructive fraud. **a.** Unintentional deception or misrepresentation that causes injury to another. **b.** See *fraud in law.*

   fraud in law. Fraud that is presumed under the circumstances, as when a debtor transfers assets and thereby impairs creditors' efforts to collect sums due.—Also termed *constructive fraud.*

   fraud in the factum. Fraud occurring when a legal instrument as actually executed differs from the one intended for execution by the person who executes it, or when the instrument may have had no legal existence. ● Compared to fraud in the inducement, fraud in the factum occurs only rarely, as when a blind person signs a mortgage when misleadingly told that it's just a letter.—Also termed *fraud in the execution*; *fraud in the making*.

fraud in the inducement. Fraud occurring when a misrepresentation leads another to enter into a transaction with a false impression of the risks, duties, or obligations involved.

insurance fraud. Fraud committed against an insurer, as when an insured lies on a policy application or fabricates a claim.

fraud on creditors. See FRAUDULENT CONVEYANCE (1).

fraud-on-the-market principle. In securities law, the doctrine that a plaintiff may presumptively establish reliance on a misstatement or omission concerning a security's market price—without proving actual knowledge of the fraudulent statement or omission—if the plaintiff's injury is caused by the purchase or sale at the deceptive price. • This doctrine recognizes that the market price of an issuer's stock reflects all available public information.

fraudulent concealment. The affirmative suppression or hiding, with the intent to deceive or defraud, of a material fact or circumstance that one is legally or morally bound to reveal.

fraudulent conveyance. 1. A transfer of property for little or no consideration, made for the purpose of hindering or delaying a creditor by putting the property beyond the creditor's reach; a transaction by which the owner of real or personal property seeks to place the property beyond the reach of creditors.—Also termed *fraud on creditors*. **2.** In bankruptcy law, a prebankruptcy transfer or obligation made or incurred by a debtor for little or no consideration or with the actual intent to hinder, delay, or defraud a creditor. • A bankruptcy trustee may recover such a conveyance from the transferee if certain statutory requirements are met.—Also termed *fraudulent transfer*. Cf. PREFERENTIAL TRANSFER.

fraudulent misrepresentation. See MISREPRESENTATION.

Freddie Mac. See FEDERAL HOME LOAN MORTGAGE CORPORATION.

free alongside ship. A mercantile term designating that the seller is responsible for delivering the goods to the dock and for paying the costs of delivery there. • As soon as the seller delivers the goods to the specified dock, the risk of loss passes to the buyer. The abbreviation F.A.S. is more common than the full phrase; it is sometimes wrongly thought to stand for *free along side* as opposed to *free*

alongside ship. Cf. FREE ON BOARD; COST, INSUR-
ANCE, AND FREIGHT.

freedom of contract. The doctrine that free
people have the right to bind themselves legally; a judicial concept that contracts are based
on mutual agreement and free choice, and
thus should not be hampered by external control such as governmental interference.

free market. See *open market* under MARKET.

free on board. A mercantile term denoting
that the seller is responsible for delivering
goods on board a ship for carriage to the
consignee. ● The seller must deliver the goods
at the location named and has the risk of loss
until the goods reach that location.—Abbr.
FOB. Cf. COST, INSURANCE, AND FREIGHT.

> *FOB destination*. A mercantile term de-
> noting that the seller is required to pay the
> freight charges as far as the buyer's named
> destination.

> *FOB shipping*. A mercantile term denoting
> that the seller is required to bear the risk of
> placing the goods on a carrier.

free rider. One who obtains an economic
benefit at another's expense without paying or
working for it.

free-trade zone. An area within a country where foreign merchandise may enter duty-free until it enters the country's market or is exported.

freeze-out, *n.* The process, usu. in a closely held corporation, by which the majority shareholders or the board of directors reduces or eliminates the power of minority shareholders in an effort to compel them to liquidate their investment on terms favorable to the controlling shareholders. Cf. SQUEEZE-OUT.

freeze-out merger. See *cash merger* under MERGER.

freight. 1. Goods transported by water or by land. **2.** The price or compensation paid to a carrier for transporting goods.

fresh start. The favorable financial status obtained by a debtor who receives a release from personal liability on prebankruptcy debts or who reorganizes debt obligations through the confirmation and completion of a bankruptcy plan.

friendly suitor. See WHITE KNIGHT.

friendly takeover. See TAKEOVER.

fringe benefit. See BENEFIT.

FRM. See *fixed-rate mortgage* under MORT-GAGE.

front-end money. See SEED MONEY.

frozen asset. See ASSET.

frozen deposit. See DEPOSIT.

frustration, *n.* **1.** The prevention or hindering of the attainment of a goal, such as contractual performance.

> *commercial frustration.* An excuse for a party's nonperformance due to some unforeseeable and uncontrollable circumstance.—Also termed *economic frustration.*

> *temporary frustration.* An occurrence that prevents performance and legally suspends the duty to perform for the duration of the event. ● If the burden or circumstance is substantially different after the event, then the duty may be discharged.

2. In contract law, the doctrine that, if the entire performance of a contract becomes fundamentally changed without any fault by either party, the contract is considered terminated.—Also termed *frustration of purpose.* Cf. IMPOSSIBILITY; IMPRACTICABILITY.

FSLIC. *abbr.* FEDERAL SAVINGS AND LOAN INSURANCE CORPORATION.

FTC. *abbr.* FEDERAL TRADE COMMISSION.

full coverage. See COVERAGE (1).

full-faith-and-credit bond. See *general-obligation bond* under BOND (1).

full indorsement. See *special indorsement* under INDORSEMENT.

full-paid stock. See STOCK.

full payout lease. See *finance lease* under LEASE.

full performance. See PERFORMANCE (1).

fully diluted earnings per share. See EARNINGS PER SHARE.

fully managed fund. See MUTUAL FUND.

fund, *n.* **1.** A sum of money or other liquid assets set apart for a specific purpose <a fund reserved for unanticipated expenses>.

> *contingent fund.* A fund set apart by a business to pay unknown costs that may

arise in the future.—Also termed *contingency reserve*.

revolving fund. A fund whose moneys are continually expended and then replenished, such as a petty-cash fund.

sinking fund. A fund consisting of regular deposits that are accumulated with interest to pay off a long-term corporate or public debt.—Abbr. SF.

2. (*usu. pl.*) Money or other assets, such as stocks, bonds, or working capital, available to pay debts, expenses, and the like <Sue invested her funds in her sister's business>.

current funds. Assets that can be readily converted into cash.

3. See MUTUAL FUND <a diverse portfolio of funds>.

fund, *vb.* **1.** To provide money to (an individual, entity, or venture), esp. to finance a particular project. **2.** To utilize resources in a manner that produces interest. **3.** To convert (a debt) into a long-term debt that bears interest at a fixed rate.

funded debt. See DEBT.

fungible (fən-jə-bəl), *adj*. Regarded as commercially interchangeable with other property of the same kind <corn and wheat are each a type of fungible goods, whereas unique property such as land is not fungible>.

fungible goods. See GOODS.

future advance. Money secured by an original security agreement even though it is lent after the security interest has attached.

futures, *n. pl*. **1.** Standardized assets (such as commodities, stocks, or foreign currencies) bought or sold for future acceptance or delivery. **2.** See FUTURES CONTRACT.

futures contract. An agreement to buy or sell a standardized asset (such as a commodity, stock, or foreign currency) at a fixed price at a future time, usu. during a particular time of a month. • Futures contracts are traded on organized exchanges such as the Chicago Board of Trade or the Chicago Mercantile Exchange.—Often shortened to *futures*. Cf. FORWARD CONTRACT; OPTION (3).

futures market. See MARKET.

futures option. See OPTION.

G

GAAP. *abbr.* GENERALLY ACCEPTED ACCOUNTING PRINCIPLES.

GAAS. *abbr.* GENERALLY ACCEPTED AUDITING STANDARDS.

gain, *n.* **1.** An increase in amount, degree, or value. **2.** Excess of receipts over expenditures or of sale price over cost. See PROFIT. **3.** In tax law, the excess of the amount realized from a sale or exchange of property over the property's adjusted basis.—Also termed *realized gain*. See CAPITAL GAIN.

> ***ordinary gain.*** The profit realized on selling or exchanging a noncapital asset. Cf. CAPITAL GAIN.

GAO. *abbr.* GENERAL ACCOUNTING OFFICE.

gap-filler. A UCC provision that supplies a contractual term that the parties failed to include in the contract. ● For example, if the contract does not contain a sales price, UCC § 2–305(1) establishes the price as being a reasonable one at the time of delivery.

gap financing. See FINANCING.

garnishee, *n.* A person or institution (such as a bank) that is indebted to or is bailee for another whose property has been subjected to garnishment.—Also termed *garnishee-defendant* (as opposed to the "principal defendant," i.e., the primary debtor).

garnisher. A creditor who initiates a garnishment action to reach the debtor's property that is thought to be held or owed by a third party (the *garnishee*).—Also spelled *garnishor*.

garnishment, *n.* A judicial proceeding in which a creditor (or potential creditor) asks the court to order a third party who is indebted to or is bailee for the debtor to turn over to the creditor any of the debtor's property (such as wages or bank accounts) held by that third party. • A plaintiff initiates a garnishment action as a means of either prejudgment seizure or postjudgment collection.

GATT. *abbr.* GENERAL AGREEMENT ON TARIFFS AND TRADE.

gender discrimination. See *sex discrimination* under DISCRIMINATION.

General Accounting Office. The federal agency that provides legal and accounting assistance to Congress, audits and investigates federal programs, and settles claims against the United States.—Abbr. GAO.

general administrative expense. See EX-
PENSE.

general agency. See AGENCY.

general agent. See AGENT.

General Agreement on Tariffs and Trade.
A multiparty international agreement—signed
originally in 1948—that promotes international trade by lowering import duties and providing equal access to markets. ● More than 100
nations are parties to the agreement.—Abbr.
GATT.

general benefit. See BENEFIT.

general contractor. See CONTRACTOR.

general counsel. See COUNSEL.

general creditor. See *unsecured creditor* under CREDITOR.

general deposit. See DEPOSIT.

general indorsement. See *blank indorsement* under INDORSEMENT.

general letter of credit. See LETTER OF CRED-
IT.

generally accepted accounting principles. The conventions, rules, and procedures that define approved accounting practices at a particular time. • These principles are issued by the Financial Accounting Standards Board for use by accountants in preparing financial statements.—Abbr. GAAP.—Also termed *generally accepted accountancy principles*.

generally accepted auditing standards. The guidelines issued by the American Institute of Certified Public Accountants establishing an auditor's professional qualities and the criteria for the auditor's examination and required reports.—Abbr. GAAS.

general mortgage bond. See BOND (1).

general-obligation bond. See BOND (1).

general partner. See PARTNER.

general partnership. See PARTNERSHIP.

general strike. See STRIKE.

generic name. In trademark law, a term that describes something generally without designating the thing's source or creator, such as the word "car" or "sink." • Generic names cannot be protected as trademarks.—Also termed *generic term*; *generic mark*.

gentlemen's agreement. An unenforceable and usu. oral agreement that depends merely on the good faith of the parties.

geographic market. See MARKET.

gift tax. See TAX.

gilt-edged, *adj.* (Of a security) having the highest rating for safety of investment; being an exceptionally safe investment.

Ginnie Mae. See GOVERNMENT NATIONAL MORTGAGE ASSOCIATION.

glamour stock. See STOCK.

GNMA. *abbr.* GOVERNMENT NATIONAL MORTGAGE ASSOCIATION.

going concern. A commercial enterprise actively engaging in business with the expectation of indefinite continuance.

going private. The process of changing a public corporation into a close corporation by terminating the corporation's publicly held status with the SEC and by having its outstanding publicly held shares acquired.

going public. The process of a company's selling stock to the investing public for the first time (after filing a registration statement under applicable securities laws), thereby becoming a public corporation. See *initial public offering* under OFFERING.

gold bond. See BOND (1).

golden parachute. An employment-contract provision that grants an upper-level executive lucrative severance benefits—including long-term salary guarantees or bonuses—if control of the company changes hands (as by a merger). Cf. TIN PARACHUTE.

good consideration. See CONSIDERATION.

good faith, *n.* **1.** A state of mind consisting in (1) honesty in belief or purpose, (2) faithfulness to one's duty or obligation, (3) observance of reasonable commercial standards of fair dealing in a given trade or business, or (4) absence of intent to defraud or to seek unconscionable advantage. **2.** In insurance law, honesty, fair dealing, and full disclosure. • An insurer must act in good faith in the settlement of claims, esp. in settling a claim within policy limits. Cf. BAD FAITH.

good-faith purchaser. See *bona fide purchaser* under PURCHASER.

goods. 1. Tangible or movable personal property <goods and services>. **2.** Things that have value, whether tangible or not <the importance of social goods varies from society to society>. **3.** Items of merchandise; supplies; raw materials; finished products <the sale of goods is governed by the UCC>.

capital goods. Goods used for the production of other goods or services, such as equipment and machinery.

consumer goods. Goods bought or used primarily for personal, family, or household purposes, and not for resale or for producing other goods.

distressed goods. Goods sold at unusually low prices or at a loss.

durable goods. Consumer goods that are designed to be used repeatedly over a long period, such as automobiles or personal computers.

fungible goods. Goods that are interchangeable with one another; goods that, by nature or trade usage, are the equivalent of any other like unit, such as coffee or grain.

nonconforming goods. Goods that fail to meet contractual specifications, allowing the buyer to reject the tender of the goods or to

revoke their acceptance. See PERFECT-TENDER
RULE.

good title. See TITLE.

goodwill. A business's reputation, patronage,
and other intangible assets that are considered
when appraising the business, esp. for purchase; the ability to earn income in excess of
the income that would be expected from the
business viewed as a mere collection of assets.

government contract. See *procurement contract* under CONTRACT.

government corporation. See *public corporation* (c) under CORPORATION.

**Government National Mortgage Associa-
tion.** A federally owned corporation that purchases, on the secondary market, residential
mortgages originated by local lenders and that
issues federally insured securities backed by
such mortgages.—Abbr. GNMA.—Also termed
Ginnie Mae.

government security. See SECURITY.

grace period. 1. A gratuitous but sometimes
legally imposed extension of time to comply
with some requirement, such as the short period beyond the premium's due date (usu. 30 or

31 days) during which an insurance policy stays in effect and payment may be made to keep the policy in good standing. **2.** A certain number of days (usu. three) given to the maker or acceptor of a bill, draft, or note to make a payment after the time specified in the paper has expired.

graduated-payment mortgage. See MORT-GAGE.

grandfather clause. A statutory or regulatory clause that exempts a class of persons or transactions because of circumstances existing before the clause takes effect.

grant, *n.* **1.** An agreement that creates a right of any description other than the one held by the grantor. ● Examples include leases, easements, charges, patents, franchises, powers, and licenses. **2.** The formal transfer of real property. **3.** The document by which a transfer is effected; esp., a deed. **4.** The property or property right so transferred.

grant, *vb.* **1.** To give or confer (a thing), with or without compensation <the parents granted the car to their daughter on her 16th birthday>. **2.** To formally transfer (real property) by deed or other writing <the Lewisons granted the townhouse to the Bufords>. **3.** To permit or agree to <the court granted the motion to dismiss>.

gratuitous bailment. See BAILMENT.

gratuitous contract. See CONTRACT.

gray market. See MARKET.

greenmail. 1. An unfriendly suitor's act of buying enough stock in a company to threaten a hostile takeover, and of then agreeing to sell the stock back to the corporation at an inflated price. **2.** The money paid for stock in the corporation's buyback.

Green River ordinance. A local licensing law that protects residents from unwanted peddlers and salespersons, typically by prohibiting door-to-door solicitations without prior consent. • The ordinance takes its name from Green River, Wyoming, which enacted the first such law in the early 20th century before others came into vogue during the 1930s and 1940s throughout the U.S.

gross income. See INCOME.

gross lease. See LEASE.

gross negligence. See NEGLIGENCE.

gross profit. See PROFIT.

ground lease. See LEASE.

ground rent. See RENT.

group annuity. See ANNUITY.

group boycott. See BOYCOTT.

group insurance. See INSURANCE.

group policy. See *master policy* under INSUR-ANCE POLICY.

growth company. See COMPANY.

growth fund. See MUTUAL FUND.

guarantee, *n*. **1.** The act of giving security; the assurance that a contract or legal act will be duly carried out. **2.** Something given or existing as security, as to fulfill a future engagement or a condition subsequent. **3.** One to whom a guaranty is made.—Also spelled *guaranty*.

guarantee clause. A provision in a contract, deed, or mortgage by which one person promises to pay the obligation of another.

guaranteed bond. See BOND (1).

guarantor. One who makes a guaranty or gives security for a debt. ● While a surety's liability begins with that of the principal, a guarantor's liability does not begin until the principal debtor is in default. Cf. SURETY.

guaranty. A promise to answer for the debt of another, usu. in finance and banking contexts. ● While a warranty relates to things (not persons), is not collateral, and need not be in writing, a guaranty is an undertaking that a person will pay or do some act, is collateral to the duty of the primary obligor, and must be in writing.

guaranty insurance. See INSURANCE.

H

haircut reorganization. See REORGANIZATION.

hard dollars. 1. Cash proceeds given to a seller. **2.** The part of an equity investment that is not deductible in the first year. Cf. SOFT DOLLARS.

Hart–Scott–Rodino Antitrust Improvement Act. A federal statute, enacted in 1976, that generally strengthens the Justice Department's antitrust enforcement powers, esp. by requiring firms to give notice to the Federal Trade Commission and the Justice Department of an intent to merge if one of the firms has annual revenues or assets exceeding $100 million, and the acquisition price or value of the acquired firm exceeds $15 million.

hazard. The risk or probability of loss or injury, esp. a loss or injury covered by an insurance policy.

hazardous contract. See *aleatory contract* under CONTRACT.

HDC. *abbr.* HOLDER IN DUE COURSE.

head of household. For income-tax purposes, an unmarried or separated person (other than a surviving spouse) who provides a home for dependents for more than one-half of the taxable year. • A head of a household is taxed at a lower rate than a single person who is not head of a household.

head-start injunction. An injunction prohibiting the defendant from using a trade secret for a period equal to the time between the date of the secret's theft and the date when the secret became public, since that period equals the "head start" that the defendant unfairly obtained over the rest of the industry.

health-maintenance organization. A group of participating healthcare providers that furnish medical services to enrolled members of a group health-insurance plan.—Abbr. HMO.

hearing officer. See ADMINISTRATIVE-LAW JUDGE.

hedge, *vb.* To make advance arrangements to safeguard oneself from loss on an investment, speculation, or bet, as when a buyer of commodities insures against unfavorable price changes by buying in advance at a fixed rate for later delivery.

hedge fund. A specialized investment group—usu. organized as a limited partnership or offshore investment company—that offers the possibility of high returns through risky techniques such as selling short or buying derivatives. • Most hedge funds are not registered with the SEC and are therefore restricted in marketing their services to the public.

hidden asset. See ASSET.

hidden defect. See DEFECT.

hidden tax. See TAX.

high-grade security. See SECURITY.

HMO. *abbr*. HEALTH-MAINTENANCE ORGANIZATION.

hoard, *vb*. To acquire and hold (goods) beyond one's reasonable needs, usu. because of an actual or anticipated shortage or price increase <hoarding food and medical supplies during wartime>.

holder. 1. A person who has legal possession of a negotiable instrument and is entitled to receive payment on it. **2.** A person with legal possession of a document of title or an investment security. **3.** A person who possesses or uses property.

holder for value. A person who has given value in exchange for a negotiable instrument. • Under the UCC, examples of "giving value" include acquiring a security interest in the instrument or accepting the instrument in payment of an antecedent claim.

holder in due course. A person who in good faith has given value for a negotiable instrument that is complete and regular on its face, is not overdue, and, to the possessor's knowledge, has not been dishonored. ● Under the UCC, a holder in due course takes the instrument free of all claims and personal defenses, but subject to real defenses.—Abbr. HDC.

hold-harmless agreement. A contract in which one party agrees to indemnify the other. See INDEMNITY.

holding company. See COMPANY.

hold out, *vb.* To represent (oneself or another) as having a certain legal status, as by claiming to be an agent or partner with authority to enter into transactions <even though he was only a promoter, Schwartz held himself out as the principal>.

home equity loan. See LOAN.

homestead. The house, outbuildings, and adjoining land owned and occupied by a person or family as its principal residence. ● As long as the homestead does not exceed in area or value the limits fixed by law, in most states it is exempt from forced sale for collection of a debt.

honor, *vb*. To accept or pay (a negotiable instrument) when presented.

horizontal merger. See MERGER.

horizontal price-fixing. See PRICE-FIXING.

horizontal restraint. See RESTRAINT OF TRADE.

hostile-environment sexual harassment. See SEXUAL HARASSMENT.

hostile takeover. See TAKEOVER.

hot-cargo contract. See CONTRACT.

hot issue. See ISSUE.

hot stock. See *hot issue* under ISSUE.

hybrid security. See SECURITY.

hypothecation (hɪ-poth-ə-**kay**-shən). The pledging of something as security without delivery of title or possession.

hypothetical creditor. See CREDITOR.

I

ICC. *abbr.* INTERSTATE COMMERCE COMMISSION.

illegal alien. See ALIEN.

illegal consideration. See CONSIDERATION.

illegal rate. See INTEREST RATE.

illusory promise. See PROMISE.

IMF. *abbr.* INTERNATIONAL MONETARY FUND.

immovable, *n.* (*usu. pl.*) Property that cannot be moved; an object so firmly attached to land that it is regarded as part of the land. See FIXTURE. Cf. MOVABLE.

impaired capital. See CAPITAL.

implied authority. See AUTHORITY.

implied contract. See CONTRACT.

implied-in-fact contract. See CONTRACT.

implied-in-law contract. See CONTRACT.

implied trust. See *constructive trust* under TRUST.

implied warranty. See WARRANTY.

implied warranty of fitness for a particular purpose. See WARRANTY.

implied warranty of merchantability. See WARRANTY.

import, *n.* **1.** A product or service brought into a country from a foreign country where it originated <imports declined in the third quarter>. **2.** The process of bringing foreign goods or services into a country <the import of products affects the domestic economy in significant ways>.

import letter of credit. See LETTER OF CREDIT.

import quota. See QUOTA.

impossibility. 1. A fact or circumstance that excuses contractual performance because (1) the subject or means of performance has deteriorated, has been destroyed, or is no longer available, (2) the method of delivery or payment has failed, (3) a law now prevents performance, or (4) death or illness prevents performance. ● Increased or unexpected difficulty and expense do not usu. qualify as an impossibility and thus do not excuse performance.— Also termed *impossibility of performance.* **2.** The doctrine by which such a fact or circumstance excuses contractual performance. Cf. FRUSTRATION; IMPRACTICABILITY.

impost. A tax or duty, esp. a customs duty <the impost was assessed when the ship reached the mainland>. See DUTY (2).

impostor rule. In commercial law, the principle that an impostor's indorsement of a negotiable instrument is not a forgery, and that the drawer or maker who issues the instrument is negligent and therefore liable to the holder for payment. • If a drawer or maker issues an instrument to an impostor, any resulting forgery of the payee's name will be effective to pass good title to later transferees.

impound account. See ACCOUNT.

impracticability (im-prak-ti-kə-**bil**-ə-tee). **1.** A fact or circumstance that excuses a party from performing an act, esp. a contractual duty, because (though possible) it would cause extreme and unreasonable difficulty. • For performance to be truly impracticable, the duty must become much more difficult or much more expensive to perform, and this difficulty or expense must have been unanticipated. **2.** The doctrine by which such a fact or circumstance excuses performance. Cf. FRUSTRATION; IMPOSSIBILITY.

commercial impracticability. In contract law, the occurrence of a contingency whose nonoccurrence was an assumption in the contract, as a result of which one party cannot perform.

improvement. An addition to real property, whether permanent or not; esp., one that increases its value or utility or that enhances its appearance. Cf. FIXTURE.

imputed income. See INCOME.

imputed interest. See INTEREST.

inactive stock. See STOCK.

in arrears, *adj*. Behind in the discharging of a debt or other obligation <the homeowners were in arrears with their mortgage payments>. See ARREAR.

in blank. (Of an indorsement) not restricted to a particular indorsee. See *blank indorsement* under INDORSEMENT.

incentive stock option. See STOCK OPTION (2).

incidental authority. See AUTHORITY.

incidental beneficiary. See BENEFICIARY.

income. The money or other form of payment that one receives, usu. periodically, from employment, business, investments, royalties, gifts, and the like. See EARNINGS. Cf. PROFIT.

accrued income. Money earned but not yet received.

adjusted gross income. Gross income minus allowable deductions specified in the tax code.

blocked income. Money earned by a foreign taxpayer but not subject to U.S. taxation because the foreign country prohibits changing the income into dollars.

current income. Income that is due within the present accounting period.

deferred income. Money received at a time later than when it was earned, such as a check received in December for commissions earned in November.

disposable income. Income that may be spent or invested after payment of taxes or other obligations.

earned income. Money derived from one's own labor or active participation; earnings from services. Cf. *unearned income* (b).

exempt income. Income that is not subject to income tax.

fixed income. Money received at a constant rate, such as payments from a pension or annuity.

gross income. Total income from all sources before deductions, exemptions, or other tax reductions.

imputed income. The benefit one receives from the use of one's own property, the performance of one's services, or the consumption of self-produced goods and services. ● Imputed income is excluded from gross income for tax purposes.

net income. Total income from all sources after calculating deductions, exemptions, and other tax reductions. ● Income tax is computed from net income.

net operating income. Income earned from running a business, calculated by subtracting operating costs from total earnings.

nonoperating income. Business income derived from investments rather than operations.

ordinary income. **a.** For business-tax purposes, earnings from the normal operations or activities of a business. ● Ordinary income is subject to regular tax rates rather than the lower rate for capital gains. **b.** For individual income-tax purposes, income that is derived from sources such as wages, commissions, and interest.

passive income. Income derived from a business activity over which the earner does not have immediate control, such as copyright royalties. See PASSIVE ACTIVITY.

real income. Income adjusted to allow for inflation or deflation so that it reflects true purchasing power.

taxable income. Gross income minus all allowable deductions and exemptions. ● Taxable income is multiplied by the applicable tax rate to compute one's tax liability.

unearned income. **a.** Earnings from investments rather than labor.—Also termed *investment income.* **b.** Income received but not yet earned; income paid in advance. Cf. *earned income.*

unrelated business income. Taxable income generated by a tax-exempt organization from a trade or business unrelated to its exempt purpose or activity.

income-basis method. A method of computing the rate of return on a security using the interest and price paid rather than the face value.

income bond. See BOND (1).

income exclusion. See EXCLUSION (1).

income fund. See MUTUAL FUND.

income property. See PROPERTY.

income-shifting. The practice of transferring income to a taxpayer in a lower tax bracket, such as a child, to reduce tax liability.

income statement. A statement of all the revenues, expenses, gains, and losses that a business incurred during a period of time.— Also termed *profit-and-loss statement*. Cf. BALANCE SHEET.

income stock. See STOCK.

income tax. See TAX.

income-tax return. See TAX RETURN.

income yield. See CAPITALIZATION RATE.

incorporation, *n*. The formation of a legal corporation. See ARTICLES OF INCORPORATION.

incremental cash flow. See CASH FLOW.

indebtedness (in-**de**-təd-nəs). **1.** The quality or state of owing money. **2.** Something owed; a debt.

indemnification. 1. The action of compensating for loss or damage sustained. **2.** The compensation so made.

indemnify, *vb.* **1.** To reimburse (a person, corporation, etc.) for a loss suffered because of a third party's act or default. **2.** To promise to reimburse (a person, corporation, etc.) for such a loss. **3.** To give (a person, corporation, etc.) security against such a loss.

indemnity (in-**dem**-nə-tee). **1.** A duty to make good any loss, damage, or liability incurred by another. **2.** The right of an injured party to claim reimbursement for its loss, damage, or liability from a person who has such a duty. **3.** Reimbursement or compensation for loss, damage, or liability. Cf. CONTRIBUTION.

indenture. A formal written instrument made by two or more persons with different interests, traditionally having the edges serrated, or indented, in a zigzag fashion to reduce the possibility of forgery and to distinguish it from a deed poll. Cf. *deed poll* under DEED.

 corporate indenture. A document containing the terms and conditions governing the issuance of debt securities, such as bonds or debentures.

independent agency. See AGENCY (3).

independent agent. See AGENT.

independent audit. See AUDIT.

independent contractor. See CONTRACTOR.

independent covenant. See COVENANT (1).

independent investigation committee. See SPECIAL LITIGATION COMMITTEE.

indeterminate bond. See BOND (1).

index fund. See MUTUAL FUND.

indexing. The practice or method of adjusting the value of wages, pension benefits, insurance, or other types of payments to account for inflation.

indirect cost. See COST.

indirect loss. See *consequential loss* under LOSS.

indirect-purchaser doctrine. In antitrust law, the doctrine holding that in litigation for price discrimination, the court will ignore sham middle parties in determining whether different prices were paid by different customers for the same good. ● This doctrine gives standing to bring an antitrust action to a party who is not an immediate buyer of a product. Thus, if a manufacturer sells a product to a retailer, but dictates the terms by which the retailer must sell the product to a consumer, a court will ignore the retailer and treat the consumer as the direct purchaser of the product.

individual retirement account. A savings account in which a person may deposit up to a specified amount of income each year ($2,000 under current law) and have the deposits be tax-deductible for that year. ● The deposits, along with any interest earned, are not taxed until the money is withdrawn when the person retires (or, with certain penalties, before retirement).—Abbr. IRA.

> *Roth IRA.* An IRA in which contributions are taxed when they are made rather than when they are withdrawn. ● No further taxes are assessed on the contributions (or accrued interest) if they are withdrawn when the account-holder retires.

indorsee (in-dor-**see**). One to whom a negotiable instrument is transferred by indorsement.—Also spelled *endorsee.*

indorsement. 1. The act of signing one's name on the back of a negotiable instrument

301

in order to transfer it to someone else (esp. in return for the cash or credit value indicated on its face). **2.** The signature itself.—Also spelled *endorsement*.

blank indorsement. An indorsement that names no specific payee, thus making the instrument payable to bearer and negotiable by delivery only.—Also termed *general indorsement*.

conditional indorsement. An indorsement by which the possession of the instrument passes to the indorsee, but the title either does not pass until the occurrence of some condition named in the indorsement or passes subject to defeat upon the happening of some condition. ● Examples of the wordings that indicate this type of indorsement are "Pay to Brad Jones if he achieves 18 years of age" and "Pay to Brigitte Turner, or order, unless before payment I give you notice to the contrary."

irregular indorsement. An indorsement made by a person who signs outside the chain of title and who therefore is not a holder or transferor of the instrument.— Also termed *anomalous indorsement*.

qualified indorsement. An indorsement that passes the title to the instrument without rendering the indorser liable to later holders if the instrument is later dishonored. • Typically, a qualified indorsement is made by writing "without recourse" or "sans recourse" over the signature.—Also termed *indorsement without recourse*. See WITHOUT RECOURSE.

restrictive indorsement. An indorsement that includes a condition (e.g., "pay Josefina Cardoza only if she has worked 8 full hours on April 13") or any other language restricting further negotiation to the check-collection system (e.g., "for deposit only").

special indorsement. An indorsement that specifies a person to whom the instrument is payable or to whom the goods named by the document should be delivered.—Also termed *full indorsement*.

unqualified indorsement. An indorsement that does not limit the indorser's liability on the paper. • It does not, for example, include the phrase "without recourse."

unrestrictive indorsement. An indorsement that includes no conditions or other language restricting further negotiation to the check-collection system.

indorser. One who transfers a negotiable instrument by indorsement.—Also spelled *endorser*.

inducement. The benefit or advantage that causes a promisor to enter into a contract.

industrial-development bond. See BOND (1).

industrial espionage. See ESPIONAGE.

industrial relations. All dealings and relationships between an employer and its employees, including collective bargaining, safety, and benefits.

industrial-revenue bond. See *industrial-development bond* under BOND (1).

industrial union. See UNION.

inflation. A general increase in prices coinciding with a fall in the real value of money. Cf. DEFLATION.

informal dividend. See DIVIDEND.

information return. See TAX RETURN.

infringement. An act that interferes with another's right or privilege, esp. an intellectual-property right (such as a patent, copyright, or trademark).

   contributory infringement. The act or fact of intentionally helping an unauthorized person make, sell, or use protected intellectual property.

copyright infringement. Unauthorized exercise of the rights reserved exclusively for the copyright owner.

innocent infringement. In copyright law, infringement by unintentionally or unconsciously borrowing from a protected work.

patent infringement. The unauthorized making, using, or selling of an invention protected by a patent. • The test for infringement is whether the allegedly infringing device performs substantially the same function to obtain substantially the same overall result as the patented product.

trademark infringement. Unauthorized use or imitation of an insignia used to identify another company's product or service. See LIKELIHOOD-OF-CONFUSION TEST.

vicarious infringement. In copyright law, infringement by controlling or supervising an infringing performance, with the potential for profiting from that performance. • For example, a concert theater can be vicariously liable for the infringing performance of a hired band.

in-house counsel. See COUNSEL.

initial margin requirement. See MARGIN RE-QUIREMENT.

initial public offering. See OFFERING.

injury. 1. The violation of another's legal right, for which the law provides a remedy; a wrong or injustice. **2.** Harm or damage.

> *compensable injury.* In workers'-compensation law, an injury caused by an accident arising from the employment and in the course of the employee's work, and for which the employee is statutorily entitled to receive compensation.

> *scheduled injury.* A partially disabling injury for which a predetermined amount of compensation is allowed under a workers'-compensation statute.

in kind, *adv*. With another (article or commodity) that is of the same type or quality, instead of cash <he made a repayment in kind>. ● The phrase is now sometimes used as an adjective <in-kind repayment>. When used in this way, the phrase should be hyphenated.

innocent infringement. See INFRINGEMENT.

in pari delicto (in-**pahr**-ee-də-**lik**-toh), *adv*. [Latin "in equal fault"] Equally at fault <courts usually deny relief when parties have

306

made an illegal agreement and both stand *in pari delicto*>.

insecurity clause. A loan-agreement provision that allows the creditor to demand immediate and full payment of the loan balance if the creditor has reason to believe that the debtor is about to default, as when the debtor suddenly loses a significant source of income. Cf. ACCELERATION CLAUSE.

inside director. See DIRECTOR.

inside information. Information about a company's financial or market situation obtained from a source within the corporation rather than from a public or published source.—Also termed *insider information*.

insider. 1. In securities law, a person who has knowledge of material facts not available to the general public.

> *temporary insider.* A person or firm that receives inside information while performing professional duties for the issuer of the shares. ● Generally, that person or firm is subject to the same prohibitions as any other insider.

2. One who takes part in the control of a corporation, such as an officer or director, or one who owns 10% or more of the corporation's stock. **3.** In bankruptcy law, an entity or person who is so closely related to a debtor that any deal between them will not be considered an arm's-length transaction and will be subject to close scrutiny.

insider trading. The use of nonpublic information to trade in the shares of a company by a corporate insider or one who owes a fiduciary duty to the company. ● This is the classic definition. The Supreme Court has also approved a broader definition, known as the "misappropriation theory": the deceitful acquisition and misuse of information that properly belongs to persons to whom one owes a duty.

insolvency. 1. The state of one who cannot pay debts as they fall due or in the usual course of business. Cf. SOLVENCY. **2.** The inability to pay debts as they mature. See BANKRUPTCY.

balance-sheet insolvency. Insolvency created when the debtor's liabilities exceed its assets. ● Under some state laws, balance-sheet insolvency prevents a corporation from making distributions to its shareholders.

equity insolvency. Insolvency created when the debtor cannot meet its obligations as they come due in the ordinary course of business. • Under most state laws, equity insolvency prevents a corporation from making distributions to its shareholders.

installment, *n.* One of several portions of a debt that is repaid periodically.

installment accounting method. See AC-COUNTING METHOD.

installment credit. See CREDIT.

installment debt. See DEBT.

installment loan. See LOAN.

installment note. See NOTE.

installment sale. See SALE.

institutional investor. One who trades in large volumes of securities, usu. by investing other people's money into large, managed funds. • Institutional investors are often pension funds, investment companies, trust managers, or insurance companies. See MUTUAL FUND.

institutional lender. A business, esp. a bank, that routinely makes loans to the general public.

institutional market. See MARKET.

instrument. A formal legal document that entails rights, duties, entitlements, and liabilities, such as a contract, will, promissory note, or share certificate. See NEGOTIABLE INSTRUMENT.

instrumentality rule. The principle that a corporation's existence will be disregarded if that corporation is controlled to such an extent by another corporation that it in reality has no separate identity.

insurable interest. The financial or legal interest that an insured must have in the person, object, or activity covered by an insurance policy. • If the policy does not have an insurable interest as its basis, it will usu. be considered a form of wagering and therefore held to be unenforceable.

insurable value. The worth of the subject of an insurance contract to the insured or the beneficiary, usu. expressed as a monetary amount.

insurance (in-**shuur**-əns). **1.** An agreement by which one party (the *insurer*) commits to do something of value for another party (the *insured*) upon the occurrence of some specified contingency; esp., a contract by which the insurer, in exchange for a paid premium, agrees to indemnify or guarantee the insured against a loss caused by a specified event or risk. **2.** The sum for which something (as a person or property) is covered by such an agreement.

accident insurance. An agreement to indemnify against expense, loss of time, suffering, or death resulting from an accident. Cf. *casualty insurance.*

all-risk insurance. Insurance that covers every kind of loss except those specifically excluded.

business-interruption insurance. An agreement to protect against one or more kinds of loss from interruption of an ongoing business, such as loss of profits while the business is shut down to repair fire damage.

casualty insurance. An agreement to indemnify against losses resulting from a broad group of causes such as legal liability, theft, accident, property damage, and workers' compensation. ● The meaning of casualty insurance has become blurred because of the rapid increase in different types of insurance coverage. Cf. *accident insurance.*

coinsurance. **a.** Insurance provided jointly by two or more insurers. **b.** Property insurance that requires the insured to bear a portion of the risk of partial or total destruction of the property if the property is not covered up to a certain percentage of its full value. • A coinsurance clause sets a minimum for which property must be insured, and anything below that amount makes the insured a coinsurer for the proportional difference between the face value of the policy and the coinsurance amount (coinsurance percentage times the fair market value of the property).

commercial insurance. An indemnity agreement in the form of a deed or bond to protect against a loss caused by a party's breach of contract.

comprehensive insurance. Insurance that combines coverage against many kinds of losses that may also be insured separately. • This is commonly used, for example, in automobile-insurance policies.

compulsory insurance. Statutorily required insurance; esp., motor-vehicle liability insurance that a state requires as a condition to registration of the vehicle.

concurrent insurance. One of two or more insurance policies that cover the same risk. • Concurrent insurance policies are stated in almost identical terms in order to allow liability to be apportioned between the insurers.

credit insurance. An agreement to indemnify against loss that may result from the death, disability, or insolvency of someone to whom credit is extended. • A debtor typically purchases this type of insurance to ensure the repayment of the loan even under the most adverse circumstances.

deposit insurance. A federally sponsored indemnification program to protect depositors against the loss of their money, up to a specified maximum, if the bank or savings-and-loan association closes.

directors' and officers' liability insurance. An agreement to indemnify corporate directors and officers against judgments, settlements, and fines arising from negligence suits, shareholder actions, and other business-related suits.—Often shortened to *D & O liability insurance.*

disability insurance. Coverage purchased to protect a person financially during periods of incapacity from working.

employers'-liability insurance. **a.** An agreement to indemnify an employer against an employee claim not covered under the workers'-compensation system. **b.** An agreement to indemnify against liability imposed on an employer for an employee's negligence that injures a third party.

313

errors-and-omissions insurance. An agreement to indemnify for loss sustained because of a mistake or oversight by the insured—though not for loss due to intentional wrongdoing. • For example, lawyers often carry this insurance as part of their malpractice coverage to protect them in suits for damages resulting from inadvertent mistakes (such as missing a procedural deadline).—Often shortened to *E & O insurance.*

excess insurance. An agreement to indemnify against any loss that exceeds the amount of coverage under another policy. Cf. EXCESS CLAUSE.

fidelity insurance. An agreement to indemnify an employer against a loss arising from the lack of integrity or honesty of an employee or of a person holding a position of trust, such as a loss from embezzlement.

fire insurance. An agreement to indemnify against property damage caused by fire, wind, rain, or other similar disasters.

floater insurance. An agreement to indemnify against a loss sustained to movable property, wherever its location within the territorial limit set by the policy.

group insurance. A form of insurance offered to a member of a group, such as the employees of a business, so long as that person remains a member of the group. • Group insurance is typically health or life insurance issued under a master policy between the insurer and the employer, who usu. pays all or part of the premium for the insured person.

guaranty insurance. An agreement to cover a loss resulting from another's default, insolvency, or specified misconduct.

key-employee insurance. Life insurance taken out by a company on an essential or valuable employee, with the company as beneficiary.—Also termed *key-man insurance*; *key-person insurance*; *key-executive insurance.*

liability insurance. An agreement to cover a loss resulting from one's liability to a third party, such as a loss incurred by a driver who injures a pedestrian. • The insured's claim under the policy arises once the insured's liability to a third party has been fixed.—Also termed *third-party insurance.*

life insurance. An agreement between an insurance company and the policyholder to pay a specified amount to a designated beneficiary on the insured's death.

Lloyd's insurance. Insurance provided by insurers as individuals, rather than as a corporation. ● The insurers' liability is several but not joint. Most states either prohibit or strictly regulate this kind of insurance.

malpractice insurance. An agreement to indemnify professionals, such as doctors or lawyers, against negligence claims.

manual-rating insurance. A type of insurance whereby the premium is set using a book that classifies certain risks on a general basis, rather than evaluating each individual case.

mortgage insurance. An agreement to provide money for mortgage payments if the insured dies or becomes disabled.

mutual insurance. A system of insurance (esp. life insurance) whereby the policyholders become members of the insurance company, each paying premiums into a common fund from which each can claim in the event of a loss.

overinsurance. An indemnification that, through the purchase of one or more policies, exceeds the value of the property insured.

participating insurance. A type of insurance that is issued by a mutual company and allows a policyholder to receive dividends.

reciprocal insurance. A system whereby several individuals or businesses act through an agent to underwrite one another's risks, making each insured an insurer of the other members of the group.

reinsurance. Insurance of all or part of one insurer's risk by a second insurer, who accepts the risk in exchange for a percentage of the original premium.

self-insurance. A plan under which a business sets aside money to cover any losses.— Also termed *first-party insurance*.

title insurance. An agreement to indemnify against damage or loss arising from a defect in title to real property, usu. issued to the buyer of the property by the title company that conducted the title search.

underinsurance. An agreement to indemnify against property damage up to a certain amount but for less than the property's full value.

insurance adjuster. One who determines the value of a loss to the insured and settles the claim against the insurer.

insurance agent. One authorized by an insurance company to sell its insurance policies.—Also termed (in property insurance) *recording agent*.

insurance broker. One who sells insurance policies without an exclusive affiliation with a particular insurance company.

insurance fraud. See FRAUD.

insurance policy. 1. A contract of insurance. **2.** The document detailing such a contract.

basic-form policy. A policy that offers limited coverage against loss. ● Basic-form policies generally cover losses from fire, windstorm, explosion, riot, aircraft, vehicles, theft, or vandalism.—Also termed *limited policy*.

blanket policy. An agreement to indemnify all property, regardless of location.

broad-form policy. A policy that offers broad protection with few limitations. ● This policy offers greater coverage than a basic-form policy, but less than an open-perils policy.

claims-made policy. An agreement to indemnify against all claims made during a specified period, regardless of when the incident that gave rise to the claims occurred.—Also termed *discovery policy*.

comprehensive general liability policy. An insurance policy, usu. obtained by a business, that covers those damages that the insured becomes legally obligated to pay to a third party because of bodily injury or property damage.—Often shortened to *CGL policy.*—Also termed *commercial general liability policy.*

master policy. An insurance policy that covers those under a group-insurance plan.—Also termed *group policy.* See *group insurance* under INSURANCE.

occurrence policy. An insurance policy that provides coverage for an incident occurring within the policy period, regardless of when the claim is made.

open-perils policy. A property insurance policy covering all risks against loss except those specifically excluded in the contract.

standard policy. An insurance policy providing insurance that is recommended or required by state law, usu. regulated by an administrative agency.

umbrella policy. An insurance policy providing supplemental insurance that exceeds the basic or usual limits of liability.

insurance pool. A group of several insurers who, in order to spread the risk, combine and share premiums and losses.

insurance premium. See PREMIUM (1).

insured, *n*. One who is covered or protected by an insurance policy.

insurer. One who agrees, under an insurance policy, to assume the risk of another's loss and to compensate for that loss.—Also termed *underwriter*; *carrier*.

intangible asset. See ASSET.

intangible property. See PROPERTY.

integrated contract. See CONTRACT.

integration. 1. In contract law, the full expression of the parties' agreement, so that all earlier agreements are superseded, the effect being that neither party may later contradict or add to the contractual terms. See PAROL-EVIDENCE RULE. **2.** In antitrust law, a firm's performance of a function that it could have purchased on the open market. ● A firm can achieve integration by entering a new market on its own, by acquiring a firm that operates in a secondary market, or by entering into a contract with a firm that operates in a second-

320

ary market.—Also termed *vertical integration*. See *vertical merger* under MERGER. **3.** In securities law, the requirement that all offerings of securities over a given period are to be considered a single offering for purposes of determining an exemption from registration.

integration clause. A contractual provision stating that the contract represents the parties' complete and final agreement and supersedes all informal understandings and oral agreements relating to the subject matter of the contract.—Also termed *merger clause*. See PAROL-EVIDENCE RULE.

intellectual property. 1. A category of intangible rights comprising primarily copyright, trademark, and patent law. **2.** A copyrightable work, a protectable trademark, or a patentable invention in which one has such intangible rights.

interchangeable bond. See BOND (1).

interest. 1. A legal share in something; all or part of a legal or equitable claim to or right in property <right, title, and interest>. **2.** The compensation fixed by agreement or allowed by law for the use or detention of money, or for the loss of money by one who is entitled to its use; esp., the cost paid to a lender in return for use of borrowed money <the components

of a monthly mortgage payment are principal, interest, insurance, and taxes>. See USURY.

> ***accrued interest.*** Interest that is earned but not yet paid, such as interest that accrues on real estate and that will be paid when the property is sold if, in the meantime, the rental income does not cover the mortgage payments.

> ***compound interest.*** Interest paid on both the principal and the previously accumulated interest. Cf. *simple interest.*

> ***imputed interest.*** An interest charge that the IRS automatically attributes to a lender regardless of whether the lender actually charged the interest to the borrower—common esp. with loans between family members.

> ***prepaid interest.*** Interest paid before it is earned.

> ***simple interest.*** Interest paid on the principal only and not on accumulated interest; interest accruing only on the original principal balance regardless of how often interest is paid. Cf. *compound interest.*

interest bond. See BOND (1).

interest-free loan. See LOAN.

interest-only mortgage. See MORTGAGE.

interest rate. The percentage that a borrower of money must pay to the lender in return for the use of the money, usu. expressed as a percentage of the principal over a one-year period.—Often shortened to *rate*.

   annual percentage rate. The actual cost of borrowing money, expressed in the form of an annualized interest rate.—Abbr. APR.

   bank rate. The rate of interest at which the Federal Reserve loans funds to member banks.

   contract rate. The interest rate printed on the face of a bond certificate.

   discount rate. **a.** The interest rate at which member banks may borrow from the Federal Reserve. ● This rate controls the supply of money available to banks for lending. **b.** The percentage of a commercial paper's face value paid by a holder who sells the instrument to a financial institution. **c.** The interest rate used in calculating discounted present value.

   effective rate. The actual annual interest rate, which incorporates compounding when calculating interest, rather than the stated rate or coupon rate.

floating rate. A varying interest charge that is tied to a financial index such as the prime rate.

illegal rate. An interest charge higher than what is allowed by law. See USURY.

legal rate. **a.** The interest rate imposed as a matter of law when none is provided for contractually. **b.** The maximum interest rate, set by statute, that may be charged on loans. See USURY.

lock rate. A mortgage-application interest rate that is established and guaranteed for a specified period.

nominal rate. The interest rate stated in a loan agreement or on a bond, with no adjustment made for inflation.—Also termed *stated rate*.

prime rate. The lowest interest rate that a commercial bank charges for short-term loans to its most creditworthy borrowers, usu. large corporations. • This rate, which can vary slightly from bank to bank, often dictates other interest rates for various personal and commercial loans.—Often shortened to *prime*.

real rate. An interest rate that has been adjusted for inflation over time.

rediscount rate. The interest rate at which member banks may borrow from the Federal Reserve on loans secured by commercial paper that has been resold by the banks.

variable rate. An interest rate that fluctuates according to the current market rate.

interest-rate swap. An agreement to swap interest-payment obligations, usu. to adjust one's risk exposure, to speculate on interest-rate changes, or to convert an instrument or obligation from a fixed to a floating rate or vice versa. ● The parties to such an agreement are termed "counterparties."

interim financing. See FINANCING.

interim statement. In accounting, a periodic financial report issued during the fiscal year (usu. quarterly) that indicates the company's current performance. ● The SEC requires the company to file such a statement if it is distributed to the company's shareholders.—Also termed *interim report*.

interlocking director. See DIRECTOR.

intermediary bank. See BANK.

internal audit. See AUDIT.

internal financing. See FINANCING.

internal rate of return. See RATE OF RETURN.

internal revenue. Governmental revenue derived from domestic taxes rather than from customs or foreign sources.

Internal Revenue Code. Title 26 of the U.S. Code, containing all current federal tax laws.—Abbr. IRC.

Internal Revenue Service. The branch of the U.S. Treasury Department responsible for enforcing the Internal Revenue Code and providing taxpayer education.—Abbr. IRS.

International Monetary Fund. A United Nations agency established to stabilize international exchange rates and promote balanced trade.—Abbr. IMF.

interstate, *adj.* Between two or more states or residents of different states.

interstate commerce. See COMMERCE.

Interstate Commerce Commission. The now-defunct federal agency established by the Interstate Commerce Act in 1887 to regulate surface transportation between states by certifying carriers and pipelines and by monitoring quality and pricing. • In December 1995, when Congress eliminated this agency, the Surface Transportation Board (STB)—a three-member board that is a division of the Department of Transportation—assumed the agency's duties.—Abbr. ICC.

intrastate commerce. See COMMERCE.

intra vires (in-trə-**veer**-eez *or* -**vI**-reez), *adj.* [Latin "within the powers (of)"] Of or referring to an action taken within a corporation's or person's scope of authority <calling a shareholders' meeting is an *intra vires* function of the board of directors>. Cf. ULTRA VIRES.

invention, *n.* A patentable device or process created through independent experimentation; a newly discovered art or operation.

inventory, *n.* **1.** A detailed list of assets <make an inventory of the estate>. **2.** In accounting, the portion of a financial statement reflecting the value of a business's raw materials, works-in-progress, and finished products <the company's reported inventory was suspiciously low>. **3.** Raw materials or goods in stock <the dealership held a sale to clear out its October inventory>. **4.** In bankruptcy law, personal property leased or furnished, held for sale or lease, or to be furnished under a contract for service, raw materials, work in process, or materials used or consumed in a business, including farm products such as crops or livestock.

inventory-turnover ratio. In accounting, the result of dividing the cost of goods by the average inventory. • This calculation is used to determine the effectiveness of the company's inventory-management policy.

inverse-floating-rate note. See NOTE.

inverse-order-of-alienation doctrine. The principle that if one has not collected on the mortgage or lien on a property sold off in successive parcels, one may collect first from the parcel still held by the original owner, then from the parcel sold last, then next to last, and so on until the amount has been satisfied.— Also termed *rule of marshaling liens*.

investment bank. See BANK.

investment banker. A person or institution that underwrites, sells, or assists in raising capital for businesses, esp. for new issues of stocks and bonds; a trader at an investment bank. See *investment bank* under BANK.

investment company. See COMPANY.

investment-grade bond. See BOND (1).

investment-grade rating. Any of the top four symbols (AAA, AA, A, or BAA) given to a bond after an appraisal of its quality by a securities-evaluation agency such as Moody's. • The rating is one factor in determining whether the bond is a worthwhile risk.

investment income. See *unearned income* (a) under INCOME.

investment trust. See *investment company* under COMPANY.

invidious discrimination. See DISCRIMINATION.

invitation to negotiate. A solicitation for one or more offers, usu. as a preliminary step to forming a contract.—Also termed *solicitation of bids*. Cf. OFFER.

invitee (in-vi-**tee**). One who has permission to enter or use another's premises, either as a business visitor or as a member of the public to whom the premises are held open. • The occupier has a duty to inspect the premises and to warn the invitee of nonobvious dangerous conditions. Cf. LICENSEE (2).

invoice, *n.* An itemized list of goods or services furnished by a seller to a buyer, usu.

specifying the price and terms of sale; a bill of costs.

involuntary bailment. See BAILMENT.

involuntary bankruptcy. See BANKRUPTCY.

involuntary dissolution. See DISSOLUTION.

IOU (I-oh-yoo). [abbr. "I owe you"] **1.** A memorandum acknowledging a debt. **2.** The debt itself.—Also termed *due-bill*.

IPO. See *initial public offering* under OFFERING.

IRA. *abbr*. INDIVIDUAL RETIREMENT ACCOUNT.

IRC. *abbr*. INTERNAL REVENUE CODE.

irregular indorsement. See INDORSEMENT.

irrevocable offer. See OFFER (1).

irrevocable trust. See TRUST.

IRS. *abbr*. INTERNAL REVENUE SERVICE.

isolated sale. See SALE.

issue. 1. A class or series of stocks or bonds that are simultaneously offered for sale. See OFFERING.

>*hot issue.* A security that, after its initial public offering, is resold in the open market at a substantially higher price.—Also termed *hot stock*.

>*new issue.* A stock or bond sold by a corporation for the first time, often to raise working capital. See BLUE-SKY LAW.

>*shelf issue.* An issue of securities that were previously registered but not all sold at that time.

2. The first delivery of a negotiable instrument by its maker or holder.

issuer. A person or entity (such as a corporation or bank) that distributes securities or other negotiable instruments for circulation.

item. In commercial transactions, a negotiable or nonnegotiable writing for the payment of money.

itemized deduction. See DEDUCTION.

J

jeopardy assessment. See ASSESSMENT.

jobber. 1. One who buys from a manufacturer and sells to a retailer; a wholesaler or middleman. **2.** A middleman in the exchange of securities among brokers.—Also termed *stockjobber*. **3.** One who works by the job; a contractor.

joint and several bond. See BOND (1).

joint and several liability. See LIABILITY.

joint bond. See BOND (1).

joint liability. See LIABILITY.

joint-stock company. See COMPANY.

joint venture. A business undertaking by two or more persons engaged in a single defined project. • The necessary elements are (1) an express or implied agreement; (2) a common purpose the group intends to carry out; (3) shared profits and losses; and (4) each member's equal voice in controlling the project.—Also termed *joint adventure*; *joint enterprise*. Cf. PARTNERSHIP; STRATEGIC ALLIANCE.

judgment. A court's final determination of the rights and obligations of the parties in a case.

judgment creditor. A person who has won a money judgment that has not yet been satisfied.

judgment debt. See DEBT.

judgment debtor. A person against whom a money judgment has been entered but not yet satisfied.

judgment lien. See LIEN.

judgment-proof, *adj.* (Of an actual or potential judgment debtor) unable to satisfy a judgment for damages because the person has no property, does not own enough property within the court's jurisdiction to satisfy the judgment, or claims the benefit of statutorily exempt property.

judicial foreclosure. See FORECLOSURE.

judicial sale. See SALE.

junior bond. See BOND (1).

junior creditor. See CREDITOR.

junior lien. See LIEN.

junior mortgage. See MORTGAGE.

junior partner. See PARTNER.

junk bond. See BOND (1).

K

Keogh plan (**kee**-oh). A tax-deferred retirement program developed for the self-employed.—Also termed *self-employed retirement plan*. See INDIVIDUAL RETIREMENT ACCOUNT.

key-employee insurance. See INSURANCE.

kickback, *n.* A return of a portion of a monetary sum received, esp. as a result of coercion or a secret agreement <the contractor paid the city official a 5% kickback on the government contract>.—Also termed *payoff*. Cf. BRIBERY.

kicker. An extra charge or penalty, esp. a charge added to a loan in addition to interest.

kick-out clause. A contractual provision allowing a party to end or modify the contract if a specified event occurs <under the kick-out clause, the company could refuse to sell the land if it were unable to complete its acquisition of the new headquarters>.

kind arbitrage. See ARBITRAGE.

kiting. See CHECK-KITING.

knockoff, *n.* An unauthorized copy or imitation of another's product, usu. for sale at a substantially lower price than the original.

335

know-how. The information, practical knowledge, techniques, and skill required to achieve some practical end, esp. in industry or technology. ● Know-how is considered intangible property in which rights may be bought and sold.

known creditor. See CREDITOR.

L

label, *n.* An informative logo, title, or similar marking affixed to a manufactured product.

labor, *n.* **1.** Work of any type, including mental exertion <the fruits of one's labor>. ● The term usu. refers to work for wages as opposed to profits. **2.** Workers considered as an economic unit or a political element <a dispute between management and labor over retirement benefits>.

labor agreement. An agreement between an employer and a union governing working conditions, wages, benefits, and grievances.—Also termed *labor contract.*

labor dispute. A controversy between an employer and its employees concerning the terms or conditions of employment, or concerning the association or representation of those who negotiate or seek to negotiate the terms or conditions of employment.

Labor Disputes Act. See NORRIS–LAGUARDIA ACT.

Labor-Management Relations Act. A federal statute, enacted in 1947, that regulates certain union activities, permits suits against unions for proscribed acts, prohibits certain strikes and boycotts, and provides steps for

settling strikes involving national emergencies.—Also termed *Taft-Hartley Act*. See NA-
TIONAL LABOR RELATIONS BOARD.

labor union. See UNION.

lagging economic indicator. See ECONOMIC
INDICATOR.

laissez-faire (le-say-**fe[ə]r**), *n.* [French "to
let (people) do (as they choose)"] **1.** Governmental abstention from interference in economic or commercial affairs. **2.** The doctrine
favoring such abstention.

land description. See LEGAL DESCRIPTION.

landlord. One who leases real property to
another.—Also termed *lessor*.

land scrip. A negotiable instrument entitling
the holder, usu. a person or company engaged
in public service, to possess specified areas of
public land.

Lanham Act. The federal trademark statute,
enacted in 1946, which provides for a national
system of trademark registration and protects
the owner of a federally registered mark
against the use of similar marks if any confu-
sion might result.

lapping. An embezzlement technique by which an employee takes funds from one customer's accounts receivable and covers it by using a second customer's payment to pay the first account, then a third customer's payment to pay the second account, and so on.

last-in, first-out. An accounting method that assumes that the most recent purchases are sold or used first, matching current costs against current revenues.—Abbr. LIFO. Cf. FIRST-IN, FIRST-OUT; NEXT-IN, FIRST-OUT.

latent ambiguity. See AMBIGUITY.

latent defect. See *hidden defect* under DEFECT.

laundering. The federal crime of transferring illegally obtained money through legitimate persons or accounts so that its original source cannot be traced.—Also termed *money-laundering*.

law. 1. The regime that orders human activities and relations through systematic application of the force of politically organized society, or through social pressure, backed by force, in such a society; the legal system <the law of the land>. **2.** The aggregate of legislation, judicial precedents, and accepted legal principles; the body of authoritative grounds of judicial and administrative action <against the law>. **3.** The set of rules or principles that make up part of a legal system <copyright law>. **4.** A statute <a lemon law>.

law and economics. (*often cap.*) **1.** A discipline advocating the economic analysis of the law, whereby legal rules are subjected to a cost-benefit analysis in order to determine whether a change from one legal rule to another will increase or decrease allocative efficiency and social wealth. • Originally developed as an approach to antitrust policy, law and economics is today used by its proponents to explain and interpret a variety of legal subjects. **2.** The field or movement in which scholars devote themselves to this discipline.

law merchant. A system of customary law that developed in Europe during the Middle Ages and regulated the dealings of mariners and merchants in all the commercial countries of the world until the 17th century. • Many of the law merchant's principles came to be incorporated into the common law, which in turn formed the basis of the Uniform Commercial Code.—Also termed *commercial law*.

lawsuit. See SUIT.

LBO. See *leveraged buyout* under BUYOUT.

LC. *abbr.* LETTER OF CREDIT.

leader. See LOSS LEADER.

leading economic indicator. See ECONOMIC INDICATOR.

lease, *n.* **1.** A temporary conveyance of the right to use and occupy real property, usu. in exchange for rent. • The lease term can be for life, for a fixed period, or for a period terminable at will. **2.** Such a conveyance plus all covenants attached to it. **3.** The written instrument memorializing such a conveyance and its covenants. **4.** The piece of real property so conveyed. **5.** A temporary conveyance of personal property in exchange for consideration.

    finance lease. A fixed-term lease used by a business to finance capital equipment. • The lessor's service is usu. limited to financing the asset, and the lessee pays maintenance costs and taxes and has the option of purchasing the asset at lease-end for a nominal price. Finance leases strongly resemble security agreements and are written almost exclusively by financial institutions as a way to help a commercial customer obtain an expensive capital item that the customer might not otherwise be able to afford.—Also termed *full payout lease.*

gross lease. A lease in which the lessee pays a flat amount for rent, out of which the lessor pays all the expenses (such as gas, water, and electricity).

ground lease. A long-term (usu. 99-year) lease of land only. • Such a lease typically involves commercial property, and any improvements built by the lessee usu. revert to the lessor.

leveraged lease. A lease that serves as collateral for the loan under which the lessor acquired the leased asset, and that provides the lender's only recourse for nonpayment of the debt; a lease in which a creditor provides nonrecourse financing to the lessor (who has substantial leverage in the property) and in which the lessor's net investment in the lease, apart from nonrecourse financing, declines during the early years and increases in later years.—Also termed *third-party equity lease*; *tax lease*.

net lease. A lease that requires the lessee to pay rent plus property expenses (such as taxes and insurance).

percentage lease. A lease in which the rent is based on a percentage of gross (or net) sales or profits, with a stipulated minimum rent.

synthetic lease. A method for financing the purchase of real estate, whereby the lender creates a special-purpose entity that buys the property and then leases it to the ultimate user (usu. a corporation). ● A synthetic lease is treated as a loan for tax purposes and as an operating lease for accounting purposes, so that the "lessee" can deduct the property's depreciation and the loan's interest yet keep both the asset and the debt off its balance sheet.

leaseback, *n.* The sale of property on the understanding, or with the express option, that the seller may lease the property from the buyer immediately upon the sale.—Also termed *sale and leaseback*.

leasehold mortgage. See MORTGAGE.

leasehold-mortgage bond. See BOND (1).

lease-purchase agreement. A rent-to-own purchase plan under which the buyer takes possession of the goods with the first payment, and ownership with the final payment.—Also termed *capital lease*.

ledger (**le**-jər). A book or series of books used for recording financial transactions in the form of debits and credits.

legal capital. See CAPITAL.

legal description. A formal description of real property, including a description of any part subject to an easement or reservation, complete enough that a particular piece of land can be located and identified. ● The description can be made by reference to a government survey, metes and bounds, or lot numbers of a recorded plat.—Also termed *land description*.

legal duty. See DUTY.

legalese (lee-gə-**leez**). The jargon characteristically used by lawyers, esp. in legal documents <the partner chided her associate about the rampant legalese in the draft sublease>.

legal owner. See OWNER.

legal person. See ARTIFICIAL PERSON.

legal rate. See INTEREST RATE.

legal reserve. See RESERVE.

legal tender. The money (bills and coins) approved in a country for the payment of debts, the purchase of goods, and other exchanges for value. See TENDER (4).

legal title. See TITLE.

lemon law. 1. A statute designed to protect consumers who buy substandard automobiles, usu. by requiring the manufacturer or dealer either to replace the vehicle or to refund the full purchase price. ● Almost all states have lemon laws in effect. **2.** By extension, a statute designed to protect consumers who buy any products of inferior quality.

lessee (le-**see**). One who has a possessory interest in real or personal property under a lease; a tenant.

lessor (le-**sor** *or* **le**-sor). One who conveys real or personal property by lease; a landlord.

let, *vb.* **1.** To offer (property) for lease; to rent out <the hospital let office space to several doctors>. **2.** To award (a contract), esp. after bids have been submitted <the federal agency let the project to the lowest bidder>.

letter of comment. See DEFICIENCY LETTER.

letter of credit. An instrument under which the issuer (usu. a bank), at a customer's request, agrees to honor a draft or other demand for payment made by a third party (the *beneficiary*), as long as the draft or demand complies with specified conditions, and regardless of whether any underlying agreement between the customer and the beneficiary is satisfied. • Letters of credit are governed by Article 5 of the UCC.—Abbr. LC; L/C.—Often shortened to *credit*.—Also termed *circular note*.

commercial letter of credit. A letter of credit used as a method of payment in a sale of goods (esp. in international transactions), with the buyer being the issuer's customer and the seller being the beneficiary, so that the seller can obtain payment directly from the issuer instead of from the buyer.

export letter of credit. A commercial letter of credit issued by a foreign bank, at a foreign buyer's request, in favor of a domestic exporter.

general letter of credit. A letter of credit addressed to any and all persons without naming anyone in particular.

import letter of credit. A commercial letter of credit issued by a domestic bank, at an importer's request, in favor of a foreign seller.

special letter of credit. A letter of credit addressed to a particular individual, firm, or corporation.

standby letter of credit. A letter of credit used to guarantee either a monetary or a nonmonetary obligation (such as the performance of construction work), whereby the issuer agrees to pay the beneficiary if the customer defaults on its obligation.

letter of intent. A written statement detailing the preliminary understanding of parties who plan to enter into a contract or some other agreement; a noncommittal writing preliminary to a contract. • A letter of intent is not meant to be binding and usu. does not hinder the parties from bargaining with a third party. Although businesspeople typically mean not to be bound by a letter of intent, and courts ordinarily do not enforce one, courts occasionally find that a commitment has been made.—Abbr. LOI. Cf. *precontract* under CON-TRACT.

letter of recall. A manufacturer's letter to a buyer of a particular product, requesting that it be brought back to the dealer for repair or replacement as a result of some defect.

letter ruling. A written statement issued by the IRS to an inquiring taxpayer, explaining the tax implications of a particular transaction.

leverage, *n.* **1.** The use of credit or borrowed funds (such as buying on margin) to improve one's speculative ability and to increase an investment's rate of return. **2.** The advantage obtained from using credit or borrowed funds rather than equity capital. **3.** The ratio between a corporation's debt and its equity capital. **4.** The effect of this ratio on common-stock prices.

leverage, *vb.* **1.** To provide (a borrower or investor) with credit or funds to improve speculative ability and to seek a high rate of return. **2.** To supplement (available capital) with credit or outside funds.

leveraged buyout. See BUYOUT.

leveraged lease. See LEASE.

leveraged recapitalization. See RECAPITALIZATION.

leverage ratio. The ratio of the amount of a firm's debt to the value of the firm's assets.

liability. 1. The quality or state of being legally obligated or responsible; the position of one who, by actual or threatened wrongdoing, is subjected to legal proceedings, whether criminal or civil in nature <subject to both civil and criminal liability>. **2.** A pecuniary obligation; a debt <assets and liabilities>.

derivative liability. Liability for a wrong that a person other than the one wronged has a right to redress. ● Examples include liability to a widow in a wrongful-death action and liability to a corporation in a shareholder's derivative suit.

enterprise liability. Liability imposed on each member of an industry responsible for manufacturing a harmful or defective product, allotted by each manufacturer's market share of the industry.

joint and several liability. Liability that may be apportioned either among two or more parties or to only one or a few select members of the group, at the adversary's discretion. ● Thus, each liable party is individually responsible for the entire obligation, but a paying party has rights of contribution and indemnity against nonpaying parties.

joint liability. Liability shared by two or more parties.

limited liability. Liability restricted by statute or contract; esp., the liability of a company's owners for nothing more than the capital they have invested in the business.

several liability. Liability that is separate and distinct from another's liability, so that the plaintiff may bring a separate action

349

against one defendant without joining the other liable parties.

strict liability. Liability that does not depend on actual negligence or intent to harm, but that is based on the breach of an absolute duty to make something safe. • Strict liability most often applies either to ultrahazardous activities or in products-liability cases.—Also termed *absolute liability*.

liability insurance. See INSURANCE.

liability limit. The maximum coverage that an insurance company has provided in an insurance policy.—Also termed *limit of liability*.

libel (lɪ-bəl), *n.* A defamatory statement expressed in a tangible medium, esp. writing but also pictures, signs, or electronic broadcasts. See DEFAMATION. Cf. SLANDER.

license, *n.* **1.** A revocable permission to commit some act that would otherwise be unlawful <buyers must obtain a license before copying and distributing copyrighted software>. **2.** The certificate or document evidencing such permission <a hunting license>.

exclusive license. A license that gives the licensee the exclusive right to perform the licensed act and that prohibits the licensor from granting that right to anyone else; esp., such a license of a copyright, patent, or trademark right.

shrink-wrap license. A license placed within the transparent wrapper of a software package, intended to limit the user's right to copy or distribute the software.— Also termed *box-top license*.

licensee. 1. One to whom a license is granted. **2.** One who has permission to enter or use another's premises, but only for his or her own purposes and not for the occupier's benefit (such as a social guest). ● The occupier has a duty to warn the licensee of any dangerous conditions known to the occupier but unknown to the licensee. Cf. INVITEE.

lien (leen *or* **lee**-ən *or* lin), *n.* A legal right or interest that a creditor has in another's property, lasting usu. until a debt or duty that it secures is satisfied. ● Typically, the creditor does not take possession of the property on which the lien has been obtained. Cf. PLEDGE (1).

first lien. A lien that takes priority over all other charges or encumbrances on the same property and that must be satisfied before other charges may share in proceeds from the property's sale.

351

floating lien. A lien that continues to exist even when the collateral changes in character, classification, or location.

judgment lien. A lien imposed on a judgment debtor's nonexempt property. • This lien gives the judgment creditor the right to attach the judgment debtor's property. See *exempt property* under PROPERTY.

junior lien. A lien that is subordinate to other liens on the same property.

mechanic's lien. A statutory lien that secures payment for labor or materials supplied in improving, repairing, or maintaining real or personal property, such as a building, an automobile, or the like.—Also termed *artisan's lien* (with respect to personal property); *construction lien* (with respect to labor); or *materialman's lien* (with respect to materials).

senior lien. A lien that has priority over other liens on the same property.

vendor's lien. **a.** A lien, equal to the unpaid portion of the purchase price, retained by a seller of real property even without a special agreement for that purpose. **b.** A lien held by a seller of goods, who retains possession of the goods until the buyer pays in full.

warehouser's lien. A lien covering storage charges for goods stored with a bailee.

lien creditor. See CREDITOR.

life annuity. See ANNUITY.

life insurance. See INSURANCE.

life-insurance trust. See TRUST.

LIFO. *abbr.* LAST-IN, FIRST-OUT.

like-kind exchange. An exchange of trade, business, or investment property (except inventory, stocks, and bonds) for other trade, business, or investment property. ● Such an exchange is not taxable unless cash or a different type of property is received.

likelihood-of-confusion test. In trademark law, the test for infringement, based on the probability that a substantial number of ordinarily prudent buyers will be misled or confused about the source of a product when its trademark allegedly infringes on that of an earlier product.

limitation-of-remedies clause. A contractual provision that restricts the remedies available to the parties in the event of breach. ● Under the UCC, such a clause is valid unless it fails of its essential purpose or (with respect to limiting consequential damages) it is unconscionable. Cf. LIQUIDATED-DAMAGES CLAUSE.

limited company. See COMPANY.

limited liability. See LIABILITY.

limited-liability company. See COMPANY.

limited-liability partnership. See PARTNER-SHIP.

limited partner. See PARTNER.

limited partnership. See PARTNERSHIP.

limited policy. See *basic-form policy* under INSURANCE POLICY.

limited warranty. See WARRANTY.

limit of liability. See LIABILITY LIMIT.

limit order. See ORDER.

line of credit. The maximum amount of credit extended to a borrower by a given lender.— Also termed *credit line*.

link financing. See FINANCING.

liquid, *adj.* **1.** (Of an asset) capable of being readily converted into cash. **2.** (Of a person or entity) possessing assets that are readily convertible into cash.

liquid asset. See *current asset* under ASSET.

liquidated amount. A figure readily computed, based on the agreement's terms.

liquidated claim. See CLAIM (2).

liquidated damages. See DAMAGES.

liquidated-damages clause. A contractual provision that determines in advance the measure of damages to be assessed if a party defaults. • Traditionally, courts have upheld such a clause unless the agreed-upon sum is determined to be a penalty for one of the following reasons: (1) the sum grossly exceeds the probable damages on breach, (2) the same sum is made payable for any variety of different breaches (some major, some minor), or (3) a mere delay in payment has been listed among the events of default. Cf. LIMITATION-OF-REMEDIES CLAUSE.

liquidated debt. See DEBT.

liquidating dividend. See *liquidation dividend* under DIVIDEND.

liquidating partner. See PARTNER.

liquidating trust. See TRUST.

liquidation, *n.* **1.** The act of determining by agreement or by litigation the exact amount of something (as a debt or damages) that before was uncertain. **2.** The act of settling a debt by payment or other satisfaction. **3.** The act of converting assets into cash, esp. for the purpose of settling debts. **4.** The process—under Chapter 7 of the Bankruptcy Code—of collecting a debtor's nonexempt property, converting that property to cash, and distributing the cash to the various creditors. ● Upon liquidation, the debtor hopes to obtain a discharge, which releases the debtor from any further personal liability for prebankruptcy debts. Cf. REHABILITATION.

liquidation dividend. See DIVIDEND.

liquidation preference. See PREFERENCE.

liquidation price. See PRICE.

liquidation value. 1. The value of an asset or business that is sold outside the ordinary course of business. **2.** See *liquidation price* under PRICE.

liquid debt. See DEBT.

liquidity ratio. The ratio between a corporation's assets that are held in cash or liquid form and the amount of its current liabilities, indicating the ability to pay current debts as they come due.

lis pendens (lis-**pen**-dənz). [Latin "a pending lawsuit"] **1.** A pending litigation. **2.** The jurisdiction, power, or control acquired by a court over property during the pendency of a legal action. **3.** A notice required in some states to warn all persons that certain property is the subject matter of litigation, and that any interests acquired during the pendency of the suit are subject to the outcome of the litigation.

listed security. See SECURITY.

listing. 1. In real estate, an agreement between a property owner and an agent, whereby the agent agrees to try to secure a buyer or tenant for a specific property at a certain price and terms in return for a fee or commission.

exclusive-agency listing. A listing providing that one agent has the right to be the only person, other than the owner, to sell the property during a specified period.

multiple listing. A listing providing that the agent will allow other agents to try to sell the property. ● Under this agreement, the original agent gives the selling agent a

357

percentage of the commission or some other stipulated amount.

net listing. A listing providing that the agent agrees to sell the owner's property for a set minimum price, any amount over the minimum being retained by the agent as commission.

open listing. A listing that allows selling rights to be given to more than one agent at a time, obligates the owner to pay a commission when a specified broker makes a sale, and reserves the owner's right to personally sell the property without paying a commission.

2. In securities trading, the contract between a firm and a stock exchange by which the trading of the firm's securities on the exchange is handled. See *listed security* under SECURITY.

dual listing. The listing of a security on more than one exchange.

3. In taxation, the creation of a schedule or inventory of a person's taxable property; the list of a person's taxable property.

listing agent. The real-estate broker's representative who obtains a listing agreement with the owner. Cf. SELLING AGENT.

list of creditors. A schedule giving the names and addresses of creditors along with amounts owed them. ● This list is required in bankruptcy proceedings.

L.L.C. See *limited-liability company* under COMPANY.

Lloyd's insurance. See INSURANCE.

Lloyd's of London. 1. A London insurance mart where individual underwriters gather to quote rates and write insurance on a wide variety of risks. **2.** A voluntary association of merchants, shipowners, underwriters, and brokers formed not to write policies but instead to issue a notice of an endeavor to members who may individually underwrite a policy by assuming shares of the total risk of insuring a client. ● The names of the bound underwriters and the attorney-in-fact appear on the policy.—Also termed *Lloyd's*.

Lloyd's underwriters. An unincorporated association of underwriters who, under a common name, engage in the insurance business through an attorney-in-fact having authority to obligate the underwriters severally, within specified limits, on insurance contracts that the attorney makes or issues in the common name.—Also termed *Lloyd's association*.

L.L.P. See *limited-liability partnership* under PARTNERSHIP.

load, *n.* An amount added to a security's price or to an insurance premium in order to cover sales commissions and expenses <the mutual fund had a high front-end load>.—Also termed *sales load*.

load fund. See MUTUAL FUND.

loan, *n.* **1.** An act of lending; a grant of something for temporary use <Trina gave him the laptop as a loan, not a gift>. **2.** A thing lent for the borrower's temporary use; esp., a sum of money lent at interest <Larry applied for a car loan>.

accommodation loan. A loan for which the lender receives no consideration in return. See ACCOMMODATION.

amortized loan. A loan calling for periodic payments that are applied first to interest and then to principal, as provided by the terms of the note. See AMORTIZATION (1).

back-to-back loan. A loan arrangement by which two firms lend each other funds denominated in different currencies for a specified period.

360

bridge loan. A short-term loan that is used to cover costs until more permanent financing is arranged.

call loan. A loan for which the lender can demand payment at any time, usu. with 24 hours' notice, because there is no fixed maturity date.—Also termed *broker call loan*; *demand loan*.

commercial loan. A loan that a financial institution gives to a business, generally for 30 to 90 days.

consolidation loan. A loan whose proceeds are used to pay off other individual loans, thereby creating a more manageable debt.

consumer loan. A loan that is given to an individual for family, household, personal, or agricultural purposes and that is generally governed by truth-in-lending statutes and regulations.

home equity loan. A line of bank credit given to a homeowner, using as collateral the homeowner's equity in the home.—Often shortened to *equity loan*. See EQUITY (1).

installment loan. A loan that is to be repaid in usu. equal portions over a specified period.

interest-free loan. Money loaned to a borrower at no charge or, under the Internal Revenue Code, with a charge that is lower than the market rate.—Also termed (in the IRC) *below-market loan*.

nonperforming loan. An outstanding loan that is not being repaid.

nonrecourse loan. A secured loan that allows the lender to attach only the collateral, not the borrower's personal assets, if the loan is not repaid.

participation loan. A loan issued by two or more lenders. See LOAN PARTICIPATION.

recourse loan. A loan that allows the lender, if the borrower defaults, not only to attach the collateral but also to seek judgment against the borrower's (or guarantor's) personal assets.

revolver loan. A single loan that a debtor takes out in lieu of several lines of credit or other loans from various creditors, and that is subject to review and approval at certain intervals. ● A revolver loan is usu. taken out in an attempt to resolve problems with creditors. Cf. *revolving credit* under CREDIT.

secured loan. A loan that is secured by property or securities.

signature loan. An unsecured loan based solely on the borrower's promise or signature. • To obtain such a loan, the borrower must usu. be highly creditworthy.

term loan. A loan with a specified due date, usu. of more than one year. • Such a loan typically cannot be repaid before maturity without incurring a penalty.

loan-amortization schedule. A schedule that divides each loan payment into an interest component and a principal component. • Typically, the interest component begins as the largest part of each payment and declines over time. See AMORTIZATION (1).

loan certificate. A certificate that a clearinghouse issues to a borrowing bank in an amount equal to a specified percentage of the value of the borrowing bank's collateral on deposit with the clearinghouse's loan committee.

loan commitment. A lender's binding promise to a borrower to lend a specified amount of money at a certain interest rate, usu. within a specified period and for a specified purpose (such as buying real estate). See MORTGAGE COMMITMENT.

loan for consumption. An agreement by which a lender delivers a given quantity of goods to a borrower who consumes them and who is obligated to return not those very goods, but goods of the same quantity, type, and quality.

loan for exchange. A contract by which a lender delivers personal property to a borrower who agrees to return similar property, usu. without compensation for its use.

loan for use. An agreement by which a lender delivers an asset to a borrower who must use it according to its normal function or according to the agreement, and who must return it when finished using it. ● No interest is charged.

loan participation. The coming together of multiple lenders to issue a large loan (called a *participation loan*) to one borrower, thereby reducing each lender's individual risk.

loan ratio. See LOAN-TO-VALUE RATIO.

loan-receipt agreement. In tort law, a settlement agreement by which the defendant lends money to the plaintiff interest-free, the plaintiff not being obligated to repay the loan unless he or she recovers money from other tortfeasors responsible for the same injury.

loansharking. The practice of lending money at excessive and esp. usurious rates, and often threatening or using extortion to enforce repayment.

loan-to-value ratio. The ratio, usu. expressed as a percentage, between the amount of a mortgage loan and the value of the property pledged as security for the mortgage. ● For example, an $80,000 loan on property worth $100,000 results in a loan-to-value ratio of 80%—which is usu. the highest ratio lenders will agree to without requiring the debtor to buy mortgage insurance.—Also termed *loan ratio*.

loan value. The maximum amount that can be safely lent on property or life insurance without damaging the lender's right to protection if the borrower defaults.

local agent. See AGENT.

local union. See UNION.

lockbox. A facility offered by a financial institution for quickly collecting and consolidating checks and other funds from a party's customers.

lockout. An employer's withholding of work and closing of a business because of a labor dispute. Cf. STRIKE.

lock rate. See INTEREST RATE.

locus sigilli. See L.S.

LOI. *abbr.* LETTER OF INTENT.

long-term debt. See DEBT.

long-term security. See SECURITY.

look-and-feel protection. Copyright protection of the images generated or revealed when one activates a computer program.

loss. **1.** A decrease in value; the amount by which a thing's original cost exceeds its subsequent selling price. **2.** The amount of financial detriment caused by an insured person's death or an insured property's damage, for which the insurer becomes liable.

    actual loss. A loss resulting from the real and substantial destruction of insured property.

    capital loss. The loss realized upon selling or exchanging a capital asset.

    casualty loss. For tax purposes, the total or partial destruction of an asset resulting from an unexpected or unusual event, such as an automobile accident or a tornado.

consequential loss. A loss arising from the results of damage rather than from the damage itself.—Also termed *indirect loss*. Cf. *direct loss*.

constructive total loss. **a.** Such serious damage to the subject matter of the insurance that the cost of repairs would exceed the value of the thing repaired. **b.** In marine underwriting, according to the traditional American rule, such serious damage to the subject matter of the insurance that the cost of repairs would exceed one-half the value of the thing repaired.

direct loss. A loss that results immediately and proximately from an event. Cf. *consequential loss*.

disaster loss. A casualty loss sustained in a geographic area that the President designates as a disaster area. ● It may be treated as having occurred during the previous tax year so that a victim may receive immediate tax benefits.

net loss. The excess of all expenses and losses over all revenues and gains.

net operating loss. The excess of operating expenses over revenues, which amount can be deducted from gross income if other deductions do not exceed gross income.—Abbr. NOL.

ordinary loss. In tax law, a loss incurred from the sale or exchange of an item that is used in a trade or business. • The loss is deductible from ordinary income, and thus is more beneficial to the taxpayer than a capital loss.

out-of-pocket loss. The difference between the value of what the buyer paid and the market value of what was received in return. • In breach-of-contract cases, out-of-pocket loss is used to measure restitution damages.

paper loss. A loss that is realized only by selling something (such as a security) that has decreased in market value.—Also termed *unrealized loss.*

passive loss. A loss, with limited tax deductibility, from an activity in which the taxpayer does not materially participate, a rental activity, or a tax-shelter activity.

pecuniary loss. A loss of money or of something having monetary value.

salvage loss. **a.** Generally, a loss that presumptively would have been a total loss if certain services had not been rendered. **b.** In marine underwriting, the difference between the salvage value, less the charges, and the original value of the insured property.

total loss. Complete loss or destruction of the subject matter of the insurance, including damage so extensive that the subject matter no longer exists in its original form.

loss leader. A good or commodity sold at a very low price, usu. below cost, to attract customers to buy other items.—Sometimes shortened to *leader*. See BAIT AND SWITCH.

loss-of-bargain rule. The doctrine that damages for breach of a contract should put the injured party in the position it would have been in if both parties had performed their contractual duties.

loss-payable clause. An insurance-policy provision that authorizes payment of proceeds to someone other than the named insured, esp. to someone with a security interest in the insured property. See MORTGAGE CLAUSE.

loss payee. A person or entity named in an insurance policy (under a loss-payable clause) to be paid if the insured property suffers a loss.

loss ratio. 1. In insurance, the ratio between premiums paid and losses incurred during a given period. **2.** In finance, a bank's loan losses compared to its loan assets; a business's receivable losses compared to its receivables.

loss reserve. The portion of a company's (esp. an insurer's) assets set aside for paying probable losses, or losses incurred but not yet paid.

lost profits. A measure of damages by which a seller may collect the profit that would have been made on the sale if the buyer had not breached.

lost-volume seller. A seller of goods who, after a buyer has breached a sales contract, resells the goods to a different buyer who would have bought identical goods from the seller's inventory even if the original buyer had not breached. ● Such a seller is entitled to lost profits, rather than contract price less market price, as damages from the original buyer's breach.

lot. 1. A parcel or article that is the subject of a separate sale or delivery, whether or not it is sufficient to perform the contract. **2.** A specified number of shares or a specific quantity of a commodity designated for trading.

odd lot. An amount of stocks or bonds that is less than a round lot.

round lot. The established unit of trading for stocks and bonds. ● A round lot of stock is usu. 100 shares, and a round lot of bonds is usu. $1,000 or $5,000 par value.—Also termed *even lot*.

lower-of-cost-or-market method. A means of inventory-costing by which inventory value is set at either acquisition cost or market cost, whichever is lower.

lowest responsible bidder. A bidder who has the lowest price conforming to the contract specifications and who is financially able and competent to complete the work, as shown by the bidder's prior performance.

low-grade security. See SECURITY.

L.P. See *limited partnership* under PARTNERSHIP.

L.S. *abbr.* [Latin *locus sigilli*] The place of the seal. • These are the traditional letters appearing on many notarial certificates to indicate where the notary public's embossed seal should be placed.

lumping sale. See SALE.

lump-sum payment. See PAYMENT.

luxury tax. See TAX.

M

M1. A measure of the money supply including cash, checking accounts, and travelers' checks.

M2. A measure of the money supply including M1 items, plus savings and time deposits, money-market accounts, and overnight-repurchase agreements.

M3. A measure of the money supply including M2 items, plus large time deposits and money-market funds held by institutions.

MACRS. *abbr*. Modified Accelerated Cost Recovery System. See ACCELERATED COST RECOVERY SYSTEM.

Magnuson-Moss Warranty Act. A federal statute requiring that a consumer product's written warranty must fully and conspicuously disclose, in plain language, the terms and conditions of the warranty, including whether the warranty is full or limited, according to standards given in the statute.

mailbox rule. In contract law, the rule that an acceptance becomes effective—and binds the offeror—once it has been properly mailed. • The mailbox rule does not apply, however, if the offer states that an acceptance is not effective until received.

main-purpose rule. In contract law, the doctrine holding that if the primary object of a promise to guarantee another's debt is the promisor's own benefit, then the statute of frauds does not apply and the promise does not have to be in writing.

maintenance call. See CALL (1).

maintenance margin requirement. See MARGIN REQUIREMENT.

majority rule. In corporate law, the principle that a director or officer owes no fiduciary duty to a shareholder with respect to stock transactions. ● This rule has been restricted by both federal insider-trading rules and state-law doctrines. Cf. SPECIAL-FACTS RULE.

majority shareholder. See SHAREHOLDER.

majority voting. See VOTING.

maker. 1. A person who makes a promise in a promissory note by signing it. See NOTE. Cf. CO-MAKER. **2.** See DRAWER.

malpractice insurance. See INSURANCE.

management buyout. See BUYOUT.

manager. A person who administers or supervises the affairs of a business, office, or other organization.

managing agent. See AGENT.

mandatory subject. In labor law, a topic that is required by the NLRB to be discussed in good faith by the parties during labor negotiations. ● Wages, hours, and working conditions are mandatory subjects. Cf. PERMISSIVE SUBJECT.

manifest, *n.* A document listing the cargo or passengers carried on a ship, plane, or other vehicle.

manipulation. The illegal practice of raising or lowering a security's price by creating the appearance of active trading.

manual-rating insurance. See INSURANCE.

manufacturing defect. See DEFECT.

margin. 1. See PROFIT MARGIN. **2.** The difference between a loan's face value and the market value of the collateral that secures the loan. **3.** Cash or collateral paid to a securities broker by an investor to protect the broker against losses from securities bought on credit. **4.** The amount of an investor's equity in securities bought on credit through the broker.

marginable security. See SECURITY.

margin account. See ACCOUNT.

marginal cost. See COST.

marginal revenue. See REVENUE.

marginal tax rate. See TAX RATE.

margin call. See CALL.

margined security. See SECURITY.

margin requirement. The percentage of the purchase price that a buyer must deposit with a broker to buy a security on margin.

    initial margin requirement. The minimum percentage of the purchase price that a buyer must deposit with a broker. • The Federal Reserve Board establishes minimum margin requirements in order to prevent excessive speculation and price volatility.

    maintenance margin requirement. The minimum equity that a buyer must keep in a margin account, expressed as a percentage of the account value.

margin transaction. A securities or commodities transaction made through a broker on a margin account.—Also termed *buying on margin*. See MARGIN (3).

maritime law. The body of law governing marine commerce and navigation, the transportation at sea of persons and property, and marine affairs in general; the rules governing contract, tort, and workers'-compensation claims arising out of commerce on or over water.—Also termed *admiralty law*.

market, *n.* **1.** A place of commercial activity in which goods or services are bought and sold <the farmers' market>. **2.** A geographic area or demographic segment considered as a place of demand for a particular good or service <the foreign market for microchips>. **3.** The opportunity for buying and selling goods or services; the extent of economic demand <a strong job market for accountants>. **4.** A securities or commodities exchange <the stock market closed early because of the blizzard>. **5.** The business of such an exchange; the enterprise of buying and selling securities or commodities <the stock market is approaching an all-time high>. **6.** The price at which the buyer and seller of a security or commodity agree <the market for oil is $16 per barrel>.

bear market. A securities market characterized by falling prices over a prolonged period.

black market. An illegal market for goods that are controlled or prohibited by the government, such as the underground market for prescription drugs.

bull market. A securities market characterized by rising prices over a prolonged period.

buyer's market. A market in which supply exceeds demand, resulting in lowered prices.

capital market. A securities market in which stock and bonds with long-term maturities are traded.

common market. An economic association formed by several nations to reduce trade barriers among them. See EUROPEAN UNION.

discount market. The portion of the money market in which banks and other financial institutions trade commercial paper.

futures market. A commodity exchange where futures contracts are traded; a market for a trade (such as commodities futures contracts and stock options) that is negotiated at the current price but calls for delivery at a future time.

geographic market. In antitrust law, the part of a relevant market that identifies the physical area in which a firm might compete. ● If a firm can raise prices or cut production without causing a quick influx of supply to the area from outside sources, that

377

firm is operating in a distinct geographic market.

gray market. A market in which legal but perhaps unethical methods are used in order to avoid a manufacturer's distribution chain and thereby sell goods (esp. imported goods) at prices lower than those intended by the manufacturer.

institutional market. The demand among large investors and corporations for short-term funds and commercial paper.

market overt. An open, legally regulated public market where buyers, with some exceptions, acquire good title to products regardless of any defects in the seller's title.

money market. The financial market for dealing in short-term negotiable instruments such as commercial paper, certificates of deposit, banker's acceptances, and U.S. Treasury securities.

open market. A market with no competitive restrictions on price or availability of products.—Also termed *free market.*

over-the-counter market. See OVER-THE-COUNTER MARKET.

primary market. The market for goods or services that are newly available for buying and selling; esp., the securities market in which new securities are issued by corporations in order to raise capital.

product market. In antitrust law, the part of a relevant market that applies to a firm's particular product by identifying all reasonable substitutes for the product and by determining whether these substitutes limit the firm's ability to affect prices.

relevant market. In antitrust law, a market that is capable of being monopolized—that is, a market in which a firm can raise prices above the competitive level without losing so many sales that the price increase would be unprofitable. ● The relevant market includes both the *product market* and the *geographic market*.

secondary market. The market for goods or services that have previously been available for buying and selling; esp., the securities market in which previously issued securities are traded among investors.

seller's market. A market in which demand exceeds supply, resulting in raised prices.

soft market. A market (esp. a stock market) characterized by falling or drifting prices and low volume.

379

thin market. A market in which the number of bids or offerings is relatively low.

marketable, *adj.* Of commercially acceptable quality; fit for sale and in demand by buyers.—Also termed *merchantable*.

marketable title. See TITLE.

marketable-title act. A state statute providing that good title to land can be established by searching the public records only back to a specified time (such as 40 years ago). See *marketable title* under TITLE.

market-making, *n.* The practice of establishing prices for over-the-counter securities by reporting bid-and-asked quotations. • A broker-dealer engaged in this practice, which is regulated by both the NASD and the SEC, buys and sells securities as a principal for its own account, and thus accepts two-way bids (both to buy and to sell). See BID AND ASKED.

market order. See ORDER.

market overt. See MARKET.

market portfolio. See PORTFOLIO.

market power. The ability to reduce output and raise prices above the competitive level—

specifically, above marginal cost—for a sustained period, and to make a profit by doing so. • In antitrust law, a large amount of market power constitutes monopoly power. See MONOPOLIZATION. Cf. MARKET SHARE.

market price. See PRICE.

market share. The percentage of the market for a product that a firm supplies, usu. calculated by dividing the firm's output by the total market output. • In antitrust law, market share is used to measure a firm's market power, and if the share is high enough—generally 70% or more—then the firm may be guilty of monopolization. See MONOPOLIZATION. Cf. MARKET POWER.

market value. See FAIR MARKET VALUE.

markup, *n.* An amount added to an item's cost to determine its selling price. See PROFIT MARGIN.

Massachusetts trust. See *business trust* under TRUST.

mass tort. See TORT.

master agreement. In labor law, an agreement between a union and industry leaders, the terms of which serve as a model for agreements between the union and individual companies within the industry.

master limited partnership. See PARTNER-SHIP.

master policy. See INSURANCE POLICY.

material breach. See BREACH OF CONTRACT.

materialman's lien. See *mechanic's lien* under LIEN.

material representation. See REPRESENTATION.

mature, *vb*. (Of a debt or obligation) to become due <the bond matures in ten years>.

matured claim. See CLAIM (2).

maturity value. The amount that is due and payable on an obligation's maturity date.

MBO. See *management buyout* under BUYOUT.

mean reserve. See RESERVE.

mechanic's lien. See LIEN.

mediation. A method of nonbinding dispute resolution involving a neutral third party who tries to help the disputing parties reach a mutually agreeable solution. Cf. ARBITRATION.

meeting. An assembly of persons, esp. to discuss and act on matters in which they have a common interest.

> *annual meeting.* A yearly meeting of shareholders for the purpose of electing directors and conducting other business. • The time and place of such a meeting are usu. specified in the corporation's articles or bylaws.—Also termed *regular meeting*.

> *creditors' meeting.* In bankruptcy law, the first meeting of a debtor's creditors and equity security holders, presided over by the U.S. Trustee and at which a bankruptcy trustee may be elected and the debtor may be examined under oath.

> *organizational meeting.* An initial meeting of a new corporation's directors to adopt bylaws, elect officers, and conduct other preparatory business.

> *special meeting.* In corporate law, a meeting called by the board of directors, an officer, or a group of shareholders for some extraordinary purpose, such as to vote on a merger.

meeting-competition defense. In antitrust law, a defense to a charge of price discrimination whereby the defendant shows that the lower price was a good-faith attempt to match what it believed to be a competitor's equally low offer.

meeting of the minds. Actual assent by both parties to the formation of a contract. • This was required under the traditional subjective theory of assent, but modern contract doctrine requires only objective manifestations of assent. See MUTUAL ASSENT.

member bank. See BANK.

member firm. A brokerage firm with at least one director, officer, or general partner who is a member of an organized securities exchange.—Also termed (if organized as a corporation) *member corporation*.

memorandum. 1. An informal written note or record outlining the terms of a transaction or contract <the memorandum indicated the developer's intent to buy the property at its appraised value>. • To satisfy the statute of frauds, a memorandum (though it can be written in any form) must (1) identify the parties to the contract, (2) indicate the contract's subject matter, (3) contain the contract's essential terms, and (4) contain the signature of the

party against whom enforcement is sought.—
Also termed *memorial*. See STATUTE OF FRAUDS.
2. An informal written communication used
esp. in offices <the firm sent a memorandum
reminding lawyers to turn in their time-
sheets>.—Often shortened to *memo*. Pl. **mem-
oranda, memorandums.**

memorandum check. See CHECK.

memorandum sale. See SALE.

mercantile (mər-kən-teel *or* -til *or* -tıl), *adj.*
Of or relating to merchants or trading; commercial <the mercantile system>.

merchandise. Goods that are bought and sold
in business; commercial wares.

merchant. One whose business is buying and
selling goods for profit; esp., a person or entity
that holds itself out as having expertise peculiar to the goods in which it deals, and is
therefore held by the law to a higher standard
than a consumer or other nonmerchant is
held. • Because the term relates solely to
goods, a supplier of services is not considered a
merchant.

merchantable. See MARKETABLE.

merchant's firm offer. See *irrevocable offer* under OFFER.

mergee. A participant in a corporate merger.

merger. 1. The act or an instance of combining or uniting. **2.** The substitution of a superior form of contract for an inferior form, as when a written contract supersedes all oral agreements and prior understandings. **3.** The absorption of one company (esp. a corporation) that ceases to exist into another that retains its own name and identity and acquires the assets and liabilities of the former. ● Corporate mergers must conform to statutory formalities and usu. must be approved by a majority of the outstanding shares. Cf. AMALGAMATION; CONSOLIDATION.

> ***bust-up merger.*** A merger in which the acquiring corporation sells off lines of business owned by the target corporation in order to repay the loans used to fund the merger.

> ***cash merger.*** A merger in which shareholders must accept cash for their shares.—Also termed *freeze-out merger.*

> ***conglomerate merger.*** A merger between unrelated businesses that are neither competitors nor customers or suppliers of each other.

de facto merger. A transaction that has the economic effect of a statutory merger but that is cast in the form of an acquisition or sale of assets or voting stock. • Although such a transaction does not meet the statutory requirements for a merger, some courts will treat it as a statutory merger for purposes of the appraisal remedy.

downstream merger. A merger of a parent corporation into its subsidiary.

horizontal merger. A merger between two or more businesses that are on the same market level because they manufacture similar products in the same geographic region; a merger of direct competitors.

product-extension merger. A merger in which the products of the acquired company are complementary to those of the acquiring company and may be produced with similar facilities, marketed through the same channels, and advertised by the same media.

reverse triangular merger. A merger in which the acquiring corporation's subsidiary is absorbed into the target corporation, which becomes a new subsidiary of the acquiring corporation.

short-form merger. A merger that is less expensive and time-consuming than an ordinary statutory merger, usu. permitted when a subsidiary merges into a parent that already owns most of the subsidiary's shares. ● Such a merger is generally accomplished when the parent adopts a merger resolution, mails a copy of the plan to the subsidiary's record shareholders, and files the executed articles of merger with the secretary of state, who issues a certificate of merger.

stock merger. A merger involving one company's purchase of another company's capital stock.

triangular merger. A merger in which the target corporation is absorbed into the acquiring corporation's subsidiary, with the target's shareholders receiving stock in the parent corporation.

upstream merger. A merger of a subsidiary corporation into its parent.

vertical merger. A merger between businesses occupying different levels of operation for the same product, such as between a manufacturer and a retailer; a merger of buyer and seller.

merger clause. See INTEGRATION CLAUSE.

merit regulation. Under state blue-sky laws, the practice of requiring securities offerings not only to have a full and adequate disclosure but also to be substantively fair, just, and equitable.

metes and bounds. The territorial limits of real property as measured by distances and angles from designated landmarks and in relation to adjoining properties. • Metes and bounds are usu. described in deeds and surveys to establish the boundary lines of land.

middleman. An intermediary or agent between two parties; esp., a dealer (such as a wholesaler) who buys from producers and sells to retailers or consumers.

mini-maxi. An underwriting arrangement for a securities transaction, whereby a broker is required to sell the minimum number of securities on an all-or-none basis and the balance on a best-efforts basis. See UNDERWRITING (2).

minimum wage. See WAGE.

minority shareholder. See SHAREHOLDER.

minute book. A record of the subjects discussed and actions authorized at a corporate directors' or shareholders' meeting.—Also termed *minutes book*.

mirror-image rule. In contract law, the rule that the acceptance of a contractual offer must be positive, unconditional, unequivocal, and unambiguous, and must not change, add to, or qualify the terms of the offer; the common-law principle requiring an acceptance's terms to correspond exactly with the offer's terms in order for a contract to be formed. • In modern commercial contexts, the mirror-image rule has been replaced by UCC § 2–207, which allows parties to enforce their agreement despite minor discrepancies between the offer and the acceptance. See BATTLE OF THE FORMS.

misappropriation. The application of another's property or money dishonestly to one's own use. See EMBEZZLEMENT.

misappropriation theory. In federal securities law, the doctrine that a person who wrongfully uses confidential information for buying or selling securities in violation of a duty owed to the information source is guilty of securities fraud.

misbranding. The act or an instance of labeling one's product falsely or in a misleading way. • Misbranding is prohibited by federal and state statutes.

miscellaneous itemized deduction. See DE-DUCTION.

misdescription. **1.** A contractual error or falsity that deceives, injures, or materially misleads one of the contracting parties. **2.** A bailee's inaccurate identification, in a document of title, of goods received from the bailor.

misrepresentation. **1.** The act of making a false or misleading statement about something, usu. with the intent to deceive. **2.** The statement so made; an assertion that does not accord with the facts.

fraudulent misrepresentation. A false statement that is known to be false or is made recklessly—without knowing or caring whether it is true or false—and that is intended to induce a party to detrimentally rely on it.

mistake. A misconception or misunderstanding; an erroneous belief.

mistake of fact. A mistake about a fact that is material to a transaction.

mistake of law. A mistake about the legal effect of a known fact or situation.

mutual mistake. A mistake that is shared and relied on by both parties to a contract. ● A court will often revise or nullify a contract based on a mutual mistake about a material term.

unilateral mistake. A mistake by only one party to a contract. ● A unilateral mistake is usu. not grounds for rescission of the contract.

mitigation-of-damages doctrine. The principle requiring a plaintiff, after an injury or breach of contract, to use ordinary care to alleviate the effects of the injury or breach. ● If the defendant can show that the plaintiff failed to mitigate damages, the plaintiff's recovery can be reduced.

Modified Accelerated Cost Recovery System. See ACCELERATED COST RECOVERY SYSTEM.

moneyed capital. See CAPITAL.

money-laundering. See LAUNDERING.

money market. See MARKET.

money-market account. An interest-bearing account at a bank or other financial institution. ● Such an account usu. pays interest competitive with money-market funds but allows a limited number of transactions per month. See *money market* under MARKET.

money-market fund. See MUTUAL FUND.

money supply. The total amount of money in circulation in the economy. See M1; M2; M3.

monopolization. The act or process of obtaining a monopoly. ● In federal antitrust law, monopolization is an offense with two elements: (1) the possession of monopoly power—that is, the power to fix prices and exclude competitors—within the relevant market; and (2) the willful acquisition or maintenance of that power, as distinguished from growth or development as a consequence of a superior product, business acumen, or historical accident.

monopoly. 1. Control or advantage obtained by one supplier or producer over the commercial market within a given region. **2.** The market condition existing when only one economic entity produces a particular product or provides a particular service. ● The term is now commonly applied also to situations that approach but do not strictly meet this definition.

> *bilateral monopoly.* A hypothetical market condition in which there is only one buyer and one seller, resulting in transactional delays because either party can hold out for a better deal without fearing that the other party will turn to a third party.

393

3. In patent law, the exclusive right to make, use, and sell an invention.

monopsony (mə-**nop**-sə-nee). A market situation in which one buyer controls the market.

moratorium. An authorized delay in the time to pay a debt or perform an obligation.

mortality table. See ACTUARIAL TABLE.

mortgage (**mor**-gij). **1.** A conveyance of real estate or some real-estate interest, voidable upon the payment of money or the performance of some other condition. **2.** A lien or charge on specific property (usu. real property) created by a document purporting to be an express transfer of title, with or without possession, but accompanied by a condition that the transfer will become void if money owed for the property is not paid in a timely fashion or the thing done to secure the transfer is not performed. **3.** An instrument (such as a deed or contract) specifying the terms of such a transaction. **4.** Loosely, the loan on which such a transaction is based.

   adjustable-rate mortgage. A mortgage in which the lender can periodically adjust the mortgage's interest rate in accordance with fluctuations in some external market index.—Abbr. ARM.

amortized mortgage. A mortgage in which the mortgagor pays the interest as well as a portion of the principal in the periodic payment. ● At maturity, the periodic payments will have completely repaid the loan. See AMORTIZATION.

balloon-payment mortgage. A mortgage requiring periodic payments for a specified time and a lump-sum payment of the outstanding balance at maturity.

blanket mortgage. A mortgage covering two or more properties that are pledged to support a debt.

chattel mortgage. A mortgage that covers the installment purchase of goods, whereby the seller transfers title to the buyer but retains a lien securing the unpaid balance. ● Chattel mortgages have generally been replaced by security agreements, which are governed by Article 9 of the UCC. Cf. *retail installment contract* under CONTRACT.

closed-end mortgage. A mortgage that does not permit either prepayment or additional borrowing against the collateral. Cf. *open-end mortgage.*

closed mortgage. A mortgage that cannot be paid in full before maturity without the lender's consent.

contingent-interest mortgage. A mortgage whose interest rate is directly related to the economic performance of the pledged property.

conventional mortgage. A mortgage, not backed by government insurance, by which the borrower transfers a lien or title to the lending bank or other financial institution. • These mortgages, which feature a fixed periodic payment of principal and interest throughout the mortgage term, are typically used for home financing.

direct-reduction mortgage. An amortized mortgage in which the principal and interest payments are paid at the same time—usu. monthly in equal amounts—with interest being computed on the remaining balance.

first mortgage. A mortgage that is senior to all other mortgages on the same property.

fixed-rate mortgage. A mortgage with an interest rate that remains the same over the life of the mortgage regardless of market conditions.—Abbr. FRM.

flip mortgage. A graduated-payment mortgage allowing the borrower to place all or some of the down payment in a savings account and to use the principal and interest to supplement lower mortgage payments in the loan's early years.

graduated-payment mortgage. A mortgage whose initial payments are lower than its later payments, which typically increase as the borrower's income increases over time.

interest-only mortgage. A balloon-payment mortgage on which the borrower must at first make only interest payments, but must make a lump-sum payment of the full principal at maturity.

junior mortgage. A mortgage that is subordinate to another mortgage on the same property.

leasehold mortgage. A mortgage secured by a lessee's leasehold interest.

open-end mortgage. A mortgage that allows the mortgagor to borrow additional funds against the same property. Cf. *closed-end mortgage.*

participation mortgage. **a.** A mortgage that permits the lender to receive profits of the venture in addition to the normal interest payments. **b.** A mortgage held by more than one lender.

price-level-adjusted mortgage. A mortgage with a fixed interest rate but the principal balance of which is adjusted to reflect inflation.

purchase-money mortgage. A mortgage that a buyer gives the seller, when the property is conveyed, to secure the unpaid balance of the purchase price. See SECURITY AGREEMENT.

renegotiable-rate mortgage. A government-sponsored mortgage that requires the mortgagee to renegotiate its terms every three to five years, based on market conditions.—Also termed *flexible-rate mortgage*.

reverse annuity mortgage. A mortgage in which the lender disburses money over a long period to provide regular income to the borrower, and in which the loan is repaid in a lump sum when the borrower dies or when the property is sold.

second mortgage. A mortgage that is junior to a first mortgage on the same property, but that is senior to any subsequent mortgages.

senior mortgage. A mortgage having priority over other mortgages on the same property.

shared-equity mortgage. A mortgage in which the lender shares in the profits from the property's resale. • Usu. the lender must first purchase a portion of the property's equity by providing a portion of the down payment.

submortgage. A mortgage used as security by someone who has rights to that mortgage only as a security; a loan to a mortgagee who puts up the mortgage as collateral or security for the loan.

wraparound mortgage. A second mortgage issued when a lender assumes the payments on the borrower's first mortgage (usu. issued through a different lender) and lends additional funds. • Such a mortgage covers both the outstanding balance of the first mortgage and the additional funds loaned.

zero-rate mortgage. A mortgage with a large down payment but no interest payments, with the balance paid in equal installments.

mortgage bond. See BOND (1).

mortgage certificate. A document evidencing part ownership of a mortgage.

mortgage clause. An insurance-policy provision that protects the rights of a mortgagee when the insured property is secured by a mortgage. • Such a clause usu. provides that any insurance proceeds must be allocated between the named insured and the mortgagee

399

"as their interests may appear." See LOSS-PAY-ABLE CLAUSE.

> ***open mortgage clause.*** A mortgage clause that does not protect the mortgagee if the insured mortgagor does something to invalidate the policy (such as committing fraud).

> ***standard mortgage clause.*** A mortgage clause that protects the mortgagee's interest even if the insured mortgagor does something to invalidate the policy. ● In effect, this clause creates a separate contract between the insurer and the mortgagee.

mortgage commitment. A lender's written agreement with a borrower stating the terms on which it will lend money for the purchase of specified real property, usu. with a time limitation.

mortgage company. A company that makes and closes mortgage loans and then sells or assigns them to investors.

mortgage-contingency clause. A real-estate-sale provision that conditions the buyer's performance on obtaining a mortgage loan.

mortgagee (mor-gə-**jee**). One to whom property is mortgaged; the mortgage-creditor, or lender.—Also termed *mortgage-holder*.

mortgagee policy. A title-insurance policy that covers only the mortgagee's title and not the owner's title. Cf. OWNER'S POLICY.

mortgage insurance. See INSURANCE.

mortgage note. See NOTE.

mortgaging out. The purchase of real property by financing 100% of the purchase price.

mortgagor (mor-gə-**jor**). One who mortgages property; the mortgage-debtor, or borrower.

most-favored-nation clause. 1. A clause in an agreement between two nations providing that each will treat the other as well as it treats any nation that is given preferential treatment. **2.** By extension, such a clause in any contract, esp. an oil-and-gas contract.— Also termed *most-favored-nations clause*.

most-favored-tenant clause. A commercial-lease provision ensuring that the tenant will be given any negotiating concessions given to other tenants.

movable, *n.* (*usu. pl.*) Property that can be moved or displaced, such as personal goods. Cf. IMMOVABLE.

multilevel-distribution program. See PYRA-MID SCHEME.

multiple listing. See LISTING (1).

municipal bond. See BOND (1).

munies. See *municipal bond* under BOND (1).

mutual assent. Agreement by both parties to a contract, usu. in the form of offer and acceptance. ● In modern contract law, mutual assent is determined by an objective standard—that is, by the apparent intention of the parties as manifested by their actions. Cf. MEETING OF THE MINDS.

mutual company. See COMPANY.

mutual contract. See *bilateral contract* under CONTRACT.

mutual fund. 1. An investment company that invests its shareholders' money in a usu. diversified selection of securities.—Often shortened to *fund*. **2.** Loosely, a share in such a company.

    balanced fund. A mutual fund that maintains a balanced investment in stocks and bonds, investing a certain percentage in senior securities.

bond fund. A mutual fund that invests primarily in specialized corporate bonds or municipal bonds.

closed-end fund. A mutual fund having a fixed number of shares that are traded on a major securities exchange or an over-the-counter market.

common-stock fund. A mutual fund that invests only in common stock.

dual fund. A closed-end mutual fund that invests in two classes of stock—stock that pays interest and dividends and stock that pays capital-gains distributions.—Also termed *split fund*.

fully managed fund. A mutual fund whose policy allows reasonable discretion in trading securities in combination or quantity.

growth fund. A mutual fund that typically invests in well-established companies whose earnings are expected to increase. • Growth funds usu. pay small dividends but offer the potential for large share-price increases.

income fund. A mutual fund that typically invests in securities that consistently produce a steady income, such as bonds or dividend-paying stocks.

index fund. A mutual fund that invests in companies constituting a specific market index, such as the Standard & Poor's 500-stock average of large companies.

load fund. A mutual fund that charges a commission, usu. ranging from 4 to 9%, either when shares are purchased (a *front-end load*) or when they are redeemed (a *back-end load*).

money-market fund. A mutual fund that invests in low-risk government securities and short-term stock.

no-load fund. A mutual fund that does not charge any sales commission (although it may charge fees to cover operating costs).

open-end fund. A mutual fund that continually offers new shares and buys back existing shares on demand. • An open-end fund will continue to grow as more shareholders invest because it does not have a fixed number of shares outstanding.

performance fund. A mutual fund characterized by aggressive purchase of stocks expected to show near-term growth.

utility fund. A mutual fund that invests only in public-utility securities.

vulture fund. An investment company that purchases bankrupt or insolvent companies to reorganize them in hopes of reselling them at a profit.

mutual insurance. See INSURANCE.

mutual insurance company. An insurer whose policyholders are its owners, as opposed to a stock insurance company owned by outside shareholders. Cf. STOCK INSURANCE COMPANY.

mutuality of obligation. The fact of both parties to a contract having agreed to be bound in some way.—Also termed *mutuality of contract*. See MUTUAL ASSENT.

mutual mistake. See MISTAKE.

mutual savings bank. See BANK.

N

NAFTA (**naf**-tə). *abbr*. NORTH AMERICAN FREE TRADE AGREEMENT.

naked authority. See AUTHORITY.

naked contract. See NUDUM PACTUM.

naked option. See OPTION.

naked promise. See PROMISE.

name partner. See PARTNER.

NASD. *abbr*. NATIONAL ASSOCIATION OF SECURITIES DEALERS.

NASDAQ (**naz**-dak). *abbr*. NATIONAL ASSOCIATION OF SECURITIES DEALERS AUTOMATED QUOTATION SYSTEM.

National Association of Securities Dealers. A group of brokers and dealers empowered by the SEC to regulate the over-the-counter securities market.—Abbr. NASD.

National Association of Securities Dealers Automated Quotation system. A computerized system for recording transactions and displaying price quotations for a group of actively traded securities on the over-the-counter market.—Abbr. NASDAQ.

national bank. See BANK.

National Daily Quotation Service. See PINK SHEET.

national debt. The total financial obligation of the federal government, including such instruments as Treasury bills, notes, and bonds, as well as foreign debt.

nationalize. To bring (an industry) under governmental control or ownership.

National Labor Relations Board. A federal agency (created by the National Labor Relations Act) that regulates employer–employee relations by establishing collective bargaining, conducting union elections, and prohibiting unfair labor practices.—Abbr. NLRB.

NAV. *abbr.* NET ASSET VALUE.

negative amortization. See AMORTIZATION.

negative cash flow. See CASH FLOW.

negative covenant. See COVENANT (1).

negative externality. See EXTERNALITY.

negligence. **1.** The failure to exercise the standard of care that a reasonably prudent person would have exercised in a similar situation; any conduct that falls below the legal standard established to protect others against unreasonable risk of harm, except for conduct that is intentionally, wantonly, or willfully disregardful of others' rights.

> *gross negligence.* A conscious, voluntary act or omission in reckless disregard of a legal duty and of the consequences to another party, who may typically recover exemplary damages.

> *negligence per se.* Negligence as a matter of law, as a result of which the breach of duty is not a jury question. ● Negligence per se usu. arises from a statutory violation.

2. A tort grounded in this failure, usu. expressed in terms of the following elements: duty, breach of duty, causation, and damages.

negligent entrustment. The act of leaving a dangerous article (such as a gun or car) with a person who the lender knows or should know is likely to use it in an unreasonably risky manner.

negotiable document of title. See DOCUMENT OF TITLE.

negotiable instrument. A written instrument that (1) is signed by the maker or drawer, (2) includes an unconditional promise or order to pay a specified sum of money, (3) is payable on demand or at a definite time, and (4) is payable to order or to bearer. • The most common types of negotiable instruments are notes and drafts.—Also termed *negotiable paper*.

negotiable order of withdrawal. A negotiable instrument (such as a check) payable on demand and issued against funds deposited with a financial institution.—Abbr. N.O.W.

negotiation. 1. A consensual bargaining process in which parties attempt to reach agreement on a disputed or potentially disputed matter. • Negotiation usu. involves complete autonomy for the parties involved, without the intervention of third parties. **2.** (*usu. pl.*) Dealings conducted between two or more parties for the purpose of reaching an understanding. **3.** The transfer of an instrument by delivery or indorsement whereby the transferee takes it for value, in good faith, and without notice of conflicting title claims or defenses. See HOLDER IN DUE COURSE.

neighborhood effect. See EXTERNALITY.

nepotism (**nep**-ə-tiz-əm). Bestowal of official favors (esp. in hiring) on one's relatives.

409

net asset value. The market value of a share in a mutual fund, computed by deducting total liabilities from total assets and dividing the difference by the number of outstanding shares.—Abbr. NAV. See MUTUAL FUND.

net cash flow. See CASH FLOW.

net cost. See COST.

net income. See INCOME.

net lease. See LEASE.

net listing. See LISTING (1).

net loss. See LOSS.

net operating income. See INCOME.

net operating loss. See LOSS.

net present value. See PRESENT VALUE.

net profit. See PROFIT.

net worth. A measure of one's wealth, usu. calculated as the excess of total assets over total liabilities.

new issue. See ISSUE.

New York Stock Exchange. An unincorporated association of member firms that handle the purchase and sale of securities both for themselves and for customers. ● This exchange, the dominant one in the U.S., trades in only large companies having at least one million outstanding shares.—Abbr. NYSE.

next-in, first-out. A method of inventory valuation (but not a generally accepted accounting principle) whereby the cost of goods is based on their replacement cost rather than their actual cost.—Abbr. NIFO. Cf. FIRST-IN, FIRST-OUT; LAST-IN, FIRST-OUT.

NIFO (**nɪ**-foh). *abbr*. NEXT-IN, FIRST-OUT.

nimble dividend. See DIVIDEND.

90-day letter. Statutory notice of a tax deficiency sent by the IRS to a taxpayer. ● During the 90 days after receiving the notice, the taxpayer must pay the taxes (and, if desired, seek a refund) or challenge the deficiency in tax court.—Also termed *notice of deficiency*.

NLRB. *abbr*. NATIONAL LABOR RELATIONS BOARD.

no-action letter. A letter from the staff of a governmental agency stating that, if the facts are as represented in a person's request for an agency ruling, the staff will advise the agency not to take action against the person. • Typically, a no-action letter is requested from the SEC on such matters as shareholder proposals, resales of stock, and marketing techniques.

Noerr-Pennington **doctrine.** The principle that the First Amendment shields from liability (esp. under antitrust laws) companies that join together to lobby the government.

NOL. See *net operating loss* under LOSS.

no-load fund. See MUTUAL FUND.

nominal asset. See ASSET.

nominal consideration. See CONSIDERATION.

nominal partner. See PARTNER.

nominal-payee rule. In commercial law, the rule that validates any person's indorsement of an instrument (such as a check) when the instrument's drawer intended for the payee to have no interest in the instrument.

nominal rate. See INTEREST RATE.

nominal yield. See YIELD.

nonassessable stock. See STOCK.

noncallable security. See SECURITY.

noncancelability clause. An insurance-policy provision that prevents the insurer from canceling the policy after an insured's loss, as long as the premium has been paid.

noncompetition covenant. See COVENANT (1).

nonconforming goods. See GOODS.

noncontribution clause. A fire-insurance-policy provision stating that only the interests of the property owner and the first mortgagee are protected under the policy.

noncumulative dividend. See DIVIDEND.

noncumulative preferred stock. See STOCK.

noncumulative voting. See VOTING.

nondelegable duty. See DUTY.

non-interest-bearing bond. See *discount bond* under BOND (1).

nonjudicial foreclosure. See FORECLOSURE.

nonnegotiable document of title. See DOCU-MENT OF TITLE.

413

nonobviousness. 1. In patent law, the fact that an invention is not obvious to a person with ordinary skill in the relevant prior art or trade. **2.** The requirement that this fact must be demonstrated for an invention to be patentable. ● Nonobviousness can be demonstrated by evidence of prior art or other objective evidence, such as commercial success or professional approval. Cf. NOVELTY.

nonoperating income. See INCOME.

nonparticipating preferred stock. See STOCK.

nonperformance. Failure to discharge an obligation (esp. a contractual one). Cf. PERFORMANCE (1).

nonperforming loan. See LOAN.

nonprofit corporation. See CORPORATION.

nonrecognition provision. A statutory rule that allows all or part of a realized gain or a loss not to be recognized for tax purposes. ● Usu. this type of provision only postpones the recognition of the gain or loss. See RECOGNITION.

nonrecourse loan. See LOAN.

nonrefund annuity. See ANNUITY.

nonshareholder constituency. A group of nonstockholders, such as employees or the public, who have an interest in the business of the corporation and whose interest may be legally considered, in addition to shareholders' interests, by the corporation when making major policy decisions.—Also termed *alternative constituency*.

nonstock corporation. See CORPORATION.

nonvoting stock. See STOCK.

nonwaiver agreement. A contract (supplementing a liability-insurance policy) in which the insured acknowledges that the insurer's investigation or defense of a claim against the insured does not waive the insurer's right to contest coverage later.—Also termed *reservation of rights*.

no-par stock. See STOCK.

Norris–LaGuardia Act. A 1932 federal law that forbids federal courts from making rules on labor policy and severely limits their powers to issue injunctions in labor disputes. • The statute was passed to curb federal-court abuses of the injunctive process, to declare the government's neutrality on labor policy, to curtail the widespread use of injunctions by employers attempting to thwart union activity, and to promote the use of collective bargaining to resolve disputes.—Also termed *Labor Disputes Act*.

North American Free Trade Agreement. A trilateral treaty—entered into on January 1, 1994 between the U.S., Canada, and Mexico—that phases out all tariffs and eliminates many nontariff barriers (such as quotas) inhibiting the free trade of goods between the participating nations.—Abbr. NAFTA.

no-shop provision. A stipulation prohibiting one or more parties to a commercial contract from pursuing or entering into a more favorable agreement with a third party.—Also termed *no-shop clause*.

no-strike clause. A labor-agreement provision that prohibits employees from striking for any reason and establishes instead an arbitration system for resolving disputes.

notary public (**noh**-də-ree). A person authorized by a state to administer oaths, certify documents, attest to the authenticity of signatures, and perform official acts in commercial matters, such as protesting negotiable instruments.—Often shortened to *notary*. Pl. **notaries public.**

notary seal. 1. The imprint or embossment made by a notary public's seal. **2.** A device, usu. a stamp or embosser, that makes an imprint on a notarized document.—Also termed *notarial seal*.

note, *n*. A written promise by one party (the *maker*) to pay money to another party (the *payee*) or to bearer. ● A note is a two-party negotiable instrument, unlike a draft (which is a three-party instrument).—Also termed *promissory note*. Cf. DRAFT.

> **balloon note.** A note requiring small periodic payments but a very large final payment. ● Usu. the periodic payments cover only interest, while the final payment (the balloon payment) represents the entire principal. Cf. *balloon payment* under PAYMENT.

> **bank note.** A note that is issued by a bank, payable to the bearer on demand, and intended to circulate as money.

> **circular note.** See LETTER OF CREDIT.

> **coupon note.** A note with attached interest coupons that the holder may present for payment as they mature.

> **demand note.** A note payable whenever the creditor wants to be paid.

installment note. A note payable at regular intervals.—Also termed *serial note.*

inverse-floating-rate note. A note structured in such a way that its interest rate moves in the opposite direction from the underlying index (such as the London Interbank Offer Rate). • Many such notes are risky investments because if interest rates rise, the securities lose their value and their coupon earnings fall.

mortgage note. A note evidencing a loan for which real property has been offered as security.

promissory note. An unconditional written promise, signed by the maker, to pay absolutely and in any event a certain sum of money either to or to the order of the bearer or a designated person.

reissuable note. A note that may again be put into circulation after having once been paid.

sale note. A broker's memorandum on the terms of a sale, given to the buyer and seller.

savings note. A short-term, interest-bearing paper issued by a bank or the U.S. Government.

secured note. A note backed by a pledge of real or personal property as collateral.

time note. A note payable only at a specified time and not on demand.

treasury note. See TREASURY NOTE.

unsecured note. A note not backed by collateral.

not-for-profit corporation. See *nonprofit corporation* under CORPORATION.

notice, *n.* **1.** Legal notification required by law or agreement, or imparted by operation of law as a result of some fact (such as the recording of instruments); definite legal cognizance, actual or constructive, of an existing right or title <under the lease, the tenant must give the landlord written notice 30 days before vacating the premises>. **2.** The condition of being so notified, whether or not actual awareness exists <all prospective buyers were on notice of the judgment lien>. **3.** A written or printed announcement <the notice of sale was posted on the courthouse bulletin board>.

actual notice. Notice given to a party directly or presumed to be received personally because the evidence within the party's knowledge is sufficient to put him or her on inquiry.

419

constructive notice. Notice arising by presumption of law from the existence of facts and circumstances that a party had a duty to take notice of, such as a pending lawsuit; notice presumed by law to have been acquired by a person and thus imputed to that person.

notice-and-comment period. In administrative law, the statutory time frame during which an administrative agency publishes a proposed regulation and receives public feedback on the regulation. • After this period expires, the regulation can take effect.—Often shortened to *comment period.*

notice of deficiency. See 90-DAY LETTER.

notice of dishonor. Notice to the indorser of an instrument that acceptance or payment has been refused. • This notice—along with presentment and actual dishonor—is a condition of an indorser's secondary liability.

notice to creditors. In bankruptcy law, formal notice to creditors that a creditors' meeting will be held, that proofs of claim must be filed, or that an order for relief has been granted.

not sufficient funds. The notation of dishonor (of a check) indicating that there are not enough funds in the drawer's account to cover payment.—Abbr. NSF.

novation (noh-**vay**-shən). The act of substituting for an old contract a new one that either replaces an existing obligation with a new obligation or replaces an original party with a new party. • A novation may substitute (1) a new obligation between the same parties, (2) a new debtor, or (3) a new creditor. Cf. AC-CORD AND SATISFACTION.

novelty. 1. In patent law, the fact that an invention is new in form and in function or performance. **2.** The requirement that this fact must be demonstrated for an invention to be patentable. • If the invention was previously patented, described in a publication, or known or used by others, it is not novel. Cf. NONOBVI-OUSNESS.

N.O.W. *abbr.* NEGOTIABLE ORDER OF WITHDRAWAL.

NPV. See *net present value* under PRESENT VAL-UE.

NSF. *abbr.* NOT SUFFICIENT FUNDS.

nudum pactum (n[y]oo-dəm-**pak**-təm). [Lat-in "nude pact"] An agreement that is unen-forceable as a contract because it is not

421

"clothed" with consideration.—Also termed *naked contract*.

nuisance. A condition or situation (such as a loud noise or foul odor) that interferes with another's use or enjoyment of property.

> *private nuisance.* A nuisance that interferes with a person's own property and that may allow the person to recover damages or obtain an injunction.

> *public nuisance.* A nuisance that interferes with a communal right and that may lead to civil injunction or criminal prosecution. ● Public nuisance is not a tort unless, in addition to injuring the public generally, it has caused actual or special damage to one or more individuals.

NYSE. *abbr.* NEW YORK STOCK EXCHANGE.

O

obligation. A formal, binding agreement or acknowledgment of a liability to pay a certain amount or to do a certain thing for a particular person or set of persons. See DUTY; LIABILITY.

> *bifactoral obligation.* An obligation created by two parties.

> *primary obligation.* A fundamental contractual term imposing a requirement on a contracting party from which other obligations may arise.

> *secondary obligation.* A duty, promise, or undertaking that is incident to a primary obligation; esp., a duty to make reparation upon a breach of contract.

> *unifactoral obligation.* An obligation created by one party.

obligee (ob-li-**jee**). One to whom an obligation is owed; a promisee or creditor.

obligor (ob-li-**gor**). One who has undertaken an obligation; a promisor or debtor.

occupancy. 1. The act of taking or fact of having possession of property; esp., the act of taking possession of something having no owner, with a view to acquiring it as property. 2. The period during which a person owns, rents, or otherwise occupies real property or premises. **3.** The socially protected legal interest in buildings and structures, including those that are not dwellings.

occupational disease. A disease that is contracted as a result of exposure to debilitating conditions or substances in the course of employment <black lung in coal miners is one of the many occupational diseases recognized by OSHA>.

occupational hazard. A danger or risk that is peculiar to a particular calling or occupation. • Asbestosis, for example, is an occupational hazard for persons who remove old insulation.

Occupational Safety and Health Administration. A federal agency that establishes and enforces health and safety standards in various industries. • This agency, created under the Occupational Safety and Health Act of 1970, routinely conducts inspections of businesses and issues citations for noncompliance with its standards.—Abbr. OSHA.

occupation tax. See TAX.

occurrence policy. See INSURANCE POLICY.

odd lot. See LOT.

offer, *n.* **1.** A promise to do or refrain from doing some specified thing in the future; a display of willingness to enter into a contract on specified terms, made in a way that would lead a reasonable person to understand that an acceptance, having been sought, will result in a binding contract <she accepted the $750 offer on the Victorian armoire>.

> *irrevocable offer.* An offer that includes a promise to keep it open for a specified period, during which the offer cannot be withdrawn without the offeror's becoming subject to liability for breach of contract. • Traditionally, such a promise must be supported by consideration to be enforceable, but under the UCC, a merchant's signed, written offer giving assurances that it will be held open—but lacking consideration—is nonetheless irrevocable for the stated period (or, if not stated, for a reasonable time not exceeding three months).—Also termed (in the UCC) *firm offer*; (if by a merchant) *merchant's firm offer*.

2. A price at which one is ready to buy or sell; a bid <she lowered her offer to $200>.

offering, *n.* **1.** The act of making an offer; something offered for sale. **2.** The sale of an issue of securities. See ISSUE (1).

425

all-or-none offering. An offering that requires the issuer to terminate the distribution if the entire block of offered securities is not sold.

initial public offering. A company's first public sale of stock; the first offering of an issuer's equity securities to the public through a registration statement.—Abbr. IPO.

primary offering. An offering of newly issued securities.

private offering. An offering made only to a small group of interested buyers.—Also termed *private placement*.

public offering. An offering made to the general public.

registered offering. A public offering of securities registered with the SEC and with appropriate state securities commissions.

rights offering. An issue of stock-purchase rights allowing shareholders to buy newly issued stock at a fixed price, usu. below market value, and in proportion to the number of shares they already own.—Also termed *privileged subscription*. Cf. PREEMPTIVE RIGHT.

secondary offering. **a.** Any offering by an issuer of securities after its initial public offering. **b.** An offering of previously issued securities by persons other than the issuer.

special offering. An offering of a large block of stock that, because of its size and the market in the particular issue, is specially handled on the floor of the stock exchange.

offering price. See *asking price* under PRICE.

office audit. See AUDIT.

officer. A person who holds an office of trust, authority, or command. ● In public affairs, the term refers esp. to a person holding public office under a national, state, or local government, and authorized by that government to exercise some specific function. In corporate law, the term refers esp. to a person elected or appointed by the board of directors to manage the daily operations of a corporation, such as a CEO, president, secretary, or treasurer. Cf. DIRECTOR (2).

of the essence. (Of a contractual requirement) so important that if the requirement is not met, the promisor will be held to have breached the contract and a rescission by the promisee will be justified <time is of the essence>.

oligopoly (oh-lə-**gop**-ə-lee *or* o-lə-). Control or domination of a market by a few large sellers, creating high prices and low output similar to those found in a monopoly. See MONOPOLY.

oligopsony (oh-lə-**gop**-sə-nee *or* o-lə-). Control or domination of a market by a few large buyers or customers.

on demand, *adv.* When presented or upon request for payment <this note is payable on demand>.—Also termed *on call.* See PAYABLE.

one-action rule. In debtor-creditor law, the principle that when a debt is secured by real property, the creditor must foreclose on the collateral before proceeding against the debtor's unsecured assets.

open account. See ACCOUNT.

open bid. See BID.

open-end fund. See MUTUAL FUND.

open-end mortgage. See MORTGAGE.

open-end mortgage bond. See BOND (1).

open listing. See LISTING (1).

open market. See MARKET.

open mortgage clause. See MORTGAGE CLAUSE.

open-perils policy. See INSURANCE POLICY.

open shop. A business where union membership is not a condition of employment. See RIGHT-TO-WORK LAW. Cf. CLOSED SHOP.

operating expense. See EXPENSE.

operating profit. See PROFIT.

opportunity cost. See COST.

oppression. **1.** In contract law, coercion to enter into an illegal contract. ● Oppression is grounds for recovery of money paid or property transferred under the illegal contract. See UNCONSCIONABILITY. **2.** In corporate law, unfair treatment of minority shareholders (esp. in a close corporation) by the directors or those in control of the corporation.—Also termed (in sense 2) *shareholder oppression*. See FREEZE-OUT.

option, *n.* **1.** A contract made to keep an offer open for a specified period, so that the offeror cannot revoke the offer during that period <the option is valid because it is supported by consideration>.—Also termed *option contract*.

See *irrevocable offer* under OFFER. **2.** The right conveyed by such a contract <Phil declined to exercise his first option to buy the house>. **3.** The right (but not the obligation) to buy or sell a given quantity of securities, commodities, or other assets at a fixed price within a specified time <trading stock options is a speculative business>. Cf. FUTURES CONTRACT.

call option. An option to buy something (esp. securities) at a fixed price even if the market rises; the right to require another to sell.—Often shortened to *call*.

cash-value option. The right of a life-insurance policyholder to take the policy's predetermined cash value at a specified point in time.

commodity option. An option to buy or sell a commodity.

futures option. An option to buy or sell a futures contract.

naked option. A call option that grants another the right to buy stock even though the option-giver does not own the stock to back up that commitment.

put option. An option to sell something (esp. securities) at a fixed price even if the market declines; the right to require another to buy.—Often shortened to *put*.

stock option. See STOCK OPTION.

option, *vb*. To grant or take an option on (something) <Ward optioned his first screenplay to the studio for $50,000>.

option agreement. In corporate law, a share-transfer restriction that commits the shareholder to sell, but not the corporation or other shareholders to buy, the shareholder's shares at a fixed price when a specified event occurs. Cf. BUY-SELL AGREEMENT (2); OPTION (1).

optional bond. See BOND (1).

option contract. See OPTION (1).

optionee (op-shə-**nee**). One who receives an option from another.—Also termed *option-holder*.

optionor (op-shə-**nor**). One who grants an option to another.—Also spelled *optioner*.—Also termed *option-giver*.

option premium. See PREMIUM (4).

oral contract. See *parol contract* (a) under CONTRACT.

order, *n*. **1.** The words in a draft (such as a check) directing one person to pay money to or deliver something to a designated person. • An order should appear to be the demand of a right as opposed to the request for a favor. See *order paper* under PAPER. **2.** In securities trading, a customer's instructions to a broker about how and when to buy or sell securities.

> ***day order.*** An order to buy or sell on one particular day only.

> ***discretionary order.*** An order to buy or sell at any price acceptable to the broker.

> ***limit order.*** An order to buy or sell only at a specified price or better.

> ***market order.*** An order to buy or sell at the best price immediately available on the market.—Also termed *order at the market*.

> ***scale order.*** An order to buy or sell a security at varying price intervals.

> ***stop order.*** An order to buy or sell when the security's price reaches a specified level (the *stop price*) on the market. ● Fixing the price beforehand cushions the investor against stock fluctuations.—Also termed *stop-loss order*.

order bill of lading. See BILL OF LADING.

order paper. See PAPER.

ordinary annuity. See ANNUITY.

ordinary course of business. See COURSE OF BUSINESS.

ordinary gain. See GAIN.

ordinary income. See INCOME.

ordinary loss. See LOSS.

organizational expense. See EXPENSE.

organizational meeting. See MEETING.

organizational picketing. See PICKETING.

original title. See TITLE.

OSHA (**oh**-shə). *abbr.* OCCUPATIONAL SAFETY AND HEALTH ADMINISTRATION.

ostensible partner. See *nominal partner* under PARTNER.

OTC. *abbr.* Over-the-counter <those stocks were traded in the OTC market>. See OVER-THE-COUNTER MARKET.

OTC market. *abbr.* OVER-THE-COUNTER MARKET.

other-insurance clause. An insurance-policy provision that attempts to limit coverage if the insured has additional insurance coverage for the same loss. • The three major other-insur-

433

ance clauses are the pro rata clause, the excess clause, and the escape clause. See ESCAPE CLAUSE; EXCESS CLAUSE; PRO RATA CLAUSE.

out-of-pocket expense. See EXPENSE.

out-of-pocket loss. See LOSS.

output contract. See CONTRACT.

outside director. See DIRECTOR.

outside financing. See FINANCING.

outstanding stock. See STOCK.

overdraft. 1. A bank depositor's withdrawal or attempted withdrawal of a sum exceeding the amount on deposit; esp., a check written for more money than is in an account. **2.** The sum overdrawn. **3.** A line of credit extended by a bank to a customer who might overdraw on an account.

overhead. Business expenses (such as rent, utilities, or support-staff salaries) that cannot be allocated to a particular product or service; fixed or ordinary operating costs.

overheated economy. See ECONOMY.

overinsurance. See INSURANCE.

overreaching. The act or an instance of tak-

434

ing unfair commercial advantage of another, esp. by fraudulent means.

override, *n.* **1.** A commission paid to a manager on a sale made by his or her subordinate. **2.** A commission paid to a real-estate broker who listed a property when, within a reasonable amount of time after the expiration of the listing, the owner sells that property directly to a buyer with whom the broker had negotiated during the term of the listing.

over-the-counter market. The market for securities that are not traded on an organized exchange. • Over-the-counter (OTC) trading usu. occurs through telephone or computer negotiations between buyers and sellers, and many of the more actively traded OTC stocks are listed on NASDAQ.—Abbr. *OTC market.*

owner. One who has the right to possess, use, and convey something; a proprietor. See OWN-ERSHIP.

　beneficial owner. **a.** One recognized as the equitable owner of something because real and beneficial use and title belong to that person, even though legal title may belong to someone else; esp., one for whom property is held in trust.—Also termed *equitable owner.* **b.** A corporate shareholder who has the power to buy or sell the shares or to direct how the shares will be voted, but who has not registered the shares on the corporation's books in his or her name.

legal owner. One recognized by law as the owner of something; esp., one who holds legal title to property for the benefit of another. See TRUSTEE.

record owner. **a.** A property owner in whose name the title appears in public records. **b.** A corporate shareholder in whose name the shares are registered on the corporation's books.

owners' equity. The aggregate of the owners' financial interests in the assets of a business entity; the capital contributed by the owners plus any retained earnings.—Also termed (in a corporation) *shareholders' equity*.

ownership. The collection of rights allowing one to use and enjoy property, including the right to convey it to others. • Ownership implies the right to possess a thing, regardless of any actual or constructive control. Ownership rights are general, permanent, and inheritable. Cf. POSSESSION; TITLE (1).

owner's policy. In real-estate law, a title-insurance policy covering the owner's title as well as the mortgagee's title. Cf. MORTGAGEE POLICY.

P

P.A. See *professional association* under ASSOCI-ATION.

Pac-Man defense. An aggressive antitake-over defense by which the target company attempts to take over the bidder company by making a cash tender offer for the bidder company's shares. ● The name derives from a video game popular in the 1980s, the object of which was to gobble up the enemy. This defense is seldom used today.

paid-in capital. See CAPITAL.

paid-in surplus. See SURPLUS.

palming off. See PASSING OFF.

paper. 1. Any written or printed document or instrument. **2.** A negotiable document or instrument evidencing a debt; esp., commercial documents or negotiable instruments considered as a group. See NEGOTIABLE INSTRUMENT.

   bearer paper. An instrument payable to the person who holds it rather than to the order of a specific person.

   chattel paper. A writing that shows both a monetary obligation and a security interest in or a lease of specific goods. ● Chattel paper is generally used in a consumer sale in which the consumer buys goods on credit. The consumer typically promises to pay for the item purchased by executing a promissory note, and the seller retains a security interest in the goods. See SECURITY AGREEMENT.

commercial paper. **a.** An instrument, other than cash, for the payment of money. • Commercial paper—typically existing in the form of a draft (as a check) or a note (as a certificate of deposit)—is governed by Article 3 of the UCC. See NEGOTIABLE INSTRUMENT. **b.** Such instruments collectively. **c.** Loosely, a short-term unsecured promissory note, usu. issued and sold by one company to meet another company's immediate cash needs.

order paper. An instrument payable to a specific payee or to any person that the payee designates.

paper loss. See LOSS.

paper profit. See PROFIT.

paper title. See TITLE.

parent corporation. See CORPORATION.

Pareto optimality (pə-**re**-doh *or* -**ray**-). An economic situation in which no person can be made better off without making someone else worse off.

Pareto superiority. An economic situation in which an exchange can be made that both benefits someone and injures no one. • When such exchanges can no longer be made, the situation becomes one of Pareto optimality.

parking. 1. The sale of securities subject to an agreement that they will be bought back by the seller at a later time for a similar price. • Parking is illegal if done to circumvent securities regulations or tax laws. **2.** The placement of assets in a safe, short-term investment while other investment opportunities are being considered.—Also termed *stock-parking*.

parol contract. See CONTRACT.

parol-evidence rule. In contract law, the principle that a writing intended by the parties to be a final embodiment of their agreement cannot be modified by evidence that adds to, varies, or contradicts the writing. • This rule usu. operates to prevent a party from introducing extrinsic evidence of negotiations that occurred before or while the agreement was being reduced to its final written form. See INTEGRATION (1); MERGER (2). Cf. FOUR-CORNERS RULE.

partial breach. See BREACH OF CONTRACT.

partially disclosed principal. See PRINCIPAL.

participating bond. See BOND (1).

participating insurance. See INSURANCE.

participating preferred stock. See STOCK.

participation loan. See LOAN.

participation mortgage. See MORTGAGE.

partner. 1. One who shares or takes part with another, esp. in a venture with shared benefits and shared risks; an associate or colleague <partners in crime>. **2.** One of two or more persons who jointly own and carry on a business for profit <the firm and its partners were sued for malpractice>. See PARTNERSHIP.

general partner. A partner who ordinarily takes part in the daily operations of the business, shares in the profits and losses, and is personally responsible for the partnership's debts and liabilities.

junior partner. A partner whose participation is limited with respect to both profits and management.

limited partner. A partner who does not take part in control of the business, receives profits from the business, and is not liable for any amount greater than his or her original investment. See *limited partnership* under PARTNERSHIP.

liquidating partner. The partner appointed to settle the accounts, collect the assets, adjust the claims, and pay the debts of a dissolving or insolvent firm.

name partner. A partner whose name appears in the name of the partnership <Mr. Tibbs is a name partner in the accounting firm of Gibbs & Tibbs>.

nominal partner. A person who by consent is held out as a partner in a firm or business but who has no actual interest in the partnership.—Also termed *ostensible partner*; *partner by estoppel*.

senior partner. A high-ranking partner, esp. in a law firm.

silent partner. A partner who shares in the profits but has no voice in the management of the firm, and whose involvement with the firm is not disclosed.

surviving partner. The partner who, upon the partnership's dissolution because of another partner's death, serves as a trustee to administer the firm's remaining affairs.

partnership. A voluntary association of two or more persons who jointly own and carry on a business for profit. ● Under the Uniform Partnership Act, a partnership is presumed to exist if the persons agree to share proportionally the business's profits or losses. Cf. JOINT VENTURE; STRATEGIC ALLIANCE.

general partnership. A partnership in which all partners participate fully in running the business and share equally in profits and losses (though the partners' monetary contributions may vary).

limited-liability partnership. A partnership in which a partner is not liable for a negligent act committed by another partner or by an employee not under the partner's supervision. ● All states have enacted statutes that allow a business (typically a law firm or accounting firm) to register as this type of partnership.—Abbr. L.L.P.

limited partnership. A partnership composed of one or more persons who control the business and are personally liable for the partnership's debts (called *general partners*), and one or more persons who contribute capital and share profits but who cannot manage the business and are liable only for the amount of their contribution (called *limited partners*). ● The chief purpose of a limited partnership is to enable investors to use their money in trade without taking an active part in managing the business, and without risking more than the sum originally contributed.—Abbr. L.P.

master limited partnership. A limited partnership whose interests or shares are publicly traded. See *publicly traded partnership*.

partnership at will. A partnership that any partner may dissolve at any time without liability. Cf. *partnership for a term*.

partnership by estoppel. A partnership implied by law when one or more persons represent themselves as partners to a third party who relies on that representation. • A person who is deemed a partner by estoppel becomes liable for any credit extended to the partnership by the third party.

partnership for a term. A partnership that exists for a specified duration or until a specified event occurs. • Such a partnership can be prematurely dissolved by any partner, but that partner may be held liable for breach of the partnership agreement. Cf. *partnership at will*.

publicly traded partnership. A partnership whose interests are traded either over-the-counter or on a securities exchange. • Such partnerships are treated as corpora-

tions for federal income-tax purposes.—
Abbr. PTP.

subpartnership. An arrangement between
a firm's partner and a nonpartner to share
the partner's profits and losses in the firm
business, but without forming a legal partnership between the partner and the nonpartner.

tiered partnership. An ownership arrangement consisting of one parent partnership
that is a partner in one or more subsidiary
partnerships.

universal partnership. A partnership
formed by persons who agree to contribute
all their individually owned property—and
to devote all their skill, labor, and services—
to the partnership.

partnership agreement. A contract defining
the partners' rights and duties toward one
another—not the partners' relationship with
third parties.

partnership association. A business organization that combines the features of a limited
partnership and a close corporation. • Partnership associations are statutorily recognized in
only a few states.

part performance. 1. The accomplishment of some but not all of one's contractual obligations. **2.** A party's execution, in reliance on an opposing party's oral promise, of enough of an oral contract's requirements that a court may hold the statute of frauds not to apply.

party. A person or entity involved in a legal transaction or court proceeding <a party to the contract> <a party to the lawsuit>.

party of the first part. *Archaic.* The party named first in a contract; esp., the owner or seller.

party of the second part. *Archaic.* The party named second in a contract; esp., the buyer.

par value. The value of an instrument or security as shown on its face; esp., the arbitrary dollar amount assigned to a stock share by the corporate charter, or the principal of a bond.—Often shortened to *par*.—Also termed *face value*; *stated value*.

passbook. A depositor's book in which a bank records all the transactions on an account.—Also termed *bankbook*.

passed dividend. See DIVIDEND.

445

passing off, *n.* The act or an instance of falsely representing one's own product as that of another in an attempt to deceive potential buyers. • Passing off is actionable in tort under the law of unfair competition.—Also termed *palming off.* Cf. MISAPPROPRIATION.

passive activity. A business activity in which the taxpayer does not materially participate and therefore does not have immediate control over the income. • A typical example is the ownership and rental of real property.

passive bond. See BOND (1).

passive debt. See DEBT.

passive income. See INCOME.

passive loss. See LOSS.

passive trust. See TRUST.

pass-through security. See SECURITY.

pass-through taxation. See TAXATION.

past consideration. See CONSIDERATION.

patent (pa-t[ə]nt). **1.** The governmental grant of a right, privilege, or authority; the official document so granting. **2.** The exclusive right

to make, use, or sell an invention for a specified period (usu. 17 years), granted by the
federal government to the inventor if the device or process is novel, useful, and nonobvious.

design patent. A patent granted for a new,
original, and ornamental design for an article of manufacture. • Design patents—
which, unlike utility patents, have a term of
only 14 years—are similar to copyrights.

utility patent. A patent granted for one of
the following types of inventions: a machine,
a composition of matter (such as a chemical
or pharmaceutical), an article of manufacture, or a process. • Utility patents are the
most commonly issued patents.

patent ambiguity. See AMBIGUITY.

Patent and Trademark Office. The Department of Commerce agency that examines
patent and trademark applications, issues patents, registers trademarks, and furnishes patent and trademark information and services to
the public.—Abbr. PTO.

patent infringement. See INFRINGEMENT.

patent pending. The designation given to an
invention while the Patent and Trademark

Office is processing the patent application. •
No protection against infringement exists,
however, until a patent has actually been
granted.—Abbr. pat. pend.

patronage (**pa**-trə-nij *or* **pay**-). **1.** The giving
of support, sponsorship, or protection. **2.** All
the customers of a business; clientele. **3.** The
power to appoint persons to governmental positions or to confer other political favors.

pawn, *n*. **1.** An item of personal property
deposited as security for payment of a debt; a
pledge or guarantee. **2.** The act of depositing
personal property in this manner. **3.** The condition of being held on deposit as a pledge.

payable, *adj*. (Of a sum of money or a negotiable instrument) that is to be paid. • An
amount may be payable without being due.
Debts are commonly payable long before they
fall due.

payable after sight. Payable after acceptance or protest of nonacceptance. See *sight
draft* under DRAFT.

payable on demand. Payable when presented or upon request for payment; payable
at any time.

payable to bearer. Payable to anyone holding the instrument.

payable to order. Payable only to a specified payee.

payable, *n*. See *account payable* under AC-COUNT.

payback method. An accounting procedure that measures the time required to recover a venture's initial cash investment.

payback period. The length of time required to recover a venture's initial cash investment, without accounting for the time value of money.

paydown. A loan payment in an amount less than the total loan principal.

payee. One to whom money is paid or payable; esp., a party named in commercial paper as the recipient of the payment.

payer. See PAYOR.

payment. 1. Performance of an obligation, usu. by the delivery of money. • Performance may occur by delivery and acceptance of things other than money, but there is a payment only if money or other valuable things are given and accepted in partial or full discharge of an obligation. **2.** The money or other valuable

449

thing so delivered in satisfaction of an obligation.

> *balloon payment.* A final loan payment that is usu. much larger than the preceding regular payments and that discharges the principal balance of the loan. See *balloon note* under NOTE.

> *constructive payment.* A payment made by the payer but not yet credited by the payee. • For example, a rent check mailed on the first of the month is a constructive payment even though the landlord does not deposit the check until ten days later.

> *down payment.* The portion of a purchase price paid in cash (or its equivalent) at the time the sale agreement is executed.

> *lump-sum payment.* A payment of a large amount all at once, as opposed to smaller payments over time.

payment bond. See BOND (2).

payment in due course. A payment to the holder of a negotiable instrument at or after its maturity date, made by the payor in good faith and without notice of the holder's defective title. See HOLDER IN DUE COURSE.

payoff. See KICKBACK.

payor. One who pays; esp., a person responsible for paying a negotiable instrument.—Also spelled *payer*. See DRAWEE.

payor bank. See BANK.

payout ratio. The ratio between a corporation's dividends per share and its earnings per share. ● Shareholders generally prefer a high payout ratio because most of them want to receive dividends consistently.

payroll. 1. A list of employees to be paid and the amount due to each of them. 2. The total compensation payable to a firm's employees for one pay period.

payroll tax. See TAX.

PBGC. *abbr.* PENSION BENEFIT GUARANTY CORPORATION.

P.C. See *professional corporation* under CORPORATION.

pecuniary benefit. See BENEFIT.

pecuniary loss. See LOSS.

penalty. 1. Punishment imposed on a wrongdoer, esp. in the form of imprisonment or a fine. ● Though usu. for crimes, penalties are

451

also sometimes imposed for civil wrongs. **2.** Excessive liquidated damages that a contract purports to impose on a party that breaches. ● If the damages are excessive enough to be considered a penalty, a court will usu. not enforce that particular provision of the contract. Some contracts specify that a given sum of damages is intended "as liquidated damages and not as a penalty"—but even that language is not foolproof.

penny stock. See STOCK.

pension. A fixed sum paid regularly to a person (or to the person's beneficiaries), esp. by an employer as a retirement benefit. Cf. ANNUITY (3).

Pension Benefit Guaranty Corporation. The federal agency that guarantees a portion of retirement benefits covered by private pension plans lacking sufficient assets to pay the promised benefits.—Abbr. PBGC.

pension plan. An employer's plan established to pay long-term retirement benefits to employees or their beneficiaries; a plan providing for the systematic payment of definitely determinable benefits to employees over a period of years, usu. for life, after retirement.

452

per annum (pər-**an**-əm), *adv*. [Latin] By the year; in each year; annually.

P/E ratio. *abbr*. PRICE-EARNINGS RATIO.

percentage lease. See LEASE.

per diem (pər-**dee**-əm), *adv*. [Latin "by the day"] Day by day; each day.

per diem, *n*. A monetary daily allowance, usu. to cover expenses.

perfect (pər-**fekt**), *vb*. To take all legal steps needed to complete, secure, or record (a claim, right, or interest); to put in final conformity with the law <perfect a security interest>.

perfect competition. A completely efficient market situation characterized by numerous buyers and sellers, a homogeneous product, perfect information for all parties, and complete freedom to move in and out of the market. ● Perfect competition rarely if ever exists, but antitrust scholars often use the theory as a standard for measuring market performance.

perfection. Validation of a security interest as against other creditors, usu. by filing a statement with some public office or by taking possession of the collateral. Cf. ATTACHMENT.

453

perfect-tender rule. The principle that a buyer may reject a seller's goods if the quality, quantity, or delivery of the goods fails to conform precisely to the contract. ● Although the perfect-tender rule was adopted by the UCC, other Code provisions—such as the seller's right to cure after rejection—have softened the rule's impact. Cf. SUBSTANTIAL-PERFORMANCE DOCTRINE.

performance. **1.** The successful completion of a contractual duty, usu. resulting in the performer's release from any past or future liability.—Also termed *full performance*. Cf. NONPERFORMANCE. **2.** The equitable doctrine by which acts consistent with an intention to fulfill an obligation are construed to be in fulfillment of that obligation, even if the party was silent on the point. **3.** A company's earnings; the ability of a corporation to maintain or increase earnings.

performance bond. See BOND (2).

performance fund. See MUTUAL FUND.

performance stock. See *glamour stock* under STOCK.

peril. See RISK (1).

permanent financing. See FINANCING.

permissive subject. In labor law, a topic that one side in labor negotiations may refuse to discuss. • According to the NLRB, union members are not allowed to strike over a permissive subject. Cf. MANDATORY SUBJECT.

perquisite (pər-kwə-zit). A privilege or benefit given in addition to one's salary or regular wages.—Often shortened to *perk*.

per se rule. In antitrust law, the judicial doctrine holding that a trade practice violates the Sherman Act simply if the practice is a restraint of trade, regardless of whether the practice actually harms anyone. Cf. RULE OF REASON.

person. 1. A human being. **2.** An entity (such as a corporation) that is recognized by law as having the rights and duties of a human being. See ARTIFICIAL PERSON.

personal defense. See DEFENSE.

personal exemption. See EXEMPTION.

personal holding company. See COMPANY.

personal property. See PROPERTY.

petition in bankruptcy. A formal written request, presented to a bankruptcy court,

seeking protection for an insolvent debtor. •
The debtor (*voluntary bankruptcy*) or the debt-
or's creditors (*involuntary bankruptcy*) can file
such a petition in order to initiate a bankruptcy proceeding. See BANKRUPTCY.

phantom stock. See STOCK.

phantom stock plan. A long-term benefit
plan under which a corporate employee is giv-
en units having the same characteristics as the
employer's stock shares. • It is termed a
"phantom" plan because the employee doesn't
actually hold any shares but instead holds the
right to the value of those shares.

physical-inventory accounting method.
See ACCOUNTING METHOD.

picketing. The gathering of persons outside a
business or organization to protest the entity's
activities or policies and to pressure the entity
to meet the protesters' demands; esp., an employees' demonstration aimed at publicizing a
labor dispute and influencing the public to
withhold business from the employer. Cf. BOY-
COTT; STRIKE.

  common-situs picketing. The illegal picketing by union workers of a construction
  site, stemming from a dispute with one of
  the subcontractors.

organizational picketing. The picketing of an employer to encourage unionization or union membership.

recognition picketing. Picketing by members of one union where the employer has already recognized another union as the bargaining agent for the company's employees.

secondary picketing. The picketing of an establishment with which the picketing party has no direct dispute in order to pressure the party with which there is a dispute. See *secondary boycott* under BOYCOTT.

piercing the corporate veil. The judicial act of imposing personal liability on otherwise immune corporate officers, directors, and active shareholders for a corporation's fraudulent or wrongful acts. See CORPORATE VEIL; ALTER EGO.

pink sheet. A daily publication listing over-the-counter stocks, their market makers, and their prices. • Printed on pink paper, pink sheets are published by the National Quotation Bureau, a private company.—Also termed *National Daily Quotation Service*.

piracy. The unauthorized and illegal reproduction or distribution of materials protected by copyright, patent, or trademark law. See INFRINGEMENT.

457

plain-language law. Legislation requiring nontechnical, readily comprehensible language in consumer contracts such as residential leases or insurance policies. • Although opponents typically rally against plain-language laws whenever they are proposed, many of these laws have genuinely simplified the needlessly obscure language in which consumer contracts have traditionally been couched.

plan of rehabilitation. See BANKRUPTCY PLAN.

plan of reorganization. See BANKRUPTCY PLAN.

pledge, *n.* **1.** A bailment or other deposit of personal property to a creditor as security for a debt or obligation; a pawn. Cf. LIEN. **2.** The item of personal property so deposited; a pawned item. **3.** Broadly, the act of providing something as security for a debt or obligation. **4.** The thing so provided.

pledged account. See ACCOUNT.

pledgee. One with whom a pledge is deposited.

pledgor. One who gives a pledge to another.

PMSI. See *purchase-money security interest* under SECURITY INTEREST.

point. 1. One percent of the face value of a loan (esp. a mortgage loan), paid up front to the lender as a service charge or placement fee <the borrower hoped for a two-point discount on the mortgage>. **2.** A unit used for quoting stock, bond, or commodity prices <the stock closed up a few points today>.

poison pill. A corporation's defense against an unwanted takeover bid whereby shareholders are granted the right to acquire equity or debt securities at a favorable price in order to increase the bidder's acquisition costs. See SHARK REPELLENT. Cf. PORCUPINE PROVISION.

policyholder. One who owns an insurance policy, regardless of whether that person is the insured party.

Ponzi scheme. A fraudulent investment scheme in which money contributed by later investors generates artificially high dividends for the original investors, whose example attracts even larger investments. • Money from the new investors is used directly to repay or pay interest to old investors, usu. without any operation or revenue-producing activity other than the continual raising of new funds. Cf. PYRAMID SCHEME.

pool. An association of individuals or entities who share resources and funds to promote their joint undertaking; esp., an association of persons engaged in buying or selling commodities. • If such an association is formed to eliminate competition throughout a single industry, it is a restraint of trade that violates federal antitrust laws.

pooling agreement. A contractual arrangement by which corporate shareholders agree that their shares will be voted as a unit.—Also termed *voting agreement*; *shareholder voting agreement*.

porcupine provision. A clause in a corporation's charter or bylaws designed to prevent a takeover without the consent of the board of directors. Cf. SHARK REPELLENT; POISON PILL.

portfolio. The various securities or other investments held by an investor at any given time, usu. for the purpose of diversifying risk.

> *market portfolio.* A value-weighted portfolio of every asset in a particular market.

positive externality. See EXTERNALITY.

possession. 1. The fact of having or holding property in one's power; the exercise of dominion over property. **2.** The right under which one may exercise control over something to the exclusion of all others. **3.** (*usu. pl.*) Something that a person owns or controls; property. Cf. OWNERSHIP; TITLE (1).

post, *vb.* To transfer (accounting entries) from an original record to a ledger <post debits and credits>.

post audit. See AUDIT.

postdate. To put a date on (something, such as an instrument) that is later than the actual date. Cf. BACKDATE.

postdated check. See CHECK.

potential Pareto superiority. See WEALTH MAXIMIZATION.

power of attorney. 1. An instrument granting someone authority to act as agent or attorney-in-fact for the grantor. **2.** The authority so granted. Pl. **powers of attorney.** See ATTORNEY (1).

> ***durable power of attorney.*** A power of attorney that remains in effect during the grantor's incompetency. ● Such instruments commonly allow an agent to make health-care decisions for a patient who has become incompetent.

power-of-sale clause. A provision in a mortgage or deed of trust permitting the mortgagee or trustee to sell the property without court authority if the payments are not made.

power-of-sale foreclosure. See FORECLOSURE.

precontract. See CONTRACT.

preemption (pree-**em[p]**-shən). **1.** The right to buy before others. See RIGHT OF PREEMPTION. **2.** The purchase of something under this right.

preemptive right. A shareholder's privilege to purchase newly issued stock—before the shares are offered to the public—in an amount proportionate to the shareholder's current holdings in order to prevent dilution of the shareholder's ownership interest. ● This right must be exercised within a fixed period, usu. 30 to 60 days. See SUBSCRIPTION RIGHT. Cf. *rights offering* under OFFERING.

preexisting duty. See DUTY.

preexisting-duty rule. In contract law, the rule that if a party does or promises to do what the party is already legally obligated to do—or promises to refrain from doing or refrains from doing what the party is already legally privileged to refrain from doing—the party has not incurred detriment; therefore, the promise does not constitute adequate consideration for contractual purposes. • For example, if a builder agrees to construct a building for a specified price but later threatens to walk off the job unless the owner promises to pay an additional sum, the owner's new promise would not be enforceable because, under the preexisting duty rule, there is no consideration for that promise.

preference. 1. Priority of payment given to one or more creditors by a debtor; a creditor's right to receive such priority. **2.** See PREFERENTIAL TRANSFER.

> *liquidation preference.* A preferred shareholder's right, once the corporation is liquidated, to receive a specified distribution before common shareholders receive anything.

> *voidable preference.* See PREFERENTIAL TRANSFER.

preferential transfer. In bankruptcy law, a prebankruptcy transfer made by an insolvent debtor to or for the benefit of a creditor, thereby allowing the creditor to receive more than its proportionate share of the debtor's assets; technically, an insolvent debtor's transfer of a property interest for the benefit of a creditor who is owed on an earlier debt, when the transfer occurs no more than 90 days before the date when the bankruptcy petition is filed or (if the creditor is an insider) within one year of the filing, so that the creditor receives more than it would otherwise receive through the distribution of the bankruptcy estate. • Under certain circumstances, the bankruptcy trustee may recover—for the estate's benefit—a preferential transfer from the transferee.—Also termed *voidable preference*. Cf. FRAUDULENT CONVEYANCE (2).

preferred dividend. See DIVIDEND.

preferred stock. See STOCK.

preliminary prospectus. See PROSPECTUS.

premises liability. A landowner's or landholder's tort liability for conditions or activities on the premises.

premium. 1. The periodic payment required to keep an insurance policy in effect.—Also termed *insurance premium*.

earned premium. The portion of an insurance premium applicable to the coverage period that has already expired. • For example, if the total premium for a one-year insurance policy is $1,200, the earned premium after three months is $300.

unearned premium. The portion of an insurance premium applicable to the coverage period that has not yet occurred. • In the same example as above, the unearned premium after three months is $900.

2. A sum of money paid in addition to a regular price, salary, or other amount; a bonus. **3.** The amount by which a security's market value exceeds its face value. Cf. DISCOUNT (3). **4.** The amount paid to buy a securities option.—Also termed (in sense 4) *option premium.*

premium bond. See BOND (1).

prepaid interest. See INTEREST.

prepayment clause. A loan-document provision that permits a borrower to satisfy a debt before its due date, usu. without paying a penalty.

prepayment penalty. A charge assessed against a borrower who elects to pay off a loan before it is due.

presenting bank. See BANK.

presentment (pri-**zent**-mənt). The formal production of a negotiable instrument for acceptance or payment.

presentment for acceptance. Production of an instrument to the drawee, acceptor, or maker for acceptance. ● This type of presentment may be made anytime before maturity, except that with bills payable at sight, after demand, or after sight, presentment must be made within a reasonable time.

presentment for payment. Production of an instrument to the drawee, acceptor, or maker for payment. ● This type of presentment must be made on the date when the instrument is due.

present value. The sum of money that, with compound interest, would amount to a specified sum at a specified future date; future value discounted to its value today.—Also termed *present worth*.

adjusted present value. An asset's value determined by adding together its present value and the value added by capital-structure effects.—Abbr. APV.

net present value. The present value of net cash flow from a project, discounted by the cost of capital. ● This value is used to evaluate the project's investment potential.—Abbr. NPV.

prevention doctrine. In contract law, the principle that each contracting party has an implied duty to not do anything that prevents the other party from performing its obligation.—Also termed *prevention-of-performance doctrine*.

price. The amount of money or other consideration asked for or given in exchange for something else; the cost at which something is bought or sold, without any deduction for the seller's cost, the cost of materials used, the cost of labor or service, or any other expense.

asked price. The lowest price at which a seller is willing to sell a security at a given time. See SPREAD (2).

asking price. The value at which a seller lists property for sale, often suggesting a willingness to sell for less.—Also termed *offering price*.

at-the-market price. A retail price that store owners in the same vicinity generally charge.

bid price. The highest price that a prospective buyer is willing to pay for a security at a given time. See SPREAD (2).

call price. **a.** The price at which a bond may be retired before its maturity. **b.** See *strike price*.

ceiling price. **a.** The highest price at which a buyer is willing to buy. **b.** The highest price allowed by a government agency or by some other regulatory institution.

closing price. The last price of a security in a trading day. ● It is usu. the price quoted by brokers and newspapers.—Also termed *close.*

fixed price. A price that is agreed upon by a wholesaler and a retailer for the sale or resale of an item. ● Agreements to fix prices are generally prohibited by state and federal statutes.

floor price. The lowest price at which a seller is willing to sell.

liquidation price. A price that is paid for property sold to liquidate a debt. ● Liquidation price is usu. below market price.—Also termed *liquidation value.*

market price. The prevailing price at which something is sold in a specific market. See FAIR MARKET VALUE.

redemption price. **a.** The price of a bond that has not reached maturity, purchased at the issuer's option. **b.** The price of shares when a mutual-fund shareholder sells shares back to the fund.

sales price. The total amount for which property is sold, often including any services that are a part of such sale. • Under sales-tax statutes, the amount is typically valued in money even if the value is not received in money.

strike price. The price for which a security will be bought or sold under an option contract if the option is exercised. See OPTION.

subscription price. See SUBSCRIPTION PRICE.

transfer price. The charge assigned to an exchange of goods or services between a corporation's organizational units.

upset price. The lowest amount a seller is willing to accept for property or goods sold at auction.

price discrimination. A price difference between two substantially contemporaneous sales of identical personal property to two different buyers. • Price discrimination can violate antitrust laws if it reduces competition. It may be either direct, as when a seller charges different prices to different purchasers, or indirect, as when a seller offers special concessions to some purchasers, such as differing credit terms.

price-earnings ratio. The ratio between a stock's current share price and the corpora-

tion's earnings per share for the last year. •
Some investors avoid stocks with high price-
earnings ratios because those stocks may be
overpriced.—Abbr. P/E ratio.

price-fixing. An unlawful cooperative effort
by competitors to interfere with trade by setting prices.

> *horizontal price-fixing.* Price-fixing
> among competitors on the same level, such
> as retailers throughout an industry.

> *vertical price-fixing.* Price-fixing among
> parties in the same chain of distribution,
> such as manufacturers and retailers at-
> tempting to control an item's resale price.

price-level-adjusted mortgage. See MORT-
GAGE.

prima facie tort. See TORT.

primary boycott. See BOYCOTT.

primary market. See MARKET.

primary obligation. See OBLIGATION.

primary offering. See OFFERING.

primary reserve ratio. See RESERVE RATIO.

prime, *n.* See *prime rate* under INTEREST RATE.

prime, *vb.* To take priority over <Watson's preferred mortgage primed Moriarty's lien>.

prime rate. See INTEREST RATE.

principal. 1. One who authorizes another to act on his or her behalf as an agent. Cf. AGENT.

> *disclosed principal.* A principal whose identity is revealed by the agent to a third party. ● A disclosed principal is always liable on the third-party contract, but the agent is usu. not liable.

> *partially disclosed principal.* A principal whose existence—but not his or her actual identity—is revealed by the agent to a third party.

> *undisclosed principal.* A principal whose identity is kept secret by the agent. ● An undisclosed principal and the agent are both liable on the third-party contract.

2. The person who has primary responsibility on an obligation, as opposed to a surety or indorser. **3.** The corpus of an estate or trust. **4.** The amount of a debt, investment, or other fund, not including interest or profits.

471

priority. 1. The status of being earlier in time, degree, or rank; precedence. **2.** An established right to such precedence; esp., a creditor's right to have a claim paid before other creditors of the same debtor receive payment.

prior-use loan. See PUBLIC-USE BAR.

private carrier. See CARRIER.

private nuisance. See NUISANCE.

private offering. See OFFERING.

private placement. See *private offering* under OFFERING.

privatization (pri-və-tə-**zay**-shən). The act or process of converting a business or industry from governmental ownership or control to private enterprise.

privileged subscription. See *rights offering* under OFFERING.

privity (**pri**-və-tee). The relationship between two contracting parties, each having a legally recognized interest in the subject matter of the contract; mutuality of interest <the buyer and seller are in privity>. ● Parties who have contracted with each other are said to be *in privity*.

proceeds (**proh**-seedz), *n*. **1.** The value of land, goods, or investments when converted into money; the amount of money received from a sale <the proceeds are subject to attachment>. **2.** Whatever is received upon selling, exchanging, collecting, or otherwise disposing of collateral. ● Proceeds differ from other types of collateral because they constitute any collateral that has changed in form. For example, if a farmer borrows credit on sheep and gives the creditor a security interest in the harvest, the harvested wheat is collateral. If the farmer exchanges the harvest for a tractor or for money, the tractor or money now becomes the proceeds of the wheat.

procurement contract. See CONTRACT.

product. Something that is distributed commercially for use or consumption and that is usu. (1) tangible personal property, (2) the result of fabrication or processing, and (3) an item that has passed through a chain of commercial distribution before ultimate use or consumption. See PRODUCTS LIABILITY.

product defect. See DEFECT.

product-extension merger. See MERGER.

product market. See MARKET.

products liability. 1. A manufacturer's or seller's tort liability for any damages or injuries suffered by a buyer, user, or bystander as a result of a defective product. ● Products liability can be based on a theory of negligence, strict liability, or breach of warranty. **2.** The legal theory by which liability is imposed on the manufacturer or seller of a defective product. **3.** The field of law dealing with this theory.

professional association. See ASSOCIATION.

professional corporation. See CORPORATION.

profit, *n.* The excess of revenues over expenditures in a business transaction; gain. Cf. EARNINGS; INCOME.

gross profit. Total sales revenue less the cost of the goods sold, excluding additional expenses and taxes.

net profit. Total sales revenue less the cost of the goods sold and all additional expenses.

operating profit. Total sales revenue less all operating expenses, excluding any nonoperating income and expenses, such as interest payments.

paper profit. An increase in the value of an investment (such as a stock), but an increase

474

that remains unrealized until the investment is sold.—Also termed *unrealized profit*.

undistributed profit. See *retained earnings* under EARNINGS.

profit-and-loss statement. See INCOME STATEMENT.

profit margin. 1. The difference between the cost of something and the price for which it is sold. **2.** The ratio, expressed as a percentage, between this difference and the selling price. ● For example, a widget costing a retailer $10 and selling for $15 has a profit margin of 33% ($5 difference divided by $15 selling price).— Often shortened to *margin*.

profit-sharing plan. An employer's benefit plan that allows an employee to share in the company's profits.

program trading. A form of computerized securities trading that usu. involves buying or selling large amounts of stocks while simultaneously selling or buying index futures in offsetting amounts.

progressive tax. See TAX.

project financing. See FINANCING.

475

promise, *n.* **1.** The manifestation of an intention to act or refrain from acting in a specified manner, conveyed in such a way that another is justified in understanding that a commitment has been made; a person's assurance that the person will or will not do something. ● A binding promise—one that the law will enforce—is the essence of a contract. **2.** The words in a promissory note expressing the maker's intention to pay a debt. ● A mere written acknowledgment that a debt is due is insufficient to constitute a promise. See CON-TRACT (3).

illusory promise. A promise that appears on its face to be so insubstantial as to impose no obligation on the promisor; an expression cloaked in promissory terms but actually containing no commitment by the promisor. ● For example, if a guarantor promises to make good on the principal debtor's obligation "as long as I think it's in my commercial interests," the promisor is not really bound.

naked promise. A promise for which the promisee has given nothing in return. ● Naked promises are not legally enforceable.

promise in restraint of trade. A promise whose performance would limit competition in any business or restrict the promisor in the exercise of a gainful occupation.

voidable promise. A promise that one party may, under the law, declare void by reason of that party's incapacity or mistake, or by reason of the fraud, breach, or other fault of the other party.

promisee. One to whom a promise is made.

promise in restraint of trade. See PROMISE.

promisor. One who makes a promise; esp., one who undertakes a contractual obligation.

promissory estoppel. See ESTOPPEL.

promissory note. See NOTE.

promoter. A founder or organizer of a corporation or business venture; one who takes the entrepreneurial initiative in founding or organizing a business or enterprise.

proof of claim. A creditor's written statement that is submitted (esp. in a bankruptcy proceeding) to show the basis and amount of the creditor's claim. Pl. **proofs of claim.**

proof of loss. An insured's formal statement of loss required by an insurance company before it will determine whether the policy covers the loss.

477

property. 1. The right to possess, use, and enjoy a determinate thing (either a tract of land or a chattel); the right of ownership <the institution of private property is protected from undue governmental interference>. **2.** Any external thing over which the rights of possession, use, and enjoyment are exercised <the airport is city property>.

distressed property. Property that must be sold because of mortgage foreclosure or because it is part of an insolvent estate.

exempt property. A debtor's holdings and possessions that, by law, a creditor cannot attach to satisfy a debt. ● All the property that creditors may lawfully reach is known as *nonexempt property*. Many states provide a homestead exemption that excludes a person's house and household items, up to a certain amount, from the liens of most creditors. The purpose of the exemption is to prevent debtors from becoming destitute. Cf. HOMESTEAD.

income property. Property that produces income, such as rental property.

intangible property. Property that lacks a physical existence. ● Examples include bank accounts, stock options, and business goodwill.

intellectual property. See INTELLECTUAL PROPERTY.

personal property. **a.** Any movable or intangible thing that is subject to ownership and not classified as real property. **b.** Property not used in a taxpayer's trade or business or held for income production or collection. Cf. *real property*.

real property. Land and anything growing on, attached to, or erected on it, excluding anything that may be severed without injury to the land. ● Real property can be either corporeal (soil and buildings) or incorporeal (easements).—Also termed *real estate*. Cf. *personal property*.

tangible property. Property that has physical form and characteristics. Cf. *intangible property*.

property tax. See TAX.

proprietary (prə-**prī**-ə-ter-ee), *adj*. **1.** Of or relating to a proprietor <the licensee's proprietary rights>. **2.** Of, relating to, or holding as property <the software designer sought to protect its proprietary data>.

proprietor. An owner, esp. one who runs a business. See SOLE PROPRIETORSHIP.

pro rata (proh-**rah**-tə *or* -**ra**-tə *or* -**ray**-tə), *adv.* Proportionately; according to an exact rate, measure, or interest <the liability will be assessed pro rata between the defendants>. See RATABLE.

pro rata clause. An insurance-policy provision—usu. contained in the "other insurance" section of the policy—that limits the insurer's liability to payment of the portion of the loss that the face amount of the policy bears to the total insurance available on the risk. Cf. ESCAPE CLAUSE; EXCESS CLAUSE.

prorate (**proh**-rayt), *vb.* To divide, assess, or distribute proportionately.

prospectus. A printed document that describes the main features of an enterprise (esp. a corporation's business) and that is distributed to prospective buyers or investors; esp., a written description of a securities offering. ● Under SEC regulations, a publicly traded corporation must provide a prospectus before anyone can buy stock in the corporation. Pl. **prospectuses.** See REGISTRATION STATEMENT.

preliminary prospectus. A prospectus for a stock issue that has been filed but not yet approved by the SEC.—Also termed *red-herring prospectus*.

480

protective tariff. See TARIFF.

protest, *n.* **1.** A notary public's written statement that, upon presentment, a negotiable instrument was neither paid nor accepted. **2.** A formal statement, usu. in writing, disputing a debt's legality or validity but agreeing to make payment while reserving the right to recover the amount at a later time. • The disputed debt is described as *under protest.*

provisional director. See DIRECTOR.

proxy. 1. One who is authorized to act as a substitute for another; esp., in corporate law, a person who is authorized to vote another's stock shares. **2.** The grant of authority by which a person is so authorized. **3.** The document granting this authority.

proxy contest. A struggle between two corporate factions to obtain the votes of uncommitted shareholders. • A proxy contest usu. occurs when a group of dissident shareholders mounts a battle against the corporation's managers.

proxy solicitation. A request that a corporate shareholder authorize another person to vote for the shareholder at a corporate meeting.

proxy statement. An informational document that accompanies a proxy solicitation and explains a proposed action (such as a merger) by the corporation.

pseudo-foreign-corporation statute. A state law regulating foreign corporations that either derive a specified high percentage of their income from that state or have a high percentage of their stock owned by people living in that state.

PTO. *abbr.* PATENT AND TRADEMARK OFFICE.

PTP. See *publicly traded partnership* under PARTNERSHIP.

public agent. See AGENT.

public carrier. See *common carrier* under CARRIER.

public corporation. See CORPORATION.

public debt. See DEBT.

public domain. The realm of publications, inventions, and processes that are not protected by copyright or patent. • Things in the public domain can be appropriated by anyone without liability for infringement.

publicly held corporation. See *public corporation* (a) under CORPORATION.

publicly traded partnership. See PARTNERSHIP.

public nuisance. See NUISANCE.

public offering. See OFFERING.

public policy. Broadly, principles and matters regarded by the legislature or by the courts as being of fundamental concern to the state and the whole of society. ● Courts sometimes use the term to justify their decisions, as when declaring a contract void because it undermines the public good.

public seal. See SEAL.

public security. See SECURITY.

public stock. See STOCK.

public-use bar. In patent law, a statutory bar that prevents the granting of a patent for an invention that was publicly used or sold in the U.S. more than one year before the application date.—Also termed *prior-use bar*.

puffing. 1. The expression of an exaggerated opinion—as opposed to a factual representa-

tion—with the intent to sell a good or service.
● Puffing involves expressing opinions, not
asserting something as a fact. Although there
is some leeway in puffing goods, a seller may
not misrepresent them or say that they have
benefits that they do not possess. **2.** See BY-BID-
DING.

punitive damages. See DAMAGES.

purchase agreement. A sales contract. Cf.
REPURCHASE AGREEMENT.

purchase-money mortgage. See MORTGAGE.

purchase-money resulting trust. See TRUST.

purchase-money security interest. See SE-
CURITY INTEREST.

purchaser. 1. One who obtains property for
money or other valuable consideration; a buyer.

> ***bona fide purchaser.*** One who buys some-
> thing for value without notice of another's
> claim to the item or of any defects in the
> seller's title; one who has in good faith paid
> valuable consideration for property without
> notice of prior adverse claims.—Abbr.
> BFP.—Also termed *good-faith purchaser*.

2. One who acquires real property by means other than descent or inheritance.

put. See *put option* under OPTION.

put bond. See BOND (1).

put option. See OPTION.

pyramiding. A speculative method used to finance a large purchase of stocks or commodities by pledging an investment's unrealized profit. See LEVERAGE; MARGIN.

pyramid scheme. A property-distribution scheme in which a participant pays for the chance to receive compensation for introducing new persons to the scheme, as well as for when those new persons themselves introduce participants. • Pyramid schemes are illegal in most states.—Also termed *multilevel-distribution program*. Cf. PONZI SCHEME.

Q

qualified indorsement. See INDORSEMENT.

qualifying share. A share of common stock purchased by someone in order to become a director of a corporation that requires its directors to be shareholders.

quantum meruit (**kwahn**-təm-**mer**-ə-wit). [Latin "as much as he or she has deserved"] **1.** The reasonable value of services; damages awarded in an amount considered reasonable to compensate a person who has rendered services in a quasi-contractual relationship. **2.** A claim or right of action for the reasonable value of services rendered.

quarterly report. A financial report issued by a corporation every three months.

quasi-contract. See *implied-in-law contract* under CONTRACT.

quasi-corporation. See CORPORATION.

quick asset. See *current asset* under ASSET.

quick-asset ratio. The ratio between an entity's current or liquid assets (such as cash and accounts receivable) and its current liabilities.

quid pro quo (**kwid**-proh-**kwoh**). [Latin "something for something"] A thing that is exchanged for another thing of more or less equal value; a substitute <the discount was given as a quid pro quo for the extra business>. Cf. CONSIDERATION.

quid-pro-quo sexual harassment. See SEXUAL HARASSMENT.

quitclaim, *n.* **1.** A formal release of one's claim or right. **2.** See *quitclaim deed* under DEED.

quitclaim, *vb.* **1.** To relinquish or release (a claim or right). **2.** To convey all of one's interest in (property), to whatever extent one has an interest.

quitclaim deed. See DEED.

quorum. The minimum number of members (usu. a majority) who must be present for a body to transact business or take a vote. Pl. **quorums.**

quota. 1. A proportional share assigned to a person or group; an allotment <the university's admission standards included a quota for in-state residents>. **2.** A quantitative restriction; a minimum or maximum number <Faldo met his sales quota for the month>.

487

import quota. A restriction on the number of a certain category of products that can be brought into a country from a foreign country.

quotation. 1. The amount stated as a stock's or commodity's current price. **2.** A contractor's estimate for a given job.—Sometimes shortened to *quote*.

R

Racketeer Influenced and Corrupt Organizations Act. A statute designed to attack organized criminal activity and preserve marketplace integrity by investigating, controlling, and prosecuting persons who participate or conspire to participate in racketeering. • Enacted in 1970, the federal Racketeer Influenced and Corrupt Organizations Act (RICO) applies only to activity involving interstate or foreign commerce. Since then, many states have adopted laws (sometimes called "little RICO" acts) based on the federal statute. The federal and most state RICO acts provide for enforcement not only by criminal prosecution but also by civil lawsuit, in which the plaintiff can sue for treble damages.

racketeering. 1. A system of organized crime traditionally involving the extortion of money by intimidation, violence, or other illegal methods. **2.** A pattern of illegal activity (such as bribery, extortion, fraud, and murder) carried out as part of an enterprise (such as a crime syndicate) that is owned or controlled by those engaged in the illegal activity. • The modern sense (sense 2) derives from the federal RICO statute, which greatly broadened the term's original sense to include such activities as mail fraud, securities fraud, and the collection of illegal gambling debts.

raider. See CORPORATE RAIDER.

raised check. See CHECK.

raising an instrument. The act of fraudulently altering a negotiable instrument, esp. a check, to increase the sum stated as being payable. See *raised check* under CHECK.

rally. A sharp rise in the general price level of the stock market or in an individual stock, following a price decline or a period of price inactivity.

R & D. *abbr.* RESEARCH AND DEVELOPMENT.

ratable (**ray**-də-bəl), *adj.* **1.** Proportionate <ratable distribution>. **2.** Capable of being estimated, appraised, or apportioned <because hundreds of angry fans ran onto the field at the same time, blame for the goalpost's destruction is not ratable>. **3.** Taxable <the government assessed the company's ratable assets>. See PRO RATA.

rate, *n.* **1.** Proportional or relative value; the proportion by which quantity or value is adjusted <rate of inflation>. **2.** An amount paid or charged for a good or service <the rate for a business-class fare is $550>. **3.** See INTEREST RATE <the rate on the loan increases by 2% after five years>.

rate base. The investment amount or property value on which a company, esp. a public utility, is allowed to earn a particular rate of return.

rate of return. The annual income from an investment, expressed as a percentage of the investment.

>*fair rate of return.* The amount of profit that a public utility is permitted to earn, as determined by a public utility commission.

>*internal rate of return.* In accounting, a discounted-cashflow method of evaluating a long-term project, used to determine the actual return on an investment.

ratification, *n.* **1.** Confirmation and acceptance of a previous act, thereby making the act valid from the moment it was done <the board of directors' ratification of the president's resolution>. **2.** In contract law, a person's binding adoption of an act already completed but either not done in a way that originally produced a legal obligation or done by a third party having at the time no authority to act as the person's agent <an adult's ratification of a contract signed during childhood is necessary to make the contract enforceable>.

readjustment. Voluntary reorganization of a financially troubled corporation by the shareholders themselves and without a trustee's or a receiver's intervention.

reaffirmation. 1. Approval of something previously agreed to; renewal <the Supreme Court's reaffirmation of this principle is long overdue>. **2.** In bankruptcy law, the revival of a preexisting debt that is dischargeable in bankruptcy <the bankruptcy court authorized the debtor's reaffirmation of prepetition debts that otherwise would have been discharged>.

real asset. See ASSET.

real covenant. See *covenant running with the land* under COVENANT (2).

real defense. See DEFENSE.

real estate. See *real property* under PROPERTY.

real-estate investment trust. A company that invests in and manages a portfolio of real estate, with the majority of the trust's income distributed to its shareholders. • Such a trust may qualify for special income-tax treatment if it distributes 95% of its income to its shareholders.—Abbr. REIT. See *investment company* under COMPANY.

    umbrella-partnership real-estate investment trust. A REIT that controls and holds most of its properties through an umbrella limited partnership, as a result of which the trust can acquire properties in exchange for the limited-partnership interests in the umbrella while triggering no immediate tax obligations for certain sellers.—Abbr. UPREIT.

real estate owned. Property acquired by a lender, usu. through foreclosure, in satisfaction of a debt.

Real Estate Settlement Procedures Act. A federal law that requires lenders to provide home buyers with information about known or estimated settlement costs.—Abbr. RESPA.

real income. See INCOME.

realization. 1. Conversion of noncash assets into cash assets. **2.** In tax law, an event or transaction, such as the sale or exchange of property, that substantially changes a taxpayer's economic position so that income tax may be imposed or a tax allowance granted. Cf. RECOGNITION.

real property. See PROPERTY.

real rate. See INTEREST RATE.

reasonable-expectation doctrine. In insurance law, the rule that resolves insurance-policy ambiguities in favor of the insured's reasonable expectations.

reasonable time. 1. In contract law, the time needed to do what a contract requires to be done, based on subjective circumstances. ● If the contracting parties do not fix a time for performance, the law will usu. presume a reasonable time. **2.** In commercial law, the time during which the UCC permits a party to accept an offer, inspect goods, substitute conforming goods for rejected goods, and the like.

rebate. A discount, deduction, or refund of money.

recapitalization. An adjustment or recasting of a corporation's capital structure—that is, its stocks, bonds, or other securities—through amendment of the articles of incorporation or merger with a parent or subsidiary. ● An example of recapitalization is the elimination of unpaid preferred dividends and the creation of a new class of senior securities. Cf. REORGANIZATION (1).

leveraged recapitalization. Recapitalization whereby the corporation substitutes debt for equity in the capital structure, usu. to make the corporation less attractive as a target for a hostile takeover.—Also termed *leveraging up*.

recapture, *n.* Recovery by the IRS of a tax benefit, such as a deduction or a credit, previously taken by a taxpayer <the tax code's rules for recapture of depreciation do not apply when the property is sold at a loss>.

recapture clause. 1. A contract provision that limits prices or allows for the recovery of goods if market conditions greatly differ from what the contract anticipated. **2.** A commercial-lease provision that grants the landlord both a percentage of the tenant's profits above a fixed amount of rent and the right to terminate the lease—and thus recapture the property—if those profits are too low.

receipt, *n.* **1.** The act of receiving something <my receipt of the document was delayed by two days>. **2.** A written acknowledgment that something has been received <keep the receipt for the gift>. **3.** (*usu. pl.*) Something received; income <post the daily receipts in the ledger>.

receipt, *vb.* **1.** To acknowledge in writing the receipt of (something, esp. money) <the bill must be receipted>. **2.** To give a receipt for (something, esp. money) <the bookkeeper receipted the payments>.

495

receivable. See *account receivable* under AC-
COUNT.

receiver. A disinterested person appointed by
a court, or by a corporation or other person,
for the protection or collection of property that
is the subject of diverse claims (for example,
because it belongs to a bankrupt or is otherwise being litigated).

receivership. 1. A legal proceeding in which
a court appoints a receiver. **2.** The state or
condition of a business or property over which
a receiver has been appointed.

recession. A period characterized by a sharp
slowdown in economic activity, declining employment, and a decrease in investment and
consumer spending. Cf. DEPRESSION.

reciprocal-dealing arrangement. A business plan between two parties whereby the
first party agrees to buy goods from the second
party only if the second party also buys goods
from the first party. • This type of arrangement often violates antitrust laws. Cf. TYING AR-
RANGEMENT.

reciprocal insurance. See INSURANCE.

recital. A preliminary statement in a contract
or deed explaining the background of the

transaction or showing the existence of particular facts <the recitals in the settlement agreement should describe the underlying dispute>.

reclamation (rek-lə-**may**-shən). In commercial law, a seller's limited right to retrieve goods delivered to a buyer when the buyer is insolvent.

recognition. The act or an instance of accounting for a realized gain or loss on current tax records. Cf. NONRECOGNITION PROVISION; REALIZATION.

recognition picketing. See PICKETING.

record date. The date on which corporate shareholders must be registered on the corporation's books to be entitled to vote and receive dividends. Cf. DIVIDEND DATE.

recording agent. See INSURANCE AGENT.

record owner. See OWNER.

record title. See TITLE.

recourse (**ree**-kors). **1.** The right of a holder of a negotiable instrument to demand payment from the drawer or indorser if the instrument is dishonored. See WITH RECOURSE; WITHOUT RE-

COURSE. **2.** The right to repayment of a loan from the borrower's personal assets, not just from the collateral that secured the loan.

recourse loan. See LOAN.

redeemable bond. See BOND (1).

redeemable security. See SECURITY.

redemption. 1. The act or an instance of reclaiming or regaining possession by paying a specific price. **2.** In bankruptcy law, a debtor's right to repurchase property from a buyer who obtained the property at a forced sale initiated by a creditor. **3.** The reacquisition of a security by the issuer. ● Redemption usu. refers to the repurchase of a bond before maturity, but it may also refer to the repurchase of stock and mutual-fund shares.—Also termed (in reference to stock) *stock redemption.* **4.** In property law, the payment of a defaulted mortgage debt by a borrower who does not want to lose the property. See EQUITY OF REDEMPTION; STATUTORY RIGHT OF REDEMPTION.

redemption period. The statutory period during which a defaulting mortgagor may recover property after a foreclosure or tax sale by paying the outstanding debt or charges.

redemption price. See PRICE.

red-herring prospectus. See *preliminary prospectus* under PROSPECTUS.

rediscount rate. See INTEREST RATE.

redlining, *n*. Unlawful credit discrimination by financial institutions that refuse to make loans on properties in allegedly bad neighborhoods.

referral sales contract. A dual agreement consisting of an agreement by the consumer to purchase goods or services (usu. at an inflated price) and an agreement by the seller to compensate the consumer for each customer (or potential customer) referred to the seller.

refinancing. An exchange of an old debt for a new debt, as by negotiating a different interest rate or by repaying the existing loan with money acquired from a new loan.

reformation (ref-ər-**may**-shən). An equitable remedy by which a court will modify a written agreement to reflect the actual intent of the parties, usu. to correct fraud or mutual mistake, such as an incomplete property description in a deed.

refund, *n*. **1.** The return of money to a person who overpaid, such as a taxpayer who overestimated tax liability or whose employer withheld too much tax from earnings. **2.** The money returned to a person who overpaid. **3.** The act of refinancing, esp. by replacing outstanding securities with a new issue of securities.

refund annuity. See ANNUITY.

re-funding bond. See BOND (1).

refusal to deal. A company's declination to do business with another company. ● A business has the right to refuse to deal only if it is not accompanied by an illegal restraint of trade.

regional securities exchange. See SECURITIES EXCHANGE.

register, *n.* An official record or list, such as a corporation's list of the names and addresses of its shareholders.

registered agent. See AGENT.

registered bond. See BOND (1).

registered check. See CHECK.

registered corporation. See CORPORATION.

registered dealer. See DEALER.

registered offering. See OFFERING.

registered representative. See REPRESENTATIVE.

registered security. See SECURITY.

registered stock. See *registered security* under SECURITY.

registration, *n.* In securities law, the complete process of preparing to sell a newly issued security to the public <the security is currently in registration>.

   shelf registration. Registration with the SEC of securities to be sold over time, the purpose being to avoid the delays and market uncertainties of individual registration.

registration statement. A document containing detailed information required by the SEC for the public sale of corporate securities. ● The statement includes the prospectus to be supplied to prospective buyers. See PROSPECTUS.

regressive tax. See TAX.

regular course of business. See COURSE OF BUSINESS.

regular meeting. See *annual meeting* under MEETING.

regulation, *n.* **1.** The act or process of controlling by rule or restriction <the federal regulation of the airline industry>. **2.** A bylaw <the CEO referred to the corporate regulation>. **3.** A rule or order, having legal force, issued by an administrative agency or a local government <Treasury regulations explain and interpret the Internal Revenue Code>. See MERIT REGULATION.

Regulation A. An SEC regulation that exempts stock offerings of up to $5 million from certain registration requirements.

Regulation D. An SEC regulation that exempts certain stock offerings (such as those offered by private sale) from registration under the Securities Act of 1933.

Regulation J. A Federal Reserve Board regulation that governs the collection of checks by and the transfer of funds through member banks.

Regulation Q. A Federal Reserve Board regulation that sets interest-rate ceilings and regulates advertising of interest on savings accounts. • This regulation, which applies to all commercial banks, was created by the Banking Act of 1933.

Regulation T. An SEC regulation that limits the amount of credit that securities brokers and dealers may extend to customers who wish to buy securities. • The Federal Reserve Board sets the limit, which usu. requires the customer to provide between 40 and 60% of the purchase price.

Regulation U. A Federal Reserve Board regulation that limits the amount of credit that banks may extend to customers who wish to buy securities.

Regulation Z. A Federal Reserve Board regulation that implements the provisions of the federal Consumer Credit Protection Act. See CONSUMER CREDIT PROTECTION ACT.

rehabilitation. In bankruptcy law, the process of reorganizing a debtor's financial affairs—under Chapter 11, 12, or 13 of the Bankruptcy Code—so that the debtor may continue to exist as a financial entity, with creditors satisfying their claims from the debtor's future earnings <the corporation's rehabilitation was successful>. Cf. LIQUIDATION (4).

reification (ree-ə-fi-**kay**-shən *or* ray-). In commercial law, embodiment of a right to payment in a writing (such as a negotiable instrument) so that a transfer of the writing also transfers the right.

reinsurance. See INSURANCE.

reissuable note. See NOTE.

REIT (reet). *abbr.* REAL-ESTATE INVESTMENT TRUST.

rejection. Refusal of a contract offer or of tendered goods. Cf. REPUDIATION; RESCISSION.

related good. In trademark law, a good that infringes a trademark because it appears to come from the same source as the marked good, despite not competing with the marked good. ● For example, a cutting tool named "McKnife" might infringe the "McDonald's" trademark as a related good.

related proceeding. In bankruptcy law, a proceeding involving claims that will affect the administration of the debtor's estate (such as a tort action between the debtor and a third party). Cf. CORE PROCEEDING.

release, *n.* **1.** Liberation from an obligation, duty, or demand; the act of giving up a right or claim to the person against whom it could have been enforced <the employee asked for a

release from the noncompete agreement>. **2.**
A written discharge, acquittance, or receipt
<Jones signed the release before accepting the
cash from Hawkins>.

release of mortgage. A written document
that discharges a mortgage upon full payment
by the borrower and that is publicly recorded
to show that the borrower has full equity in
the property.

relevant market. See MARKET.

reliance. Dependence or trust by a person,
esp. when combined with action based on that
dependence or trust.

 detrimental reliance. Reliance by one party on the acts or representations of another,
 causing a worsening of the first party's position. ● Detrimental reliance may serve as a
 substitute for consideration and thus make a
 promise enforceable as a contract. See *promissory estoppel* under ESTOPPEL.

remargining. In securities law, the act or
process of depositing additional cash or collateral with a broker when the equity in a margin
account falls to an insufficient level. See *margin account* under ACCOUNT.

remedy, *n.* The means of enforcing a right or preventing or redressing a wrong; legal or equitable relief.

> *administrative remedy.* A nonjudicial remedy provided by an administrative agency. • Ordinarily, if an administrative remedy is available, it must be exhausted before a court will hear the case.

> *equitable remedy.* A nonmonetary remedy, such as an injunction or specific performance, obtained when monetary damages cannot adequately redress the injury.

> *extrajudicial remedy.* A remedy not obtained from a court, such as repossession.

> *specific remedy.* A remedy for breach of contract whereby the injured party is awarded the very performance that was contractually promised, as when the court orders a defaulting seller of goods to deliver the specified goods to the buyer (as opposed to paying damages).

> *substitutional remedy.* A remedy for breach of contract intended to give the promisee something as a replacement for the promised performance, as when the court orders a defaulting seller of goods to pay the buyer damages (as opposed to delivering the goods).

remit, *vb.* To transmit (as money) <upon receiving the demand letter, she promptly remitted the amount due>.

remuneration (ri-myoo-nə-**ray**-shən). **1.** Payment; compensation. **2.** The act of paying or compensating.

renegotiable-rate mortgage. See MORTGAGE.

renegotiation. The negotiation of terms in a previously signed contract. ● Renegotiation often occurs as part of a review of contracts by the government to determine whether contractors have made excessive profits.

rent, *n.* Consideration paid, usu. periodically, for the use or occupancy of property.

economic rent. See ECONOMIC RENT.

ground rent. Rent paid by a tenant under a long-term lease for the use of undeveloped land, usu. for the construction of a commercial building. See *ground lease* under LEASE.

renunciation (ri-nən[t]-see-**ay**-shən). The express or tacit abandonment of a right without transferring it to another.

reorganization. 1. In corporate tax law, a restructuring of a corporation, such as by a merger or recapitalization. • The Internal Revenue Code classifies the different types of reorganizations for tax purposes <a Class A reorganization>. Cf. RECAPITALIZATION. **2.** In bankruptcy law, a financial restructuring of a corporation, esp. in the repayment of debts, under a plan created by a trustee and approved by a court. See CHAPTER 11.

> *haircut reorganization.* In bankruptcy, a restructuring of the indebtedness that remains after a creditor forgives a portion of the debtor's loan.

reorganization bond. See *adjustment bond* under BOND (1).

replacement cost. See COST.

replacement-cost depreciation method. See DEPRECIATION METHOD.

repo (ree-poh). **1.** See REPOSSESSION. **2.** See REPURCHASE AGREEMENT.

reporting company. A company that, because it issues publicly traded securities, must comply with the reporting requirements of the Securities Exchange Act of 1934.

repossession. The act or an instance of retaking property; esp., a seller's retaking of goods sold on credit when the buyer has failed to pay for them.—Often shortened to *repo*. Cf. FORE-CLOSURE.

representation. A presentation of fact—either by words or by conduct—made to induce someone to act, esp. to enter into a contract <the buyer relied on the seller's representation that the roof did not leak>. Cf. MISREPRE-SENTATION.

 material representation. A representation that relates directly to the matter in issue or that actually causes an event to occur (such as a party's relying on the representation in entering into a contract). • Material representation is a necessary element of an action for fraud.

representative. One who stands for or acts on behalf of another <the owner was the football team's representative at the labor negotiations>. See AGENT.

 accredited representative. A person with designated authority to act on behalf of another person, group, or organization, usu. by being granted that authority by law or by the rules of the group or organization <as an officer of the union, she was the accredited representative of the employees in the wage dispute>.

class representative. A person who sues on behalf of a group of plaintiffs in a class action. See CLASS ACTION.

registered representative. A person approved by the SEC and stock exchanges to sell securities to the public.

representative action. 1. See CLASS ACTION. **2.** See DERIVATIVE ACTION.

reproduction right. A copyright holder's exclusive right to make copies or phonorecords of the protected work. ● Unauthorized copying by others constitutes infringement.

repudiation (ri-pyoo-dee-**ay**-shən). A contracting party's words or actions that indicate an intention not to perform the contract in the future; a threatened breach of contract. Cf. REJECTION; RESCISSION.

anticipatory repudiation. Repudiation of a contractual duty before the time for performance, giving the injured party an immediate right to damages for total breach, as well as discharging the injured party's remaining duties of performance. See *anticipatory breach* under BREACH OF CONTRACT.

total repudiation. An unconditional refusal by a party to perform the acts required by a contract. ● This type of repudiation justifies the other party in refraining from performance.

repurchase agreement. A short-term loan agreement by which one party sells a security to another party but promises to buy back the security on a specified date at a specified price.—Often shortened to *repo*.

required reserve. See RESERVE.

requirements contract. See CONTRACT.

res (rays *or* reez *or* rez). [Latin "thing"] **1.** An object, interest, or status, as opposed to a person <jurisdiction of the res—the real property in Colorado>. **2.** A trust corpus <the stock certificate is the res of the trust>. See CORPUS. Pl. **res.**

resale. 1. The act of selling goods or property—previously sold to a buyer who breached the sales contract—to someone else. **2.** A retailer's selling of goods, previously purchased from a manufacturer or wholesaler, to consumers.

resale-price maintenance. An agreement between a manufacturer and a retailer—or the manufacturer's unilateral requirement—that the retailer will not sell the manufacturer's product below a specified minimum price. See *vertical price-fixing* under PRICE-FIXING.

rescission (ri-**sizh**-ən). **1.** A party's unilateral unmaking of a contract for a legally sufficient reason, such as the other party's material breach. ● Rescission is generally available as a remedy or defense for the nonbreaching party and restores the parties to their precontractual positions. **2.** An agreement by contracting parties to discharge all remaining duties of performance and terminate the contract.—Also termed (in sense 2) *abandonment*. Cf. REJECTION; REPUDIATION.

research and development. A company's effort to develop new products and services.— Abbr. R & D.

reservation of rights. See NONWAIVER AGREEMENT.

reserve, *n.* Something retained or stored for future use; esp., a fund of money set aside by a bank or an insurance company to cover future liabilities.

> **bad-debt reserve.** A reserve to cover losses on uncollectible accounts receivable.

> **legal reserve.** The amount of liquid assets that a bank or an insurance company must

maintain in order to meet depositors' or claimants' demands.

mean reserve. In insurance, the average of the beginning reserve (after the premium has been paid for the policy year) and the ending reserve of the policy year.

required reserve. The minimum amount of money, as required by the Federal Reserve Board, that a bank must hold in the form of vault cash and deposits with regional Federal Reserve Banks.

sinking-fund reserve. A reserve used to pay long-term debt. See SINKING FUND.

reserve bank. See *member bank* under BANK.

reserve ratio. The Federal Reserve Board's measurement of a member bank's required reserves. See *required reserve* under RESERVE.

primary reserve ratio. The ratio between a bank's required reserves (cash in vault plus deposits with Federal Reserve Banks) and its demand and time deposits.

secondary reserve ratio. The ratio between a bank's government securities and its demand and time deposits.

resident agent. See *registered agent* under AGENT.

residual. 1. The profit on a sale. **2.** The cash available after the refinancing of an investment.

residual value. The value of an asset after depreciation charges have been deducted from the original cost. See DEPRECIATION.

resolution. A formal expression of an official body's opinion or decision <the corporate resolution declared a stock dividend>.

Resolution Trust Corporation. A federal agency established to act as a receiver for insolvent federal savings-and-loan associations and to transfer or liquidate those associations' assets. • The agency was created when the Federal Savings and Loan Insurance Corporation was abolished in 1989.—Abbr. RTC.

RESPA (**res**-pə). *abbr.* REAL ESTATE SETTLEMENT PROCEDURES ACT.

respondeat superior (ri-**spon**-dee-at-sə-peer-ee-**or**). [Latin "let the master respond"] The common-law doctrine holding an employer or principal liable for the employee's or agent's actions (including torts) committed within the scope of employment. See SCOPE OF EMPLOYMENT.

514

respondent bank. See BANK.

restitution. 1. Return or restoration of some specific thing or condition. **2.** Compensation for benefits derived from a wrong done to another. **3.** Compensation or reparation for the loss caused to another.

restraint of trade. In antitrust law, an agreement between or combination of businesses intended to eliminate competition, create a monopoly, artificially raise prices, or otherwise adversely affect the free market. ● Restraints of trade are usu. illegal, but may be declared reasonable if they are in the best interests of both the parties and the public. See PER SE RULE; RULE OF REASON.

horizontal restraint. A restraint of trade imposed by agreement between competitors at the same level of distribution. ● The restraint is horizontal not because it has horizontal effects, but because it is the product of a horizontal agreement.

vertical restraint. A restraint of trade imposed by agreement between firms at different levels of distribution (as between manufacturer and retailer).

restricted security. See SECURITY.

restrictive covenant. See COVENANT (2).

restrictive indorsement. See INDORSEMENT.

resulting trust. See TRUST.

retail, *n.* The sale of goods or commodities to ultimate consumers, as opposed to the sale for further distribution or processing. Cf. WHOLE-SALE.

retailer. A person or entity engaged in the business of selling personal property to the public or to consumers, as opposed to selling to those who intend to resell the items.

retail installment contract. See CONTRACT.

retainage (ri-**tay**-nij). A percentage of what a landowner pays a contractor, withheld until the construction has been satisfactorily completed and all mechanic's liens are released or have expired.

retained earnings. See EARNINGS.

retaliatory eviction. See EVICTION.

retaliatory law. A state law restraining another state's businesses—as by levying taxes—in response to similar restraints imposed by the second state on the first state's businesses.

retaliatory tariff. See TARIFF.

retired stock. See *treasury stock* under STOCK.

retirement. 1. Voluntary termination of one's own employment or career, esp. upon reaching a certain age <she traveled around the world after her retirement>. **2.** Withdrawal from circulation; payment of a debt <retirement of a series of bonds>. See REDEMPTION (3).

retirement plan. A benefit plan—such as a pension plan or Keogh plan—provided by an employer (or a self-employed person) for an employee's retirement.

return, *n*. **1.** See TAX RETURN <file your return before April 15>. **2.** Yield or profit <return on an investment>. See RATE OF RETURN.

revaluation. An increase in the value of one currency in relation to another currency. Cf. DEVALUATION.

revaluation surplus. See SURPLUS.

revenue. Gross income or receipts from a given source.

   marginal revenue. The amount of revenue earned from the sale of one additional unit.

revenue bond. See BOND (1).

Revenue Procedure. An official published statement by the IRS regarding the administration and procedures of the tax laws.—Abbr. Rev. Proc.

Revenue Ruling. An official interpretation by the IRS of the proper application of the tax law to a specific transaction. • Revenue Rulings carry some authoritative weight and may be relied on by the taxpayer.—Abbr. Rev. Rul.

revenue tariff. See TARIFF.

reverse annuity mortgage. See MORTGAGE.

reverse discrimination. See DISCRIMINATION.

reverse stock split. See STOCK SPLIT.

reverse triangular merger. See MERGER.

revocable trust. See TRUST.

revocation (rev-ə-**kay**-shən). **1.** An annulment, cancellation, or reversal, usu. of an act or power. **2.** In contract law, withdrawal of an offer by the offeror.

revolver loan. See LOAN.

revolving credit. See CREDIT.

revolving fund. See FUND (1).

Rev. Proc. *abbr*. REVENUE PROCEDURE.

Rev. Rul. *abbr*. REVENUE RULING.

RICO. *abbr*. RACKETEER INFLUENCED AND CORRUPT ORGANIZATIONS ACT.

rigging the market. The practice of artificially inflating stock prices, by a series of bids, so that the demand for those stocks appears to be high and investors will therefore be enticed into buying the stocks. See MANIPULATION.

right of action. 1. The right to bring a specific case to court. **2.** A right that can be enforced by legal action. Cf. CAUSE OF ACTION.

right of dissent and appraisal. See APPRAISAL REMEDY.

right of first refusal. A potential buyer's contractual right to meet the terms of a third party's offer if the seller intends to accept that offer. ● For example, if Beth has a right of first refusal on the purchase of Sam's house, and if Sam intends to accept Terry's offer to buy the house for $300,000, Beth can match this offer and prevent Terry from buying it. Cf. RIGHT OF PREEMPTION.

right of preemption. A potential buyer's contractual right to have the first opportunity to buy, at a specified price, if the seller chooses to sell. ● For example, if Beth has a right of preemption on Sam's house for five years at $100,000, Sam can either keep the house for five years (in which case Beth's right expires) or, if he wishes to sell during those five years, offer the house to Beth, who can either buy it for $100,000 or refuse to buy, but if she refuses, Sam can sell to someone else.—Also termed *first option to buy*. Cf. RIGHT OF FIRST REFUSAL.

right of redemption. See EQUITY OF REDEMPTION.

rights offering. See OFFERING.

right-to-work law. A state law that prevents labor-management agreements requiring a person to join a union as a condition of employment. See OPEN SHOP; CLOSED SHOP.

risk, *n*. **1.** The hazard of property loss covered by an insurance contract, or the degree of such a hazard.—Also termed *peril*. **2.** A person or thing that an insurer considers a hazard.

    absorbable risk. A potential loss that a corporation believes that it can cover either with available capital or with self-insurance.

risk arbitrage. See ARBITRAGE.

risk capital. See CAPITAL.

risk management. A business's plan for the reduction of losses caused by unpredictable events.

risk of loss. The danger or possibility that a party will have to bear the costs and expenses for the damage, destruction, or inability to locate goods or other property.

Robinson-Patman Act. A federal statute (specifically, an amendment to the Clayton Act) prohibiting price discrimination that hinders competition or tends to create a monopoly. See ANTITRUST LAW; CLAYTON ACT.

rolling over. 1. The extending or renewing of a short-term loan for another term. **2.** The transfer of funds, esp. retirement-plan funds, from one type of investment to another.

Roth IRA. See INDIVIDUAL RETIREMENT ACCOUNT.

round lot. See LOT.

royalty. 1. A payment made to an author or inventor for each copy of a work or article sold under a copyright or patent. **2.** A share of the

product or profit from real property, reserved
by the grantor of a mineral lease, in exchange
for the lessee's right to mine or drill on the
land.

RTC. *abbr.* RESOLUTION TRUST CORPORATION.

Rule 10b–5. The SEC rule that prohibits deceptive or manipulative practices (such as material misrepresentations or omissions) in the
buying or selling of securities.

rule of 72. A method for determining how
many years it takes to double money invested
at a compound interest rate. ● For example, at
a compound rate of 6%, it takes 12 years (72
divided by 6) for principal to double.

rule of 78. A method for computing the
amount of interest that a borrower saves by
paying off a loan early, when the interest
payments are higher at the beginning of the
loan period. ● For example, to determine how
much interest is saved by prepaying a
12-month loan after 6 months, divide the sum
of the digits for the remaining six payments
(21) by the sum of the digits for all twelve
payments (78) and multiply that percentage by
the total interest.

rule of marshaling assets. An equitable doctrine that requires a senior creditor, having

two or more funds to satisfy its debt, to first dispose of the fund not available to a junior creditor. ● It prevents the inequity that would result if the senior creditor could choose to satisfy its debt out of the only fund available to the junior creditor and thereby exclude the junior creditor from any satisfaction.

rule of marshaling liens. See INVERSE-ORDER-OF-ALIENATION DOCTRINE.

rule of reason. In antitrust law, the judicial doctrine holding that a trade practice violates the Sherman Act only if the practice is an unreasonable restraint of trade, based on economic factors. Cf. PER SE RULE.

running account. See ACCOUNT.

S

safe-deposit box. A lockbox stored in a bank's vault and used by a customer to secure valuables. ● It usu. takes two keys (one held by the bank and one held by the customer) to open the box.—Also termed *safety-deposit box*.

safe harbor. A provision (as in a statute or regulation) that affords protection from liability or penalty. ● SEC regulations, for example, provide a safe harbor for an issuer's business forecasts that are made in good faith.

salable (**say**-lə-bəl), *adj.* Fit for sale in the usual course of trade at the usual selling price.

sale. 1. The transfer of property for a price. **2.** The agreement by which such a transfer takes place. ● The four elements are (1) parties competent to contract, (2) mutual assent, (3) a thing capable of being transferred, and (4) a price in money paid or promised.

> ***bootstrap sale. a.*** A sale in which the purchase price is financed by earnings and profits of the thing sold; esp., a leveraged buyout. See BUYOUT. **b.** A seller's tax-saving conversion of a business's ordinary income into a capital gain from the sale of corporate stock.

> ***bulk sale.*** See BULK TRANSFER.

cash sale. **a.** A transaction that calls for cash payment and delivery usu. on the same day. **b.** A securities transaction on the stock-exchange floor requiring cash payment and same-day delivery.

conditional sale. **a.** A sale in which the buyer gains immediate possession but the seller retains title until the buyer performs a condition, esp. payment of the full purchase price. **b.** A sale accompanied by an agreement to resell upon specified terms.

consignment sale. A sale of an owner's property (such as clothing or furniture) by a third party entrusted to make the sale.

credit sale. A sale of goods to a buyer who is allowed to pay for the goods at a later time.

distress sale. **a.** A form of liquidation in which the seller receives less for the goods than what would be received under normal sales conditions; esp., a going-out-of-business sale. **b.** A foreclosure or tax sale.

documentary sale. A sale in which the buyer pays upon the seller's tender of documents of title covering the goods, plus a sight draft requiring the buyer to pay "at sight." • This type of sale typically occurs before delivery of the goods, which might be en route when the buyer pays.

execution sale. A forced sale of a debtor's property by a government official carrying out a writ of execution.—Also termed *forced sale*; *sheriff's sale*.

forced sale. **a.** See *execution sale.* **b.** A hurried sale by a debtor because of financial hardship or a creditor's action.

foreclosure sale. The sale of mortgaged property authorized by court decree or a power-of-sale clause, the proceeds of which are used to satisfy the debt. See DEFICIENCY JUDGMENT.

installment sale. A conditional sale in which the buyer makes a down payment followed by periodic payments and the seller retains the title until all payments have been received.

isolated sale. An infrequent or one-time sale that does not carry an implied warranty of merchantability.

judicial sale. A sale conducted under the authority of a judgment or court order, such as an execution sale.

lumping sale. A court-ordered sale in which several distinct pieces of property are sold together for a single sum.

memorandum sale. A conditional sale in which the buyer takes possession but does not accept title until he or she approves the property.

sale and leaseback. See LEASEBACK.

sale as is. A sale in which the buyer must accept the property in its existing condition unless the seller has misrepresented its quality.

sale in gross. A sale of a tract of land made with no guarantee about the exact amount or size of the land being sold.

sale on approval. A sale whose completion hinges on the buyer's satisfaction, regardless of whether the goods conform to the contract. • Title and risk of loss remain with the seller until the buyer approves.

sale or return. A sale in which the buyer may return the goods to the seller, regardless of whether they conform to the contract, if the goods were delivered primarily for resale. • This transaction is a type of consignment in which the seller (usu. a distributor) sells goods to the buyer (often a retailer), who then tries to resell the goods, but a buyer who cannot resell is allowed to return them to the seller. Title and risk of loss are with the buyer until the goods are returned.—Also termed *sale and return*.

sale with right of redemption. A sale in which the seller reserves the right to retake the goods by refunding the purchase price.

short sale. A sale of a security that the seller does not possess or has not contracted for at the time of sale, and that the seller must borrow to make delivery. ● Such a sale is usu. made when the seller expects the security's price to drop. If the price does drop, the seller can make a profit on the difference between the price of the shares sold and the lower price of the shares bought to pay back the borrowed shares.

short sale against the box. A short sale of a security by a seller who owns enough shares of the security to cover the sale but borrows shares anyway because the seller wants to keep ownership a secret or because the owned shares are not easily accessible. ● Delivery may be made with either the owned or the borrowed shares, so it is less risky than an ordinary short sale. The phrase *against the box* refers to the owned shares that are in safekeeping; formerly, the "box" was a container used to store stock certificates.

simulated sale. A contrived sale lacking consideration and intended to put property beyond the reach of creditors.

wash sale. The simultaneous, or nearly simultaneous, selling and buying of the same asset, esp. stock, by the same person to create the impression of market activity. See MANIPULATION.

sale and return. See *sale or return* under SALE.

sale note. See NOTE.

sale on approval. See SALE.

sale or return. See SALE.

sales load. See LOAD.

sales price. See PRICE.

sales tax. See TAX.

sale with right of redemption. See SALE.

salvage loss. See LOSS.

salvage value. The value of an asset after it has become useless to the owner. ● Salvage value is used, under some depreciation methods, to determine the allowable tax deduction for depreciation.

S & L. *abbr.* SAVINGS-AND-LOAN ASSOCIATION.

SAR. *abbr.* STOCK-APPRECIATION RIGHT.

satisfaction. 1. The giving of something with the intention, express or implied, that it is to extinguish some existing legal or moral obligation. ● Satisfaction differs from performance because it is always something given as a substitute for or equivalent of something else, while performance is the identical thing promised to be done. **2.** The fulfillment of an obligation; esp., the payment in full of a debt. See ACCORD AND SATISFACTION. **3.** See SATISFACTION PIECE.

satisfaction piece. A written statement that one party (esp. a debtor) has discharged its obligation to another party, who accepts the discharge.—Also termed *satisfaction*.

saving clause. See SEVERABILITY CLAUSE.

savings-and-loan association. A financial institution—often organized and chartered like a bank—that is designed primarily to make home-mortgage loans but that also usu. maintains checking accounts and provides other banking services.—Abbr. *S & L.*—Also termed *thrift institution*; *thrift.* Cf. BUILDING-AND-LOAN ASSOCIATION.

savings bank. See BANK.

savings bond. See BOND (1).

savings note. See NOTE.

SBA. *abbr.* SMALL BUSINESS ADMINISTRATION.

scab. A person who works under conditions contrary to a union contract; esp., a worker who crosses a union picket line to replace a union worker during a strike.

scale order. See ORDER.

scalping. **1.** The purchase of a security by an investment adviser before recommending that customers buy the same security. • This practice is usu. considered unethical because the customers' purchase will increase the security's price, thus enabling the investment adviser to sell at a profit. **2.** The excessive markup or markdown on a transaction by a market-maker. • This action violates NASD guidelines. **3.** The practice of selling something (esp. a ticket) at a price above face value once it becomes scarce (usu. just before a high-demand event begins).

schedule, *n.* A written list or inventory; esp., a statement that is attached to a document and that details various matters referred to in the document <Schedule B to the title policy lists the encumbrances on the property>.

scheduled injury. See INJURY.

scope of employment. The range of reasonable and foreseeable activities that an employee engages in while carrying out the employer's business. See RESPONDEAT SUPERIOR.

scorched-earth defense. An antitakeover device by which a target corporation sells its most valuable assets or divisions, or otherwise destroys the character of the corporation, in order to defeat the bidder's tender offer. See CROWN JEWEL.

S corporation. See CORPORATION.

scrip. 1. A document that entitles the holder to receive something of value. **2.** Paper money issued for temporary use.

scrip dividend. See DIVIDEND.

seal, *n.* An impression or sign that has legal consequence when applied to an instrument.

   corporate seal. A seal adopted by a corporation for executing and authenticating its corporate and legal instruments.

   public seal. A seal that is used to certify documents belonging to a public authority or government bureau.

sealed bid. See BID.

sealed contract. See *contract under seal* under CONTRACT.

seasonable, *adj.* Within the time agreed upon; within a reasonable time <seasonable performance of the contract>.

SEC. *abbr.* SECURITIES AND EXCHANGE COMMISSION.

secondary boycott. See BOYCOTT.

secondary market. See MARKET.

secondary meaning. A special sense that a trademark or tradename for a business, goods, or services has acquired even though the trademark or tradename was not originally protectable.—Also termed *trade meaning*.

secondary obligation. See OBLIGATION.

secondary offering. See OFFERING.

secondary reserve ratio. See RESERVE RATIO.

secondary strike. See STRIKE.

secondary trading. The buying and selling of securities in the market between members of the public, usu. involving neither the issuer nor the underwriter of the securities.

second mortgage. See MORTGAGE.

secretary. A corporate officer in charge of official correspondence, minutes of meetings, and records of stock ownership and transfer.

secretary of state. A state government official who is responsible for the licensing and incorporation of businesses, the administration of elections, and other formal duties.

secured bond. See BOND (1).

secured claim. See CLAIM (4).

secured creditor. See CREDITOR.

secured debt. See DEBT.

secured loan. See LOAN.

secured note. See NOTE.

secured transaction. A business arrangement by which a buyer or borrower gives collateral to the seller or lender to guarantee payment of an obligation. See SECURITY AGREEMENT.

Securities Act of 1933. The federal securities act regulating the initial public offering of securities, with an emphasis on full public disclosure.—Also termed *Securities Act*; *1933 Act*.

Securities and Exchange Commission. The federal agency that regulates the issuance and trading of securities in an effort to protect investors against fraudulent or unfair practices.—Abbr. SEC.

securities exchange. 1. A facility for the organized purchase and sale of securities, esp. stocks. **2.** A group of individuals and entities that are members of such a facility.—Often shortened to *exchange*.—Also termed *stock exchange*.

> *regional securities exchange.* A securities exchange that focuses on stocks and bonds of local interest, such as the Boston, Philadelphia, and Midwest stock exchanges.

Securities Exchange Act of 1934. The federal securities act regulating the public trading of securities. • This statute provides for the registration and supervision of securities exchanges and brokers, and regulates proxy solicitations. The Act also established the SEC.—Also termed *Exchange Act*; *1934 Act*.

security, *n.* **1.** Collateral given or pledged to guarantee the fulfillment of an obligation. **2.** An instrument that evidences the holder's ownership rights in a firm (e.g., a stock), the holder's creditor relationship with a firm or government (e.g., a bond), or the holder's other rights (e.g., an option). • A security indicates an interest based on an investment in a common enterprise rather than direct participation in the enterprise.

adjustment security. A stock or bond that is issued during a corporate reorganization. • The security holders' relative interests are readjusted during this process.

certificated security. A security that is a recognized investment vehicle, belongs to or is divisible into a class or series of shares, and is represented on an instrument payable to the bearer or a named person.

collateral security. A security, subordinate to and given in addition to a primary security, that is intended to guarantee the validity or convertibility of the primary security.

conversion security. The security into which a convertible security may be converted, usu. common stock.

convertible security. A security (usu. a bond or preferred stock) that may be exchanged by the owner for another security, esp. common stock from the same company, and usu. at a fixed price on a specified date.

coupon security. A security with attached interest coupons that the holder may present for payment as they mature. • Coupon securities are usu. in denominations of $1,000, and they are negotiable.

debt security. A security representing funds borrowed by the corporation from the holder of the debt obligation; esp., a bond, note, or debenture. • Generally, a debt security is any security that is not an equity security. See BOND.

equity security. A security representing an ownership interest in the corporation, such as a share of stock, rather than a debt interest, such as a bond; any stock or similar security, or any security that is convertible into stock or similar security or carrying a warrant or right to subscribe to or purchase stock or a similar security, and any such warrant or right.

exempt security. A security that is not required to be registered under the provisions of the Securities Act of 1933 and is exempt from the margin requirements of the Securities Exchange Act of 1934.

government security. A security whose principal or interest is guaranteed by the government or its agents.—Also termed *agency security*.

high-grade security. A security issued by a company of sound financial condition and having the ability to maintain good earnings (e.g., a utility-company security).

hybrid security. A security with features of both a debt instrument (such as a bond) and an equity interest (such as a share of stock). • An example of a hybrid security is a convertible bond, which can be exchanged for shares in the issuing corporation and is subject to stock-price fluctuations.

listed security. A security accepted for trading on a securities exchange. • The issuing company must have met the SEC's registration requirements and complied with the rules of the particular exchange. See DE-LISTING.

long-term security. **a.** A new securities issue with an initial maturity of ten years or more. **b.** On a balance sheet, a security with a remaining maturity of one year or more.

low-grade security. A security with low investment quality. • Low-grade securities usu. offer higher yields to attract capital. See *junk bond* under BOND.

marginable security. A security that can be bought on margin. See MARGIN.

margined security. A security that is bought on margin and that serves as collateral in a margin account. See MARGIN.

marketable security. A security that the holder can readily sell on a stock exchange or an over-the-counter market.

noncallable security. A security that cannot be redeemed, or bought back, at the issuer's option.

pass-through security. A security that passes through payments from debtors to investors. ● Pass-through securities are usu. assembled and sold in packages to investors by private lenders who deduct a service fee before passing the principal and interest payments through to the investors. See COLLATERALIZED MORTGAGE OBLIGATION.

public security. A negotiable or transferable security that is evidence of government debt.

redeemable security. Any security, other than a short-term note, that, when presented to the issuer, entitles the holder to receive a share of the issuer's assets or the cash equivalent.—Also termed *callable security*.

539

registered security. **a.** A security with the owner's name printed on the face of the certificate. ● The issuer keeps a record of the current owners for purposes of sending checks, proxies, and the like.—Also termed (depending on the type of security) *registered stock*; *registered bond*. **b.** A security that was registered with the SEC at the time of its initial sale, or was later sold publicly in accordance with SEC rules.—Also termed *registered stock*.

restricted security. A security that is not registered with the SEC and therefore may not be sold publicly unless specified conditions are met. ● A restricted security is usu. acquired in a nonpublic transaction in which the buyer gives the seller a letter stating the buyer's intent to hold the security as an investment rather than resell it.

short-term security. A bond or note that matures and is payable within a brief period (usu. less than one year).

speculative security. A security that, as an investment, involves a risk of loss greater than would be involved in an ordinary investment; esp., a security whose value depends on proposed or promised future promotion or development, rather than on present tangible assets or conditions.

unlisted security. An over-the-counter security that is not registered with a stock exchange.—Also termed *unlisted stock*.

voting security. See *voting stock* under STOCK.

when-issued security. A security that can be traded even though it has not yet been issued. • Any transactions that take place do not become final until the security is issued.

zero-coupon security. A security (esp. a bond) that is issued at a large discount but that pays no interest.

security agreement. An agreement that creates or provides for an interest in specified real or personal property to guarantee the performance of an obligation.

security interest. A property interest created by agreement or by operation of law to secure performance of an obligation (esp. repayment of a debt). • Although the UCC limits the creation of a security interest to personal property, the Bankruptcy Code defines the term to mean "a lien created by an agreement."

purchase-money security interest. A security interest that is created when a buyer uses the lender's money to make the purchase and immediately gives the lender security; a security interest that is either (1) taken or retained by the seller of the collateral to secure all or part of its price, or (2) taken by a person who by making advances or incurring an obligation gives value to enable the debtor to acquire rights in or the use of collateral if that value is in fact so used. • If a buyer's purchase of a boat, for example, is financed by a bank that loans the purchase price paid to the seller, the bank's security interest in the boat that secures the loan is a purchase-money security interest.—Abbr. PMSI.

security rating. 1. The system for grading or classifying a security by financial strength, stability, or risk. • Firms such as *Standard and Poor's* and *Moody's* grade securities. **2.** The classification that a given security is assigned to under this system.

seed money. Start-up money for a business venture.—Also termed *front-end money*.

self-dealing. Participation in a transaction that benefits oneself instead of another who is owed a fiduciary duty. • For example, a corporate director might engage in self-dealing by participating in a competing business to the corporation's detriment.

self-employed retirement plan. See KEOGH PLAN.

self-employment tax. See TAX.

self-insurance. See INSURANCE.

seller's market. See MARKET.

selling agent. The real-estate broker's representative who sells the property, as opposed to the agent who lists the property for sale. Cf. LISTING AGENT.

senior lien. See LIEN.

senior mortgage. See MORTGAGE.

senior partner. See PARTNER.

sequestration (see-kwes-**tray**-shən). The seizure, under court order, of a defendant's property either to satisfy a debt or to preserve the property until trial.

serial bond. See BOND (1).

serial note. See *installment note* under NOTE.

series bonds. See BOND (1).

service, *vb.* **1.** To provide service for <the copy machine needed to be serviced>. **2.** To pay interest on <service a debt>. **3.** To perform services for <the firm focused on servicing its new clients>.

servicemark. A name, phrase, or other device used to identify and distinguish the services of a certain provider. ● Servicemarks identify and afford protection to intangible things such as services, as distinguished from the protection already provided for marks affixed to tangible things such as goods and products. Cf. TRADE-MARK (1).

setoff, *n*. A debtor's right to reduce the amount of a debt by any sum the creditor owes the debtor; the counterbalancing sum owed by the creditor.

settlement. 1. An agreement to end a dispute or lawsuit <the parties reached a settlement the day before trial>. **2.** Payment, satisfaction, or final adjustment <the seller shipped the goods after confirming the buyer's settlement of the account>. **3.** A real-estate closing <the settlement on their first home is next Friday>. See CLOSING.

settlement sheet. See CLOSING STATEMENT.

settlement statement. See CLOSING STATE-MENT.

severability clause. A provision that keeps the remaining provisions of a contract in force if any portion of that contract is judicially declared void.—Also termed *saving clause*. See *severable contract* under CONTRACT.

severable contract. See CONTRACT.

several liability. See LIABILITY.

severance pay. Money (apart from back wages or salary) paid by an employer to an employee who is dismissed. ● Such a payment is often made in exchange for a release of any claims that the employee might have against the employer.

severance tax. See TAX.

sex discrimination. See DISCRIMINATION.

sexual harassment. A type of employment discrimination consisting in verbal or physical abuse of a sexual nature.

　hostile-environment sexual harassment. Sexual harassment in which a work environment is created where an employee is subject to unwelcome verbal or physical sexual behavior that is either severe or pervasive. ● This type of harassment might occur, for example, if a group of coworkers repeatedly e-mailed pornographic pictures to a colleague who found the pictures offensive.

quid-pro-quo sexual harassment. Sexual harassment in which the satisfaction of a sexual demand is used as the basis of an employment decision. • This type of harassment might occur, for example, if a boss fired or demoted an employee who refused to go on a date with the boss.

SF. See SINKING FUND under FUND (1).

S/F. *abbr.* STATUTE OF FRAUDS.

share, *n.* **1.** An allotted portion owned by, contributed by, or due to someone <Sean's share of the partnership's profits>. **2.** One of the definite number of equal parts into which the capital stock of a corporation or joint-stock company is divided <the broker advised her customer to sell the stock shares when the price reached $29>. • A share represents an ownership interest in the corporation or joint-stock company or in its equity.

share acquisition. The acquisition of a corporation by purchasing all or most of its outstanding shares directly from the shareholders. Cf. ASSET ACQUISITION.

share certificate. See STOCK CERTIFICATE.

shared-equity mortgage. See MORTGAGE.

share draft. See DRAFT.

shareholder. One who owns or holds a share or shares in a company, esp. a corporation.— Also termed (in a corporation) *stockholder*. Cf. STAKEHOLDER (3).

> *controlling shareholder.* A shareholder who is in a position to influence the corporation's activities because the shareholder either owns a majority of outstanding shares or owns a smaller percentage but a significant number of the remaining shares are widely distributed among many others.

> *dummy shareholder.* A shareholder who owns stock in name only for the benefit of the true owner, whose identity is generally concealed.

> *majority shareholder.* A shareholder who owns or controls more than half the corporation's stock.

> *minority shareholder.* **a.** Generally, a shareholder who owns less than half the total shares outstanding. **b.** A shareholder who holds such a small percentage of the total shares outstanding that he or she cannot control the corporation's management or singlehandedly elect directors.

547

shareholder derivative suit. See DERIVATIVE ACTION.

shareholder oppression. See OPPRESSION (2).

shareholder proposal. A proposal by one or more corporate stockholders to change company policies or procedures. • Ordinarily, the corporate managers inform all stockholders about the proposal before the next shareholder meeting.

shareholders' equity. See OWNERS' EQUITY.

shareholder voting agreement. See POOLING AGREEMENT.

shark repellent. A measure taken by a corporation to discourage hostile takeover attempts. • Examples include issuing new shares of stock, acquiring expensive assets, and adopting a poison-pill defense.—Also termed *takeover defense*. See POISON PILL. Cf. PORCUPINE PROVISION.

shelf issue. See ISSUE.

shelf registration. See REGISTRATION.

shell corporation. See CORPORATION.

shelter, *n.* See TAX SHELTER <the shelter saved the taxpayer over $2,000 in taxes>.

shelter doctrine. In commercial law, the rule providing that a person to whom a holder in due course has transferred commercial paper, as well as any later transferees, will succeed to the rights of the holder in due course. • As a result, transferees of holders in due course are generally not subject to most defenses against the payment of an instrument. This doctrine ensures the free transferability of commercial paper. Its name derives from the idea that the transferees "take shelter" in the rights of the holder in due course.

sheriff's sale. See *execution sale* under SALE.

Sherman Antitrust Act. A federal statute, passed in 1890, that prohibits direct or indirect interference with the freely competitive interstate movement of goods. • This Act was amended by the Clayton Act in 1914.—Often shortened to *Sherman Act*.

shingle theory. In securities law, the notion that a broker-dealer must be held to a high standard of conduct because by the very act of engaging in the securities business ("hanging out a shingle"), the broker-dealer implicitly represents to the world that the conduct of all its employees will be fair and meets professional norms.

shipper. 1. One who ships goods to another. 2. One who tenders goods to a carrier for transportation.

shipping document. Any paper that covers a shipment in trade, such as a bill of lading or letter of credit.

shop steward. See STEWARD.

short-form merger. See MERGER.

short sale. See SALE.

short sale against the box. See SALE.

short-swing profits. Profits made by an insider on the purchase and sale (or sale and purchase) of company stock within a six-month period. ● These profits are subject to being returned to the company.

short-term debt. See DEBT.

short-term security. See SECURITY.

short-term trading. Investment in securities only to hold them long enough to take profit from market-price fluctuations.

shrinkage. The reduction in inventory caused by theft, breakage, or waste.

shrink-wrap license. See LICENSE.

sight draft. See DRAFT.

signatory (**sig**-nə-tor-ee). A party that signs a document, personally or through an agent, and thereby becomes a party to an agreement <eight companies are signatories to the agreement>.

signature. 1. A person's name or mark written by that person or at his or her direction. 2. In commercial law, any name, mark, or writing used with the intention of authenticating a document.

signature loan. See LOAN.

silent partner. See PARTNER.

simple contract. See *parol contract* (b) under CONTRACT.

simple interest. See INTEREST.

simple trust. See TRUST.

simulated sale. See SALE.

single-name paper. A negotiable instrument signed by only one maker and not backed by a surety.

sinking fund. See FUND (1).

sinking-fund bond. See BOND (1).

sinking-fund debenture. See DEBENTURE.

sinking-fund depreciation method. See DE-PRECIATION METHOD.

sinking-fund reserve. See RESERVE.

sister corporation. See CORPORATION.

sit-down strike. See STRIKE.

slander, *n.* **1.** A defamatory statement expressed in a transitory form, esp. speech. ● Unlike damages from libel, damages from slander are not presumed and thus must be proved by the plaintiff (unless the defamation is slander per se). **2.** The act of making such a statement. See DEFAMATION. Cf. LIBEL.

SLAPP. *abbr.* Strategic Lawsuit Against Public Participation—a suit brought by a developer, corporate executive, or elected official to stifle those who protest against some type of high-dollar initiative or who take an adverse

552

position on a public-interest issue (often involving the environment).—Also termed *SLAPP suit*.

SLC. *abbr*. SPECIAL LITIGATION COMMITTEE.

sleeper. A potentially strong security that is underpriced and lacks public interest.

slush fund. Money that is set aside for undesignated purposes, often corrupt ones.

Small Business Administration. A federal agency that assists and protects the interests of small businesses, often by making low-interest loans.—Abbr. SBA.

smart money. Funds held by sophisticated, usu. large investors who are considered capable of minimizing risks and maximizing profits <the smart money has now left this market>.

soft dollars. **1.** In the securities industry, the credits that brokers give their clients in return for the clients' stock-trading business. **2.** The portion of an equity investment that is tax-deductible in the first year. Cf. HARD DOLLARS.

soft market. See MARKET.

solemnity of contract. The concept that two people may enter into any contract they wish and that the resulting contract is enforceable if formalities are observed and no defenses exist.

sole proprietorship. A form of business in which one person owns all the assets, owes all the liabilities, and conducts affairs in his or her own capacity, often under an assumed name.

solicitation. 1. The act or an instance of seeking to obtain something; a request or petition. **2.** An attempt or effort to gain business.

solicitation of bids. See INVITATION TO NEGOTIATE.

solicitor. 1. A person who seeks business or contributions from others; an advertiser or promoter. **2.** A person who conducts matters on another's behalf; an agent or representative.

solvency. The ability to pay debts as they come due. Cf. INSOLVENCY (1).

S–1. An SEC form that a company usu. must file before listing and trading its securities on a national exchange. ● Used primarily by first-time issuers of securities, this form is the basic, full-length registration statement that requires a great deal of information about the issuer and the securities being sold. The SEC also has adopted modified forms for smaller enterprises, such as Forms SB–1 and SB–2.

SPE. *abbr.* SPECIAL-PURPOSE ENTITY.

special agency. See AGENCY.

special agent. See AGENT.

special assessment. See ASSESSMENT.

special-circumstances rule. See SPECIAL-FACTS RULE.

special contract. See CONTRACT.

special deposit. See DEPOSIT.

special-facts rule. In corporate law, the principle that a director or officer has a fiduciary duty to disclose material inside information to a shareholder when engaging in stock transactions under special circumstances, as when the shareholder lacks business acumen, the shares are closely held with no readily ascertainable market value, or the director or officer instigated the transaction. ● This is an exception to the "majority rule."—Also termed *special-circumstances rule*. Cf. MAJORITY RULE.

special indorsement. See INDORSEMENT.

specialist. A securities-exchange member who makes a market in one or more listed securities. ● The exchange assigns securities to various specialists and expects them to maintain a fair and orderly market as provided by SEC standards.

special letter of credit. See LETTER OF CREDIT.

special litigation committee. In corporate law, a committee of independent corporate directors assigned to investigate the merits of a shareholder derivative suit and, if appropriate, to recommend maintaining or dismissing the suit.—Abbr. SLC.—Also termed *independent investigation committee*; *authorized committee*. See DERIVATIVE ACTION.

special meeting. See MEETING.

special offering. See OFFERING.

special-purpose entity. A business established to perform one function, usu. for the purpose of facilitating a transaction by limiting the number of creditors the business will have. ● This is often required by lenders funding single-purpose and other large, complex projects. A special-purpose entity, which is usu. permitted to perform no function other than to develop, own, and operate the project, is established to limit the number of creditors who will have an interest in the entity's business. This provides additional protection for project lenders, which are usu. paid solely out of the money generated by the entity's business, because there will be fewer competing claims for that money and because the entity will be less likely to be forced into bankruptcy. A special-purpose entity will sometimes issue securities instead of just receiving a direct loan.—Abbr. SPE.—Also termed *special-purpose vehicle* (SPV). See BANKRUPTCY-REMOTE ENTITY.

special-tax bond. See BOND (1).

special trust. See *active trust* under TRUST.

special warranty deed. See DEED.

specific performance. A court-ordered remedy that requires precise fulfillment of a legal or contractual obligation when monetary damages are inappropriate or inadequate, as when the sale of real estate or rare articles is involved.

specific remedy. See REMEDY.

speculation. The buying or selling of something with the expectation of profiting from price fluctuations <he engaged in speculation in the stock market>.

speculative security. See SECURITY.

speculator. A knowledgeable, aggressive investor who trades securities to profit from fluctuating market prices.

spendthrift trust. See TRUST.

spin-off, *n.* **1.** A corporate divestiture in which a division of a corporation becomes an independent company and stock of the new company is distributed to the original corporation's shareholders. **2.** The corporation created by this divestiture. Cf. SPLIT-OFF; SPLIT-UP.

split-off, *n.* **1.** The creation of a new corporation by an existing corporation that gives its shareholders stock in the new corporation in return for their stock in the original corporation. **2.** The corporation created by this process. Cf. SPIN-OFF; SPLIT-UP.

split-up, *n.* The division of a corporation into two or more new corporations. • The shareholders in the original corporation typically receive shares in the new corporation, and the original corporation goes out of business. Cf. SPIN-OFF; SPLIT-OFF.

spread, *n*. **1.** The difference between the interest rate that a financial institution must pay to attract deposits and the rate at which money can be loaned. **2.** The difference between the highest price a buyer is willing to pay for a security (the *bid price*) and the lowest price at which a seller is willing to sell a security (the *asked price*). **3.** The simultaneous buying and selling of one or more options or futures contracts on the same security in order to profit from the price difference. **4.** The difference between the price the underwriter pays the issuer of the security and the price paid by the public in the initial offering.

spread eagle. See STRADDLE.

SPV. *abbr*. Special-purpose vehicle. See SPE-CIAL-PURPOSE ENTITY.

squeeze-out, *n*. An action taken in an attempt to eliminate or reduce the minority interest in a corporation. Cf. FREEZE-OUT.

staggered board of directors. See BOARD OF DIRECTORS.

stakeholder. 1. One who holds the money or valuables placed as bets when people are wagering. **2.** A disinterested third party who holds money or property, the right or possession of which is disputed between two other parties. **3.** A member of a group having an interest (or stake) in a company's actions, though not as owners. • In this sense, *stakeholder* is opposed to *shareholder*. Cf. SHAREHOLDER.

stale check. See CHECK.

stamp tax. See TAX.

standard deduction. See DEDUCTION.

standard mortgage clause. See MORTGAGE CLAUSE.

standard policy. See INSURANCE POLICY.

standby commitment. An arrangement between an underwriter and an issuer of securities whereby the underwriter agrees, for a fee, to buy any unsold shares remaining after the public offering.—Also termed *standby underwriting agreement*. See *standby underwriting* under UNDERWRITING.

standby letter of credit. See LETTER OF CREDIT.

standby underwriting. See UNDERWRITING.

standby underwriting agreement. See STANDBY COMMITMENT.

state bank. See BANK.

stated capital. See CAPITAL.

stated interest rate. See *nominal rate* under INTEREST RATE.

stated value. See PAR VALUE.

statement of financial affairs. In bankruptcy, a document that an individual or corporate debtor must file to answer questions about its past and present financial status.

statement of financial position. See BALANCE SHEET.

statute. A law passed by a legislative body.

statute of frauds. A statute designed to prevent fraud and perjury by requiring certain contracts to be in writing and signed by the parties. • Statutes of frauds traditionally apply to the following types of contracts: (1) a contract for the sale or transfer of an interest in land, (2) a contract that cannot be performed within one year of its making, (3) a contract for the sale of goods valued at $500 or more, (4) a contract of an executor or administrator to answer for a decedent's debt, (5) a contract to guarantee the debt or duty of another, and

(6) a contract made in consideration of marriage.—Abbr. S/F.

statute of limitations. A statute establishing a time limit for suing or for prosecuting a crime, based on the date when the claim accrues (usu. when the injury occurs). • The purpose of such a statute is to require diligent prosecution of known claims, thereby providing finality and predictability in legal affairs and ensuring that claims will be resolved while evidence is reasonably available and fresh.

statutory agent. See AGENT.

statutory right of redemption. The right of a mortgagor in default to recover property after a foreclosure sale by paying the principal, interest, and other costs that are owed, together with any other measure required to cure the default. • This statutory right exists in many states but is not uniform.

stay, *n.* **1.** The postponement or halting of a proceeding, judgment, or the like. **2.** An order to suspend all or part of a judicial proceeding or judgment resulting from that proceeding.

    automatic stay. In bankruptcy law, a bar to all judicial and extrajudicial collection efforts against the debtor or the debtor's property. • The policy behind the automatic stay, which is effective upon the filing of the bankruptcy petition, is that all actions against the debtor should be halted pending the determination of creditors' rights and the orderly administration of the debtor's assets free from creditors' interference.

stepped-up basis. See BASIS.

steward. **1.** A person appointed in place of another. **2.** A union official who represents union employees and who oversees the carrying out of union contracts.—Also termed (in sense 2) *shop steward.*

stickering. The practice of updating an SEC registration statement to account for material changes. ● The prospectus supplement is termed a "sticker," hence the name for this practice. See REGISTRATION STATEMENT.

stock, *n.* **1.** A merchant's goods that are kept for sale or trade <the car dealer put last year's models on sale to reduce its stock>. **2.** The capital or principal fund raised by a corporation through subscribers' contributions or the sale of shares <Acme's stock is worth far more today than it was 20 years ago>. **3.** A proportional part of a corporation's capital, represented by the number of units (or shares) that one owns, and granting the holder the right to participate in the company's general management and to share in its net profits or earnings <Julia sold her stock in Pantheon Corporation>.

authorized stock. The total number of shares of stock that the charter or articles of incorporation permit a corporation to sell. • A corporation may increase the amount of authorized stock if a majority of the outstanding shares consent.—Also termed *authorized shares*.

blue-chip stock. See BLUE CHIP.

bonus stock. A stock share that is issued for no consideration, as an enticement to buy some other type or class of security. • It is considered a type of watered stock.—Also termed *bonus share*.

book-value stock. Stock offered to executives at a book-value price, rather than at its market value. • The stock is offered with the understanding that when its book value has risen, the company will buy back the stock at the increased price or will make payments in stock equal to the increased price.

capital stock. **a.** The total amount of stock authorized for issuance by a corporation, including common stock and preferred stock. **b.** The total par value or stated value of this stock.

common stock. Ownership shares in a corporation entitling the holder to vote and to
receive dividends after other claims and dividends have been paid (esp. to preferred
shareholders). • Common stock is often
called *capital stock* if it is the corporation's
only class of stock outstanding.

corporate stock. An equity security issued
by a corporation.

cumulative preferred stock. Preferred
stock that must pay dividends in full before
common shareholders may receive any dividend. • If the corporation passes a dividend
in a particular year or period, it is carried
over to the next year or period and must be
paid before the common shareholders receive any payment.

deferred stock. Stock whose dividends are
paid only after the corporation meets some
other specified obligation, such as the discharge of a liability or the payment of a
dividend to preferred shareholders.

discount stock. A stock share issued for
less than par value. • Discount stock is
considered a type of watered stock, the issuance of which may impose liability on the
recipient for the difference between the par
value and the cash amount paid.—Also
termed *discount share.*

full-paid stock. Stock on which no further payments can be demanded by the issuing company.

glamour stock. A stock with great public interest because of a real or imagined potential for fast growth or high earnings.—Also termed *performance stock*.

inactive stock. A low-volume stock.

income stock. A stock with a history of high yields or dividend incomes (e.g., public utilities and well-established corporations).

nonassessable stock. Stock owned by a holder whose potential liability is limited to the amount paid for the stock and who cannot be charged additional funds to pay the issuer's debts. • Stock issued in the United States is usu. nonassessable.

noncumulative preferred stock. Preferred stock that does not have to pay dividends that are in arrears. • Once a period's dividends are passed, they will not be paid.

nonparticipating preferred stock. Preferred stock that does not give the shareholder the right to additional earnings—usu. surplus common-stock dividends—beyond those stated in the preferred contract.

nonvoting stock. Stock that has no voting rights attached to it under most situations.

no-par stock. Stock issued without a specific value assigned to it. • For accounting purposes, it is often given a legal or stated value that has little or no connection to the stock's market value.

outstanding stock. Stock that is held by an investor and has not been redeemed by the issuing corporation.

participating preferred stock. Preferred stock whose holder is entitled to priority in receiving stated dividends or in sharing with the common shareholders in any additional distributions of earnings.

penny stock. An equity security that is not traded in established markets or that has average revenues of less than specified amounts. • Generally, a penny stock is highly speculative and can be purchased for under $5 a share.

phantom stock. Imaginary stock that is credited to a corporate executive's account as part of the executive's compensation package.

preferred stock. Stock that gives its holders a preferential claim to dividends and to corporate assets upon liquidation but that usu. carries no voting rights.

public stock. **a.** See *public security* under SECURITY. **b.** Stock of a publicly traded corporation.

registered stock. See *registered security* under SECURITY.

restricted stock. See *restricted security* under SECURITY.

treasury stock. Stock issued by a company but then reacquired and either canceled or held. • Some states have eliminated this classification and treat such stock as if it is authorized but unissued.—Also termed *retired stock.*

unissued stock. Stock that is authorized by the corporate charter but not yet distributed.

unlisted stock. See *unlisted security* under SECURITY.

voting stock. Stock that entitles the holder to vote in the corporation's election of its officers and on other matters put to a vote.—Also termed *voting security.*

watered stock. Stock issued for no or little consideration, usu. in exchange for overvalued property or services.

whisper stock. The stock of a company that is rumored to be the target of a takeover attempt.

stock-appreciation right. (*usu. pl.*) A right, typically granted in tandem with a stock option, to be paid the option value (usu. in cash) when exercised along with the simultaneous cancellation of the option.—Abbr. SAR.

stock bonus plan. A special type of profit-sharing plan in which the distribution of benefits is in the form of the employer-company's own stock.

stockbroker. One who buys or sells stock as agent for another.

stock certificate. An instrument evidencing ownership of a bond or shares of stock.—Also termed *share certificate*.

stock clearing. The actual physical delivery of money and stocks between buyer and seller.

stock clearing corporation. A New York Stock Exchange subsidiary that is a central agency for securities deliveries and payments between member firms.

stock corporation. See CORPORATION.

stock dividend. See DIVIDEND.

stock exchange. See SECURITIES EXCHANGE.

stockholder. See SHAREHOLDER.

stock insurance company. An insurance company operated as a private corporation and owned by stockholders who share in the company's profits and losses. Cf. MUTUAL INSURANCE COMPANY.

stockjobber. See JOBBER (2).

stockjobbing, *n.* The business of dealing in stocks or shares; esp., the buying and selling of stocks and bonds by jobbers who operate on their own account.—Also termed *stockjobbery*.

stock market. See MARKET (4) & (5).

stock merger. See MERGER.

stock option. 1. An option to buy or sell stock at a designated price for a specified period regardless of shifts in market value during the period. **2.** An option that allows a corporate employee to buy shares of corporate stock at a fixed price. • Such an option is usu. granted as a form of compensation and can qualify for special tax treatment under the Internal Revenue Code.—Also termed (in sense 2) *incentive stock option*; *employee stock option*.

stock-parking. See PARKING (2).

stock redemption. See REDEMPTION (3).

stock split. The issuing of two or more new shares for each old share without changing the proportional ownership interests of each shareholder. • For example, a 3–for–1 split would give an owner of 100 shares a total of 300 shares, or 3 shares for each share previously owned. A stock split lowers the price per share and thus makes the stock more attractive to potential investors.

> *reverse stock split.* A reduction in the number of a corporation's shares by calling in all outstanding shares and reissuing fewer shares having greater value.

stock subscription. See SUBSCRIPTION (2).

stock swap. See SWAP.

stock-transfer agent. See AGENT.

stock warrant. SUBSCRIPTION WARRANT.

stop-loss order. See *stop order* under ORDER.

stop order. 1. See ORDER. **2.** An SEC order that suspends a registration statement containing false, incomplete, or misleading information. **3.** A bank customer's order instructing the bank not to honor one of the customer's checks.—Also termed (in sense 3) *stop-payment order*.

straddle, *n.* A situation in which an investor holds contracts to buy and to sell the same security or commodity, thus ensuring a loss on one of the contracts. ● The aim of this strategy is to defer gains and use losses to offset other taxable income.—Also termed *spread eagle*.

straight annuity. See ANNUITY.

straight bankruptcy. See CHAPTER 7.

straight bill of lading. See BILL OF LADING.

straight life annuity. See *nonrefund annuity* under ANNUITY.

straight-line depreciation method. See DEPRECIATION METHOD.

straight voting. See *noncumulative voting* under VOTING.

strategic alliance. A coalition formed by two or more persons in the same or complementa-

ry businesses to gain long-term financial, operational, and marketing advantages without
jeopardizing   competitive   independence
<through their strategic alliance, the manu-
facturer and distributor of a co-developed
product shared development costs>. Cf. JOINT
VENTURE; PARTNERSHIP.

straw man. A third party used in some transactions as a temporary transferee so that the
principal parties can accomplish something
that is otherwise impermissible.

street name. The registered name of securities that are held in the name of the broker
instead of in the name of the owner. • A
security is held by a broker in street name (at
the customer's request) to simplify trading because no signature on the stock certificate is
required. A street name may also be used for
securities purchased on margin.

strict foreclosure. See FORECLOSURE.

strict liability. See LIABILITY.

strike, *n*. An organized cessation or slowdown
of work by employees to compel the employer
to meet the employees' demands. Cf. LOCKOUT;
BOYCOTT; PICKETING.

general strike. A strike organized to affect an entire industry.

secondary strike. A strike against an employer because that employer has business dealings with another employer directly involved in a dispute with the union.

sit-down strike. A strike in which employees appear at the workplace but do not work.

wildcat strike. A strike not authorized by a union or in violation of a collective-bargaining agreement.

strike price. See PRICE.

strike suit. See SUIT.

subagent. See AGENT.

subcontract. See CONTRACT.

subcontractor. See CONTRACTOR.

sublease, *n.* A lease by a lessee to a third party, conveying some or all of the leased property for a shorter term than that of the lessee, who retains a reversion in the lease.— Also termed *subtenancy.*

sublessee. A third party who receives by lease some or all of the leased property from a lessee.—Also termed *subtenant*.

sublessor. A lessee who leases some or all of the leased property to a third party.

submortgage. See MORTGAGE.

subordinate debenture. See DEBENTURE.

subordination agreement. An agreement by which one who holds an otherwise senior interest agrees to subordinate that interest to a normally lesser interest, usu. when a seller agrees to subordinate a purchase-money mortgage so that the buyer can obtain a first-mortgage loan to improve the property.

subordination clause. A covenant in a junior mortgage enabling the first lien to keep its priority in case of renewal or refinancing.

subpartnership. See PARTNERSHIP.

subpoena (sə-**pee**-nə), *n.* A court order commanding the appearance of a witness, subject to penalty for noncompliance. Pl. **subpoenas.**

subpoena duces tecum (doo-səs-**tee**-kəm *or* -**tay**-kəm). A subpoena ordering the witness not only to appear but also to bring specified books, papers, or records.

subrogation (səb-rə-**gay**-shən), *n.* **1.** The substitution of one party for another whose debts the party pays, entitling the paying party to rights, remedies, or securities that would otherwise go to the debtor. ● For example, a surety who has paid on the principal debtor's debt is entitled to subrogation to all the securities held by the creditor and to any judgment in which the debt has been merged, and the surety may enforce those securities and rights against the debtor in any way in which the creditor might have enforced them. **2.** The principle under which an insurer that has paid the loss under an indemnity policy is entitled to take on all the rights and remedies belonging to the insured against a third party with respect to any injuries or breaches covered by the policy.

subrogee (səb-rə-**jee**). One who is substituted for another in having a right, duty, or claim. ● Insurance companies frequently become subrogees after paying a policy claim, as a result of which they are then in a position to sue a tortfeasor who injured the insured or otherwise caused damages.

subrogor (səb-rə-**gor**). One who allows another to be substituted for oneself as creditor, with a transfer of rights and duties.

subscribed capital. See CAPITAL.

subscription. **1.** The act of signing one's name on a document; the signature so affixed. **2.** In securities law, a written contract to purchase newly issued shares of stock or bonds.— Also termed (in connection with stock) *stock subscription*. **3.** An oral or written agreement to contribute a sum of money or property, gratuitously or with consideration, to a specific person or for a specific purpose.

subscription price. The price at which investors can buy shares in a new stock offering before the shares are offered to the public.

subscription right. A certificate evidencing a shareholder's right to purchase newly issued stock before the stock is offered to the public. • Subscription rights have a market value and are actively traded because they allow the holder to purchase stock at favorable prices. See PREEMPTIVE RIGHT.

subscription warrant. An instrument granting the holder a long-term (usu. a five- to ten-year) option to buy shares at a fixed price. • It is commonly attached to preferred stocks or bonds.—Also termed *stock warrant*.

subsidiary corporation. See CORPORATION.

substantial-certainty test. In copyright law, the test for deciding whether a second work was copied from the first. • The question is whether a reasonable observer would conclude with substantial certainty that the second work is a copy.

substantial-performance doctrine. The equitable rule that, if a good-faith attempt to perform does not precisely meet the terms of the agreement, the agreement will still be considered complete if the substantial purpose of the contract is accomplished. • Courts may allow a remedy for minimal damages caused by the deviance.

substantial similarity. In copyright law, a strong resemblance between a copyrighted work and an alleged infringement, thereby creating an inference of unauthorized copying. • The standard for substantial similarity is whether an ordinary person would conclude that the alleged infringement has appropriated nontrivial amounts of the copyrighted work's expressions.

substituted basis. See BASIS.

substitutional remedy. See REMEDY.

subtenancy. See SUBLEASE.

subtenant. See SUBLESSEE.

succession. The right by which one group, in replacing another group, acquires all the goods, movables, and other chattels of a corporation.

successor. A corporation that, through amalgamation, consolidation, or other assumption of interests, is vested with the rights and duties of an earlier corporation.

successor in interest. One who follows another in ownership or control of property. ● A successor in interest retains the same rights as the original owner, with no change in substance.

suit. Any proceeding by a party or parties against another in a court of law.—Also termed *lawsuit*.

> *blackmail suit.* A suit filed by a party having no genuine claim but hoping to extract a favorable settlement from a defendant who would rather avoid the expenses and hassles of litigation.

> *strike suit.* A derivative action, usu. based on no valid claim, brought either for nuisance value or to obtain a settlement.

suitor. A corporation or individual who offers to buy the corporation's voting stock in order to take over the corporation.

sum certain. 1. Any amount that is fixed, settled, or exact. **2.** In negotiable instruments, a sum that is agreed on in the instrument or a sum that can be ascertained from the document.

sum–of–the–years' –digits depreciation method. See DEPRECIATION METHOD.

sunk cost. See COST.

Superfund. 1. The program that funds and administers the cleanup of hazardous-waste sites through a trust fund (financed by taxes on petroleum and chemicals and a new tax on corporations) created to pay for cleanup pending reimbursement from the liable parties. **2.** The popular name for the act that established this program—the Comprehensive Environmental Response, Compensation, and Liability Act of 1980 (CERCLA). See CERCLA.

superpriority. In bankruptcy, the special priority status granted by the court to a creditor for extending credit to a debtor or trustee that cannot obtain unsecured credit from a willing lender. • This priority may be either an administrative claim outranking other adminis-

trative claims or, if certain statutory requirements are met, a security interest in property.

supplier. A person engaged, directly or indirectly, in the business of making a product
available to consumers.

supply, *n.* The amount of goods produced or
available at a given price.

  aggregate supply. The total amount of
  goods and services generated in an economy
  during a specific period.

supply curve. A line on a price-output graph
showing the relationship between a good's
price and the quantity supplied at a given
time.

surcharge. 1. An additional tax, charge, or
cost, usu. one that is excessive. **2.** An additional load or burden. **3.** A second or further
mortgage. **4.** The omission of a proper credit
on an account.

surety (**shuur**[-ə]-tee). **1.** A person who is
primarily liable for the payment of another's
debt or the performance of another's obligation. • Although a surety is similar to an
insurer, one important difference is that a
surety often receives no compensation for assuming liability. A surety differs from a guar-

581

antor, who is liable to the creditor only if the debtor does not meet the duties owed to the creditor; the surety is directly liable. Cf. GUAR-ANTOR. **2.** A formal assurance; esp., a pledge, bond, guarantee, or security given for the fulfillment of an undertaking.

surety bond. See *performance bond* under BOND (2).

suretyship. 1. The legal relation that arises when one party assumes with a second the liability for a debt, default, or other failing of that second party. ● The liability of both parties begins simultaneously. **2.** The lending of credit to aid a principal who does not have sufficient credit. ● The purpose is to guard against loss if the principal debtor were to default. **3.** The position or status of a surety.

surplus. 1. The excess of receipts over disbursements. **2.** Funds that remain after a partnership has been dissolved and all its debts paid. **3.** A corporation's net worth beyond the par value of capital stock.

  acquired surplus. The surplus gained by the purchase of another business.

  earned surplus. See *retained earnings* under EARNINGS.

paid-in surplus. The surplus gained by the sale, exchange, or issuance of capital stock at a price above par value.—Also termed *capital surplus*.

revaluation surplus. Surplus that is gained when assets are reappraised at a higher value.—Also termed *appreciation surplus*.

surplus earnings. See EARNINGS.

surplus revenue. See *appropriated retained earnings* under EARNINGS.

surrender, *n.* In commercial law, the delivery of an instrument so that the delivery releases the deliverer from all liability.

surrender value. See CASH SURRENDER VALUE.

surtax. See TAX.

surviving partner. See PARTNER.

survivorship annuity. See ANNUITY.

swap, *n.* An exchange of one security for another.

currency swap. An agreement to swap specified payment obligations denominated in one currency for specified payment obligations denominated in a different currency.

stock swap. In a corporate reorganization, an exchange of one corporation's stock for another corporation's stock.

sweat equity. Financial equity created in property by the owner's labor in improving the property <the lender required the homeowner to put 300 hours of sweat equity into the property>. Cf. EQUITY (2).

symbolic delivery. See DELIVERY.

syndicalism (**sin**-di-kə-liz-əm). A direct plan or practice implemented by trade-union workers seeking to control the means of production and distribution, esp. by using a general strike.

syndicate (**sin**-di-kət), *n.* A group organized for some common purpose; esp., an association formed to promote a common interest, carry out some particular business transaction, or (in a negative sense) organize criminal enterprises.

synthetic lease. See LEASE.

T

tacking. The joining of a junior lien with the first lien in order to acquire priority over an intermediate one.

Taft-Hartley Act. See LABOR-MANAGEMENT RELATIONS ACT.

take-or-pay contract. See CONTRACT.

takeover. The acquisition of ownership or control of another corporation. ● A corporate takeover is typically accomplished by a purchase of shares or assets, a tender offer, or a merger.

> *friendly takeover.* A takeover that is favored or approved by the target corporation's board of directors.

> *hostile takeover.* A takeover that is resisted by the target corporation's board of directors.

takeover bid. An attempt by an outside corporation or group to wrest control away from the incumbent management of a target corporation.

takeover defense. See SHARK REPELLENT.

takeover offer. See TENDER OFFER.

TAM. *abbr*. TECHNICAL ADVICE MEMORANDUM.

tangible property. See PROPERTY.

target corporation. See CORPORATION.

tariff, *n*. **1.** A schedule or system of duties imposed by a government on imported or exported goods. ● In the U.S., tariffs are imposed on imported goods only. **2.** A duty imposed on imported or exported goods under such a system.

   protective tariff. A tariff designed primarily to give domestic manufacturers economic protection against price competition from abroad, rather than to generate revenue.

   retaliatory tariff. A tariff imposed to pressure another country into removing its own tariffs or making trade concessions.

   revenue tariff. A tariff enacted solely or primarily to raise revenue.

tax, *n*. A monetary charge imposed by the government on persons, entities, or property to yield public revenue. ● Most broadly, the term embraces all governmental impositions on the person, property, privileges, occupations, and enjoyment of the people, and includes duties, imposts, and excises.

accumulated-earnings tax. A penalty tax imposed on a corporation that has retained its earnings in an effort to avoid the income-tax liability arising once the earnings are distributed to shareholders as dividends.

ad valorem tax. [Latin "according to value"] A tax imposed proportionally on the value of something (esp. real property), rather than on its quantity or some other measure.

alternative minimum tax. A flat tax potentially imposed on corporations and high-income individuals to ensure that those taxpayers do not fully avoid income-tax liability by using exclusions, deductions, and credits.

capital-gains tax. A tax on income derived from the sale of a capital asset. ● The federal income tax on capital gains typically has a more favorable maximum tax rate—now 28% for individuals and 34% for corporations—than the maximum tax rate on ordinary income. See CAPITAL GAIN.

capital-stock tax. A tax on capital stock in the hands of a stockholder.

estimated tax. A tax paid quarterly by taxpayers not subject to withholding (such as self-employed persons) based on either the previous year's tax liability or an estimation of the current year's tax liability.

excise tax. A tax imposed on the manufacture, sale, or use of goods (such as a cigarette tax), or on an occupation or activity (such as a license tax).

flat tax. A tax in which the tax rate remains fixed regardless of the amount of the tax base. • Most sales taxes are flat taxes.

franchise tax. A state tax imposed on the privilege of carrying on a business (esp. as a corporation), usu. measured by the business's income.

gift tax. A tax imposed when property is voluntarily and gratuitously transferred. • Under federal law, the gift tax is imposed on the donor, but some states tax the donee.

hidden tax. A tax that is unknowingly paid by someone other than the person or entity on whom it is levied; esp., a tax imposed on a manufacturer or seller (such as a gasoline producer) who passes it on to consumers in the form of higher sales prices.

income tax. A tax on an individual's or entity's net income. • The federal income tax—governed by the Internal Revenue Code—is the federal government's primary source of revenue, and many states have income taxes as well.

luxury tax. An excise tax imposed on high-priced items that are not necessities (such as cars costing more than a specified amount).

occupation tax. An excise tax imposed on persons for the privilege of carrying on a business, trade, or profession. • For example, many states require lawyers to pay an occupation tax.

payroll tax. **a.** A tax owed by an employer on its payroll (such as social-security tax and unemployment tax). **b.** A tax collected by an employer from its employees' paychecks (such as income tax and social-security tax).

progressive tax. A tax structured so that the tax rate increases as the tax base increases. • Most income taxes are progressive, meaning that those with higher income pay at a higher rate.

property tax. A tax levied on the owner of property (esp. real property), usu. based on the property's value. • Local governments often impose property taxes to finance school districts, municipal projects, and the like.

regressive tax. A tax structured so that the tax rate decreases as the tax base increases. • A flat tax (such as the typical sales tax) is usu. considered regressive—despite its constant rate—because it is more burdensome for low-income taxpayers than high-income taxpayers.

sales tax. A tax imposed on the sale of goods and services, usu. measured as a percentage of their price.

self-employment tax. The social-security tax imposed on the net earnings of a self-employed person.

severance tax. A tax imposed on the value of oil, gas, timber, or other natural resources extracted from the earth.

stamp tax. A tax imposed by requiring the purchase of revenue stamps that must be affixed to legal documents (such as deeds or notes) before the documents can be recorded.

surtax. An additional tax imposed on the thing being taxed or on the primary tax itself.

use tax. A tax imposed on the use of certain goods that are bought outside of the taxing authority's jurisdiction. • Use taxes are designed to discourage the purchase of products that are not subject to the sales tax.

value-added tax. A tax assessed at each step in the production process of a commodity, based on the value added at each step by the difference between the commodity's production cost and its selling price. • Value-added taxes—which are popular in several European countries—effectively act as a sales tax on the ultimate consumer.—Abbr. VAT.

withholding tax. A portion of income tax that is deducted from salary, wages, dividends, or other income before the earner receives payment. • The most common example is the income tax and social-security tax withheld by an employer from an employee's paycheck.

taxable, *adj.* Subject to taxation <interest earned on a checking account is taxable income>.

taxable income. See INCOME.

tax-anticipation bill. A short-term obligation issued by the U.S. Treasury to meet the cash-flow needs of the government. • Corporations can tender these bills at par value to make quarterly tax payments.

taxation. The imposition or assessment of a tax; the means by which the state obtains the revenue essential to its activities.

double taxation. **a.** The imposition of two taxes on the same property during the same period and for the same taxing purpose. **b.** The imposition of two taxes on one corporate profit; esp., the structure of taxation employed by Subchapter C, under which corporate profits are first taxed to the corporation when earned and also taxed to the shareholders when the earnings are distributed as dividends. See *C corporation* under CORPORATION. **c.** In international law, the imposition of comparable taxes in two or more countries on the same taxpayer for the same subject matter or identical goods.

pass-through taxation. The taxation of an entity's owners for the entity's income without taxing the entity itself. ● Partnerships and S corporations are taxed under this method.

tax audit. See AUDIT.

tax avoidance. The act of taking advantage of legally available tax-planning opportunities in order to minimize one's tax liability. Cf. TAX EVASION.

tax base. The total property, income, or wealth subject to taxation in a given jurisdiction. Cf. BASIS.

tax basis. See BASIS.

tax-benefit rule. The principle that if a taxpayer recovers a loss or expense that was deducted in a previous year, the recovery must be included in the current year's gross income to the extent that it was previously deducted.

tax bracket. A categorized level of income subject to a particular tax rate under federal or state law <28% tax bracket>.

tax credit. An amount subtracted directly from one's total tax liability, dollar for dollar, as opposed to a deduction from gross income. Cf. DEDUCTION.

child- and dependent-care tax credit. A tax credit available to a person who is employed full-time and who maintains a household for a dependent child or a disabled spouse or dependent.

earned-income credit. A refundable federal tax credit on earned income of low-income workers with dependent children. ● The credit is paid to the taxpayer even if it exceeds the total tax liability.

foreign tax credit. A tax credit against U.S. income taxes for taxpayers who earn income overseas and have paid foreign taxes on that income. See FOREIGN-EARNED-INCOME EXCLUSION.

tax deduction. See DEDUCTION.

tax-deferred annuity. See ANNUITY.

tax evasion. The willful attempt to defeat or circumvent the tax law in order to minimize one's tax liability. • Tax evasion is punishable by both civil and criminal penalties.—Also termed *tax fraud*. Cf. TAX AVOIDANCE.

tax-exempt, *adj.* **1.** Not legally subject to taxation <a tax-exempt charity>. **2.** Bearing interest that is free from income tax <tax-exempt municipal bonds>.—Also termed *tax-free*.

tax-exempt bond. See BOND (1).

tax fraud. See TAX EVASION.

tax lease. See *leveraged lease* under LEASE.

tax liability. The amount that a taxpayer legally owes after multiplying his or her tax base by the applicable tax rate; the amount of unpaid taxes.

taxpayer. One who pays or is subject to a tax.

tax rate. The proportion at which a tax base is taxed, usu. expressed as a percentage.

average tax rate. A rate calculated by dividing tax liability by taxable income.

marginal tax rate. In a progressive-tax scheme, the rate applicable to the last dollar of income earned by the taxpayer. • This concept is useful in calculating the tax effect of additional income or deductions. See TAX BRACKET.

tax return. An income-tax form on which a person or entity reports income, deductions, and exemptions, and on which tax liability is calculated.—Often shortened to *return*.—Also termed *income-tax return*.

amended return. A return filed after the original return, usu. to correct an error in the original.

consolidated return. A return that reflects the combined financial interests of a group of affiliated corporations.

false return. A return on which taxable income is incorrectly reported or the tax is incorrectly computed.

information return. A return filed by an entity to report some economic information other than tax liability, such as a W–2.

tax shelter, *n.* A financial operation or investment strategy (such as a partnership or real-estate investment trust) that is created primarily for the purpose of reducing or deferring income-tax payments. • The Tax Reform Act of 1986—by restricting the deductibility of passive losses—sharply limited the effectiveness of tax shelters.—Often shortened to *shelter.*

tax year. The period used for computing federal or state income-tax liability, usu. either the calendar year or a fiscal year of 12 months ending on the last day of a month other than December.

T-bill. *abbr.* TREASURY BILL.

T-bond. *abbr.* TREASURY BOND.

technical adjustment. A brief change (e.g., rally) in the direction of stock-market-price trends if it contradicts the general trend.

Technical Advice Memorandum. A publication issued by the national office of the IRS, usu. at a taxpayer's request, to explain some complex or novel tax-law issue.—Abbr. TAM.

temporary frustration. See FRUSTRATION.

temporary insider. See INSIDER.

tenant. One who pays rent for the temporary use and occupation of another's land under a lease or similar arrangement. See LESSEE.

tender, *n.* **1.** An unconditional offer of money or performance to satisfy a debt or obligation <a tender of delivery>. ● The tender may save the tendering party from a penalty for nonpayment or nonperformance or may, if the other party unjustifiably refuses the tender, place the other party in default. **2.** An offer or bid put forward for acceptance <a tender for the construction contract>. **3.** Something that serves as a means of payment, such as coin, bank notes, or other circulating medium; money <legal tender>.

tender offer. A public offer to buy a specified number of shares from a corporation's shareholders at a fixed price, usu. at a substantial premium over the market price and usu. in an attempt to take control of the corporation.—Also termed *takeover offer*.

   cash tender offer. A tender offer in which the bidder corporation offers to pay cash for the target's shares, as opposed to offering its own shares in exchange. ● Most tender offers involve cash.

597

creeping tender offer. The gradual purchase of a corporation's stock at varying prices in the open market. • This takeover method does not involve a formal tender offer, although the SEC may classify it as such for regulatory purposes.

10–K. A financial report filed annually with the SEC by registered corporations. • The report typically includes audited financial statements, a description of the corporation's business and financial condition, and summaries of other financial data.

10–Q. An unaudited financial report filed quarterly with the SEC by registered corporations. • The 10–Q is less detailed than the 10–K.

term bond. See BOND (1).

term loan. See LOAN.

thin capitalization. See CAPITALIZATION.

thin corporation. See CORPORATION.

thin market. See MARKET.

third party. One who is not a party to a lawsuit, agreement, or other transaction but who is somehow involved in the transaction;

someone other than the principal parties. See PARTY.

third-party beneficiary. See BENEFICIARY.

third-party equity lease. See *leveraged lease* under LEASE.

third-party insurance. See *liability insurance* under INSURANCE.

thrift institution. See SAVINGS-AND-LOAN ASSOCIATION.

tiered partnership. See PARTNERSHIP.

time arbitrage. See ARBITRAGE.

time deposit. See DEPOSIT.

time draft. See DRAFT.

time note. See NOTE.

tin parachute. An employment-contract provision that grants a corporate employee (esp. one below executive level) severance benefits in the event of a takeover. ● These benefits are typically less lucrative than those provided under a golden parachute. Cf. GOLDEN PARACHUTE.

tip, *n*. A piece of special information; esp., in securities law, advance or inside information passed from one person to another. See INSIDE INFORMATION; INSIDER TRADING.

tippee. In securities law, a person who acquires material nonpublic information from someone who enjoys a fiduciary relationship with the company to which that information pertains.

tipper. In securities law, a person who possesses material inside information and who selectively discloses that information for trading or other personal purposes <the tippee traded 5,000 shares after her conversation with the tipper>.

title. 1. The union of all elements (as ownership, possession, and custody) constituting the legal right to control and dispose of property; the legal link between a person who owns property and the property itself <no one has title to that land>. **2.** Legal evidence of a person's ownership rights in property; an instrument (such as a deed) that constitutes such evidence <title was recorded with the county clerk>.

after-acquired title. See AFTER-ACQUIRED-TITLE DOCTRINE.

bad title. **a.** See *defective title*. **b.** See *unmarketable title*.

clear title. **a.** Title that is free from any encumbrances, burdens, or other limitations. **b.** See *marketable title*.—Also termed *good title*.

defective title. Title that cannot legally convey the property to which it applies, usu. because of some conflicting claim to that property.—Also termed *bad title*.

derivative title. A title that results when an already existing right is transferred to a new owner.

doubtful title. Title that exposes the party holding it to the risk of litigation with an adverse claimant. See *unmarketable title*.

equitable title. Title that indicates a beneficial interest in property and that gives the holder the right to receive formal legal title. Cf. *legal title*.

good title. **a.** Title that is legally valid or effective. **b.** See *clear title* (a). **c.** See *marketable title*.

legal title. Title that evidences apparent ownership but does not necessarily signify full and complete title or a beneficial interest. Cf. *equitable title*.

marketable title. Title that a reasonable buyer would accept because it appears to lack material defects and to cover the entire property that the seller has purported to sell.—Also termed *clear title*; *good title*.

original title. A title that creates a right anew.

paper title. Title supported by a mere series of conveyances rather than by a proper chain of title. See CHAIN OF TITLE.

record title. Title as it appears in the public records after being properly recorded.

unmarketable title. Title that a reasonable buyer would refuse to accept because of possible conflicting interests in or litigation over the property.—Also termed *bad title*.

title company. See COMPANY.

title insurance. See INSURANCE.

title search. An examination of the public records to determine whether any defects or encumbrances exist in a given property's chain of title. ● Title searches are typically conducted by title companies or real-estate lawyers at a prospective buyer's or lender's request.

T-note. See TREASURY NOTE.

tombstone. An advertisement (esp. in a newspaper) for a public securities offering, stating some of the security's details as well as the parties who are selling the issue. ● The term gets its name from the ad's traditional black border and plain print.—Also termed *tombstone ad*. Cf. PROSPECTUS.

tort. **1.** A civil wrong for which a remedy may be obtained, usu. in the form of damages; a breach of a duty that the law imposes on everyone. **2.** (*pl.*) The branch of law dealing with such wrongs.

mass tort. A large number of tort claims with a common cause that has injured many victims. ● Examples include a single-accident disaster, a defective product that injures many people, or environmental contamination at a single site.

prima facie tort. An unjustified, intentional infliction of harm on another person, resulting in damages, by one or more acts that would otherwise be lawful. ● Some jurisdictions have established this tort to provide a remedy for malicious deeds—esp. in business and trade contexts—that are not covered under traditional tort law.

toxic tort. A tort caused by exposure to a toxic substance, such as asbestos, radiation, or hazardous waste. ● Toxic torts can be remedied by civil lawsuits (esp. class actions) or administrative actions.

tortfeasor. One who commits a tort; a wrong-doer.

tortious interference with contractual relations. A third party's intentional induce-ment of a contracting party to break a con-tract, causing damage to the relationship be-tween the contracting parties.

tortious interference with prospective advantage. An intentional, damaging intru-sion on another's potential business relation-ship, such as the opportunity of obtaining cus-tomers or employment.

tort reform. A movement to reduce the amount of tort litigation in the judicial system, usu. involving legislation that restricts legal theories in tort or that caps damage awards (esp. for punitive damages). ● Advocates of tort reform argue that it lowers insurance and healthcare costs, while opponents contend that it denies plaintiffs the recovery they deserve for their injuries.

total breach. See BREACH OF CONTRACT.

total loss. See LOSS.

total repudiation. See REPUDIATION.

Totten trust. See TRUST.

toxic tort. See TORT.

trade acceptance. See ACCEPTANCE.

trade deficit. See DEFICIT.

trade dress. The overall appearance and image of a product (such as its packaging and labeling) or commercial enterprise (such as its design and decor) in the marketplace. • If a trade dress is distinctive and nonfunctional, it may be protected under trademark law.

trade fixture. See FIXTURE.

trade gap. See *trade deficit* under DEFICIT.

trade libel. A false statement that disparages the quality or reputation of another's product or business. See DISPARAGEMENT.

trademark, *n.* **1.** A word, phrase, logo, or other graphic symbol used by a manufacturer or seller to distinguish its products from those of others. • To receive federal protection, a trademark must be (1) distinctive rather than merely descriptive, (2) affixed to a product that is actually sold in the marketplace, and

(3) registered with the U.S. Patent and Trademark Office. Cf. SERVICEMARK. **2.** The body of law dealing with how businesses distinguish their products from those of others. See LANHAM ACT.

trademark infringement. See INFRINGEMENT.

trade meaning. See SECONDARY MEANING.

tradename. 1. A name, style, or symbol used to distinguish a company, partnership, or business (as opposed to a product or service); the name under which a business operates. ● A tradename is a means of identifying a business—or its products or services—and of establishing goodwill. It symbolizes the business's reputation. **2.** A trademark that was not originally susceptible to exclusive appropriation but has acquired a secondary meaning.

trade secret. A formula, process, device, or other business information that is kept confidential in order to maintain an advantage over competitors; information—including a formula, pattern, compilation, program, device, method, technique, or process—that derives independent economic value, actual or potential, from not being generally known to and not being readily ascertainable by proper means by other persons who can obtain economic value from its disclosure or use, and is the subject of efforts that are reasonable under the circumstances to maintain its secrecy.

trade usage. See USAGE.

tranche (transh), *n.* **1.** A bond issue derived from a pooling of similar debt obligations. • A tranche usu. differs from other issues by maturity date or rate of return. **2.** A block of bonds designated for sale in a foreign country.—Also spelled *tranch.* See COLLATERALIZED MORTGAGE OBLIGATION.

transaction. 1. The act or an instance of conducting business or other dealings.

    closed transaction. In tax law, a transaction in which an amount realized on a sale can be established for the purpose of stating a gain or loss.

    colorable transaction. A sham transaction having the appearance of authenticity; a pretended transaction.

2. Something performed or carried out; a business agreement or exchange. **3.** Any activity involving two or more persons.

transaction cost. See COST.

transfer, *n.* **1.** A conveyance of property or title from one person to another. **2.** Any mode of disposing of or parting with an asset or an interest in an asset, including the payment of money, release, lease, or creation of a lien or other encumbrance. • The term embraces every method of disposing of or parting with property or with an interest in property, including retention of title as a security interest and foreclosure of the debtor's equity of redemption. **3.** Negotiation of an instrument according to the forms of law. • The four methods of transfer are by indorsement, by delivery, by assignment, and by operation of law.

transfer agent. See AGENT.

transfer price. See PRICE.

Treasury bill. A short-term debt security issued by the federal government, with a maturity of 13, 26, or 52 weeks. • These bills—auctioned weekly or quarterly—pay interest in the form of the difference between their discounted purchase price and their par value at maturity.—Abbr. T-bill.

Treasury bond. A long-term debt security issued by the federal government, with a maturity of 10 to 30 years. • These bonds are considered risk-free, but they pay relatively little interest.—Abbr. T-bond.

Treasury note. An intermediate-term debt security issued by the federal government, with a maturity of 2 to 10 years. ● These notes are considered risk-free, but they pay relatively little interest.—Abbr. T-note.

Treasury Regulation. A regulation promulgated by the U.S. Treasury Department to explain or interpret a section of the Internal Revenue Code. ● Treasury Regulations are binding on all taxpayers.—Abbr. Treas. Reg.

treasury stock. See STOCK.

treasury warrant. See WARRANT.

treble damages. See DAMAGES.

triangular merger. See MERGER.

trust. 1. The right, enforceable solely in equity, to the beneficial enjoyment of property to which another person holds the legal title; a property interest held by one person (the *trustee*) at the request of another (the *settlor*) for the benefit of a third party (the *beneficiary*). **2.** A fiduciary relationship regarding property and subjecting the person with title to the property to equitable duties to deal with it for another's benefit; the confidence placed in a trustee, together with the trustee's obligations toward the property and the beneficiary. ● A trust arises as a result of a manifestation of an intention to create it. See FIDUCIARY RELATION-SHIP. **3.** The property so held; a trust fund. **4.** A business combination that aims at monopoly. See ANTITRUST.

active trust. A trust in which the trustee has some affirmative duty of management or administration besides the obligation to transfer the property to the beneficiary.— Also termed *special trust.* Cf. *passive trust.*

business trust. A form of business organization, similar to a corporation, in which investors receive transferable certificates of beneficial interest (instead of stock shares).—Also termed *Massachusetts trust.*

constructive trust. A trust imposed by a court on equitable grounds against one who has obtained property by wrongdoing, thereby preventing the wrongful holder from being unjustly enriched. ● Such a trust creates no fiduciary relationship.—Also termed *implied trust.* Cf. *resulting trust.*

express trust. A trust created with the settlor's express intent, usu. declared in writing; an ordinary trust as opposed to a resulting trust or a constructive trust.

investment trust. See *investment company* under COMPANY.

irrevocable trust. A trust that cannot be terminated by the settlor once it is created. • In most states, a trust will be deemed irrevocable unless the settlor specifies otherwise.

life-insurance trust. A trust consisting of one or more life-insurance policies payable to the trust when the insured dies.

liquidating trust. A trust designed to be liquidated as soon as possible. • An example is a trust into which a decedent's business is placed to safeguard the business until it can be sold off.

passive trust. A trust in which the trustee has no duty other than to transfer the property to the beneficiary. Cf. *active trust.*

purchase-money resulting trust. A resulting trust that arises when one person buys property but directs the seller to transfer the property and its title to another. • The buyer is the beneficiary, and the holder is the trustee.

real-estate investment trust. See REAL-ESTATE INVESTMENT TRUST.

resulting trust. A trust imposed by law when someone transfers property under circumstances suggesting that he or she did not intend the transferee to have the benefi-

611

cial interest in the property. Cf. *constructive trust*.

revocable trust. A trust in which the settlor reserves the right to terminate the trust and recover the corpus.

simple trust. **a.** A trust that must distribute all income as it accrues. **b.** See *passive trust*.

spendthrift trust. A trust that prohibits the beneficiary from assigning his or her equitable interest and also prevents a creditor from attaching that interest.

Totten trust. A revocable trust created by one's deposit of money in one's own name as a trustee for another. • Totten trusts are commonly used to indicate a successor to the account without having to create a will.

voting trust. A trust in which corporate shareholders transfer their shares to a trustee for the purpose of creating a voting bloc. • The shareholders still receive dividends under such an arrangement.

trust company. See COMPANY.

trustee (trǝs-**tee**), *n.* **1.** One who, having legal title to property, holds it in trust for the benefit of another and owes a fiduciary duty to that beneficiary. **2.** In bankruptcy law, an officer of the court who is elected by creditors or appointed by a judge to act as the representative of a bankruptcy estate.—Also termed (in sense 2) *bankruptcy trustee*; *trustee in bankruptcy*.

Truth in Lending Act. See CONSUMER CREDIT PROTECTION ACT.

turnkey, *adj*. **1.** (Of a product) provided in a state of being ready for immediate use <a turnkey computer network>. **2.** Of, relating to, or involving a product provided in this manner <a turnkey contract>.

two-tier offer. A two-step technique by which a bidder tries to acquire a target corporation, the first step involving a cash tender offer and the second usu. a merger in which the target company's remaining shareholders receive securities from the bidder (these securities ordinarily being less favorable than the cash given in the first step).

tying arrangement. In antitrust law, an arrangement by which a seller will let a buyer obtain a desired product (the *tying product*) only if the buyer agrees to take an additional product (the *tied product*) that may or may not be desired. ● Tying arrangements may be illegal under the Sherman Act or Clayton Act if their effect is unduly anticompetitive. Cf. RECIPROCAL-DEALING ARRANGEMENT.

U

U3C. *abbr.* UNIFORM CONSUMER CREDIT CODE.

UCC. *abbr.* UNIFORM COMMERCIAL CODE.

UCCC. *abbr.* UNIFORM CONSUMER CREDIT CODE.

ultra vires (əl-trə-**veer**-eez *or* -**vɪ**-reez), *adj.* Unauthorized; beyond the scope of power allowed or granted by a corporate charter or by law <the officer was liable for the firm's ultra vires actions>. Cf. INTRA VIRES.

umbrella-partnership real-estate investment trust. See REAL-ESTATE INVESTMENT TRUST.

umbrella policy. See INSURANCE POLICY.

unconscionability. **1.** Extreme unfairness. **2.** The principle that courts may refuse to enforce contracts that are unfair or oppressive because of procedural abuses during contract formation or because of overreaching contractual terms, esp. terms that are unreasonably favorable to one party while precluding meaningful choice for the other party.

unconscionable (ən-**konsh**-[ə-]nə-bəl), *adj.* **1.** (Of a person) having no conscience; unscrupulous <an unconscionable used-car salesman>. **2.** (Of an act or transaction) showing no regard for conscience; affronting the sense

614

of justice, decency, or reasonableness <the contract is void as unconscionable>. Cf. CON-SCIONABLE.

undercapitalization. See CAPITALIZATION.

underinsurance. See INSURANCE.

under protest. See PROTEST (2).

underwriter. 1. See INSURER. **2.** One who purchases stock from the issuer with an intent to resell it to the public; a person or entity, esp. an investment banker, who guarantees the sale of newly issued securities by purchasing all or part of the shares for resale to the public.

underwriting, *n.* **1.** The act of assuming a risk by insuring it; the insurance of life or property. See INSURANCE. **2.** The act of agreeing to buy all or part of a new issue of securities to be offered for public sale.

best-efforts underwriting. Underwriting whereby an investment banker agrees to direct, but not guarantee, the public sale of the issuer's securities. • The underwriter, or selling group, sells the securities as agent for the issuer, and any unsold securities are never issued.

firm-commitment underwriting. Underwriting whereby the underwriter agrees to purchase all the shares to be issued and remain financially responsible for any securities not purchased. ● The underwriter, or underwriting group, purchases the securities from the issuer and resells as principal. In this type of underwriting, securities that cannot be sold to the public are owned by the underwriter, and the issuer receives funds for those securities as well as the others.

standby underwriting. Underwriting whereby the underwriter agrees, for a fee, to buy from the issuer any unsold shares remaining after the public offering.

undisclosed agency. See AGENCY (1).

undisclosed principal. See PRINCIPAL.

undistributed profit. See *retained earnings* under EARNINGS.

undocumented alien. See *illegal alien* under ALIEN.

undue influence. The improper use of power or trust in a way that deprives a person of free will and substitutes another's objective. ● Consent to a contract, transaction, or relationship is voidable if the consent is obtained through undue influence.

unearned income. See INCOME.

unearned premium. See PREMIUM.

unfair competition. 1. Dishonest or fraudulent rivalry in trade and commerce; esp., the practice of trying to substitute one's own goods or products in the market for those of another by means of imitating or counterfeiting the name, brand, size, shape, or other distinctive characteristic of the article or packaging. **2.** The body of law protecting the first user of such a name, brand, size, shape, or other distinctive characteristic against an imitating or counterfeiting competitor.

unfair labor practice. Any act by a union or employer in violation of the National Labor Relations Act. • Examples include an employer's act that interferes with or restrains the ability of its workers to organize or bargain collectively, and a union's coercion of employers to discriminate against employees.

unfair persuasion. In contract law, a type of undue influence in which a stronger party achieves a result by means that seriously impaired the weaker party's free and competent exercise of judgment. • Unfair persuasion is a lesser form of undue influence than duress and misrepresentation. The two primary factors to be considered are the unavailability of independent advice and the susceptibility of the person persuaded. See UNDUE INFLUENCE.

unifactoral obligation. See OBLIGATION.

Uniform Commercial Code. A uniform law that governs commercial transactions, including sales of goods, secured transactions, and negotiable instruments. • The Code has been adopted in some form by every state.—Abbr. UCC.

Uniform Consumer Credit Code. A uniform law designed to simplify and modernize the consumer credit and usury laws, to further consumer understanding of the terms of credit transactions, to protect consumers against unfair practices, and the like. • This Code has been adopted by only a few states.—Abbr. UCCC; U3C. Cf. CONSUMER CREDIT PROTECTION ACT.

Uniform Deceptive Trade Practices Act. A type of Baby FTC Act that provides monetary and injunctive relief for a variety of unfair and deceptive acts, such as false advertising and disparagement. See BABY FTC ACT.

unilateral contract. See CONTRACT.

unilateral mistake. See MISTAKE.

unincorporated association. See ASSOCIATION.

union. A workers' organization formed to collectively negotiate with employers about such issues as salary, benefits, hours, and working conditions.—Also termed *labor union*.

>   *company union.* **a.** A union whose membership is limited to the employees of a single company. **b.** A union under company domination.

>   *craft union.* A union composed of workers in the same trade or craft, such as carpentry or plumbing, regardless of the industry in which they work.

>   *industrial union.* A union composed of workers in the same industry, such as shipbuilding or automobile manufacturing, regardless of their particular trade or craft.

>   *local union.* A union that serves as the local bargaining unit for a national or international union.

union certification. The determination by the National Labor Relations Board or a state agency that a particular union qualifies as the bargaining unit for a company's or an indus-

619

try's workers because it has the support of a majority of the workers.

union shop. See CLOSED SHOP.

unissued stock. See STOCK.

unit cost. See COST.

unit depreciation method. See DEPRECIATION METHOD.

United States Code Annotated. A multi-volume publication of the complete text of the United States Code (the codification of federal statutory law) with historical notes, cross-references, and casenotes of federal and state decisions construing specific Code sections.— Abbr. USCA.

units-of-output depreciation method. See DEPRECIATION METHOD.

universal agent. See AGENT.

universal partnership. See PARTNERSHIP.

unjust enrichment. **1.** A benefit obtained from another, not intended as a gift and not legally justifiable, for which the beneficiary must make restitution or recompense. **2.** The area of law dealing with unjustifiable benefits of this kind.

unliquidated claim. See CLAIM (2).

unliquidated debt. See DEBT.

unlisted security. See SECURITY.

unlisted stock. See *unlisted security* under SECURITY.

unmarketable title. See TITLE.

unqualified indorsement. See INDORSEMENT.

unrealized loss. See *paper loss* under LOSS.

unrealized profit. See *paper profit* under PROFIT.

unreasonable compensation. See COMPENSATION.

unrelated business income. See INCOME.

unrestrictive indorsement. See INDORSEMENT.

unsecured claim. See CLAIM (4).

unsecured creditor. See CREDITOR.

unsecured debt. See DEBT.

unsecured note. See NOTE.

UPREIT. See *umbrella-partnership real-estate investment trust* under REAL-ESTATE INVESTMENT TRUST.

upset price. See PRICE.

upstreaming. A parent corporation's use of a subsidiary's cash flow or assets for purposes unrelated to the subsidiary.

upstream merger. See MERGER.

usage. A well-known, customary, and uniform practice, usu. in a specific profession or business. See CUSTOM (1).

trade usage. A practice or method of dealing having such regularity of observance in a region, vocation, or trade as to justify an expectation that it will be observed in a given transaction; a customary practice or set of practices relied on by persons conversant in, or connected with, a trade or business.

USCA. *abbr.* UNITED STATES CODE ANNOTATED.

useful life. The estimated length of time that depreciable property will generate income. ● Useful life is used to calculate depreciation and amortization deductions. See DEPRECIATION METHOD.

use tax. See TAX.

usury (**yoo**-zə-ree *or* **yoozh**-[ə-]ree). **1.** Historically, the lending of money with interest. **2.** Today, the charging of an illegal rate of interest. **3.** An illegally high rate of interest.

utility fund. See MUTUAL FUND.

utility patent. See PATENT.

V

valuation. 1. The process of determining the value of a thing or entity. **2.** The estimated worth of a thing or entity.

value, *n*. The monetary worth or price of something; the amount of goods, services, or money that something will command in an exchange.

value-added tax. See TAX.

variable annuity. See ANNUITY.

variable cost. See COST.

variable rate. See INTEREST RATE.

VAT. See *value-added tax* under TAX.

vendor's lien. See LIEN.

venture capital. See CAPITAL.

verification, *n*. **1.** A formal declaration made in the presence of an authorized officer, such as a notary public, by which one swears to the truth of the statements in the document. Cf. ACKNOWLEDGMENT (1). **2.** An oath or affirmation that an authorized officer administers to an affiant or deponent. **3.** See ACKNOWLEDGMENT (2).

vertical integration. See INTEGRATION (2).

vertical merger. See MERGER.

vertical price-fixing. See PRICE-FIXING.

vertical restraint. See RESTRAINT OF TRADE.

vicarious infringement. See INFRINGEMENT.

vindictive damages. See *punitive damages* under DAMAGES.

voidable preference. See PREFERENTIAL TRANS-FER.

voidable promise. See PROMISE.

voluntary bankruptcy. See BANKRUPTCY.

voluntary dissolution. See DISSOLUTION.

voting. The casting of votes for the purpose of deciding an issue.

   class voting. A method of shareholder voting by which different classes of shares vote separately on fundamental corporate changes that adversely affect the rights and privileges of that class.

   cumulative voting. A system for electing corporate directors whereby a shareholder may multiply his or her number of shares by the number of open directorships and cast the total for a single candidate or a select few candidates. • Cumulative voting enhances the ability of minority shareholders to elect at least one director.

majority voting. A system for electing corporate directors whereby each shareholder is allowed one vote for each director, who can win with a simple majority.

noncumulative voting. A corporate voting system in which a shareholder is limited in board elections to voting no more than the number of shares he or she owns for a single candidate. • The result is that a majority shareholder will elect the entire board of directors.—Also termed *straight voting*.

voting agreement. See POOLING AGREEMENT.

voting security. See *voting stock* under STOCK.

voting stock. See STOCK.

voting trust. See TRUST.

voucher. 1. Confirmation of the payment or discharge of a debt; a receipt. **2.** A written or printed authorization to disburse money.

vulture fund. See MUTUAL FUND.

W

wage, *n.* (*usu. pl.*) Payment for labor or services, usu. based on time worked or quantity produced.

> ***minimum wage.*** The lowest hourly rate of compensation for labor, as established by federal statute and required of employers engaged in interstate commerce.

wage-and-hour law. A law, such as the federal Fair Labor Standards Act, governing the minimum wages and maximum working hours for employees.

waiver. 1. The voluntary relinquishment or abandonment—express or implied—of a legal right or advantage <waiver of notice>. ● The party alleged to have waived a right must have had both knowledge of the existing right and the intention of forgoing it. Cf. ESTOPPEL. **2.** The instrument by which a person relinquishes or abandons a legal right or advantage <the plaintiff must sign a waiver when the funds are delivered>.

warehouser. One who, as a business, keeps or stores the goods of another for a fee. ● The transaction that a warehouser engages in is a bailment for the benefit of both parties, and the bailee is liable for ordinary negligence.

warehouse receipt. A document evidencing title to goods stored with someone else. • A warehouse receipt may be a negotiable instrument and is often used for financing with inventory as security. See BAILMENT.

warehouser's lien. See LIEN.

warehousing. **1.** A mortgage banker's holding of mortgages until the resale market improves. **2.** A corporation's giving of advance notice of a tender offer to institutional investors, who can then buy stock in the target company before public awareness of the takeover inflates the stock's price. See TENDER OFFER.

warrant, *n*. **1.** A document conferring authority, esp. to pay or receive money.

treasury warrant. An order in the form of a check on which government disbursements are paid.

2. An order by which a drawer authorizes someone to pay a particular sum of money to another. **3.** See SUBSCRIPTION WARRANT.

warrant, *vb.* **1.** To give warranty of (title); to give warranty of title to (a person) <the seller warrants the property's title to the buyer>. **2.** To promise or guarantee <warrant payment>.

warranty. 1. An express or implied undertaking that something in furtherance of a contract is guaranteed by one of the contracting parties; esp., a seller's undertaking that the thing being sold is as represented or promised.

express warranty. A warranty created by the overt words or actions of the seller.

implied warranty. A warranty arising by operation of law because of the circumstances of a sale, rather than by the seller's express promise.

implied warranty of fitness for a particular purpose. A warranty—implied by law if the seller has reason to know of the buyer's special purposes for the property—that the property is suitable for those purposes.

implied warranty of merchantability. A warranty that the property is fit for the ordinary purposes for which it is used.— Sometimes shortened to *warranty of merchantability.*

limited warranty. A warranty that does not fully cover labor and materials for repairs. ● Under federal law, a limited warranty must be clearly labeled as such on the face of the warranty.

warranty of title. A warranty that the seller or assigner of property has title to that property, that the transfer is rightful, and that there are no liens or other encumbrances that the buyer or assignee was unaware of at the time of contracting. ● This warranty arises automatically whenever anyone sells goods.—Also termed *warranty of actual title*.

2. In insurance law, a pledge or stipulation by the insured that the facts relating to the person insured, the thing insured, or the risk insured are as stated.

warranty deed. See DEED.

warranty of title. See WARRANTY.

wash sale. See SALE.

wasting asset. See ASSET.

watered stock. See STOCK.

waybill. See BILL OF LADING.

wealth maximization. An economic situation in which a change in the allocation of resources benefits the winner—i.e., the one who gains from the allocation—more than it harms the loser.—Also termed *potential Pareto superiority*.

630

wear and tear. Deterioration caused by ordinary use <the tenant is not liable for normal wear and tear to the leased premises>.

when-issued security. See SECURITY.

whisper stock. See STOCK.

whistleblower. An employee who reports employer misconduct to a government or law-enforcement agency. ● Federal and state laws protect whistleblowers from employer retaliation.

white-collar crime. A nonviolent crime usu. involving cheating or dishonesty in commercial matters. ● Examples include fraud, bribery, and insider trading.

white knight. A person or corporation that rescues the target of an unfriendly corporate takeover, esp. by acquiring a controlling interest in the target corporation or by making a competing tender offer.—Also termed *friendly suitor*. See TAKEOVER. Cf. CORPORATE RAIDER.

wholesale, *n.* The sale of goods or commodities usu. for resale by retailers, as opposed to a sale to the ultimate consumer. Cf. RETAIL.

wholesaler. One who buys large quantities of goods and resells them in smaller quantities to retailers or other merchants, who in turn sell to the ultimate consumer.

wildcat strike. See STRIKE.

Williams Act. A federal statute, enacted in 1968, that amended the Securities Exchange Act of 1934 by requiring investors who own more than 5% of a company's stock to furnish certain information to the SEC and to comply with certain requirements when making a tender offer.

winding up, *n.* The process of settling accounts and liquidating assets in anticipation of a partnership's or a corporation's dissolution. Cf. DISSOLUTION (3).

with all faults. See AS IS.

withdrawal. The removal of money from a depository <withdrawal of funds from the checking account>.

withholding, *n.* The practice of deducting a certain amount from a person's salary, wages, dividends, winnings, or other income, usu. for tax purposes; esp., an employer's practice of taking out a portion of an employee's gross earnings and paying that portion to the government for income-tax and social-security purposes.

withholding tax. See TAX.

without recourse, *adv*. (In an indorsement) with no liability to subsequent holders. ● With this stipulation, one who indorses an instrument repudiates any liability to anyone who may later hold the instrument. See *qualified indorsement* under INDORSEMENT.

with recourse, *adv*. (In an indorsement) with liability to subsequent holders. ● With this stipulation, one who indorses an instrument indicates that he or she remains liable to the holder for payment.

workers' compensation. A system of providing benefits to an employee for injuries occurring in the scope of employment. ● Most workers'-compensation statutes hold the employer strictly liable and bar the employee from suing in tort.

work for hire. A copyrightable work produced either by an employee within the scope of employment or by an independent contractor under a written agreement; esp., a work specially ordered or commissioned for use as (1) a contribution to a collective work, (2) a translation, (3) a supplementary work, (4) a part of a movie or other audiovisual work, (5) a compilation, (6) an instructional text, (7) a test, (8) answer material for a test, or (9) an atlas. ● If the work is produced by an independent contractor, the parties must agree expressly in writing that the work will be a work for hire. The employer or commissioning party owns the copyright.

working capital. See CAPITAL.

workout, *n.* **1.** The act of restructuring or refinancing overdue loans. **2.** In bankruptcy law, a debtor's agreement, negotiated out of court, with a creditor or creditors to discharge debt.

World Bank. A United Nations bank established in 1945 to provide loans that aid in economic development, through economically sustainable enterprises. ● Its capital derives from U.N. member states' subscriptions and loans on the open market.

wraparound mortgage. See MORTGAGE.

write off, *vb.* To remove (an asset) from the books, esp. as a loss or expense <the partnership wrote off the bad debt>.

writ of attachment. See ATTACHMENT (3).

writ of execution. See EXECUTION (3).

wrongful-discharge action. A lawsuit brought by a person against his or her former employer, alleging that the person's termination from employment violated a contract or statute.—Also termed *wrongful-termination action*.

XYZ

XD. *abbr.* EX DIVIDEND.

year-end dividend. See DIVIDEND.

yellow-dog contract. An employment contract forbidding membership in a labor union. ● Such a contract is generally illegal under federal and state statutes.

yield, *n.* Profit expressed as a percentage of investment.—Also termed *return*. See RATE OF RETURN.

    coupon yield. The annual interest paid on a security (esp. a bond) divided by the security's par value.

    current yield. The annual interest paid on a security (esp. a bond) divided by the security's current market price.

    earnings yield. The earnings per share of a security divided by its market price. ● The higher the ratio, the better the investment yield. Cf. PRICE-EARNINGS RATIO.

    nominal yield. The annual income received from a security (esp. a bond) divided by the security's par value.

yield to maturity. The rate of return from an investment if the investment is held until it matures.—Abbr. YTM.

z-bond. See *accrual bond* under BOND (1).

zero-coupon bond. See BOND (1).

zero-coupon security. See SECURITY.

zero-rate mortgage. See MORTGAGE.

zipper clause. An integration clause, esp. in a labor agreement. See INTEGRATION CLAUSE.

zoning. The legislative division of a region, esp. a municipality, into separate districts with different regulations within the districts as to land use, building size, and the like.